MUSI

and

LITERATURE

A Comparison of the Arts

By
CALVIN S. BROWN

Contents

I.	Science and Art	1
II.	The Fine Arts	7
III.	Rhythm and Pitch	15
IV.	Timbre, Harmony, and Counterpoint	31
V.	Vocal Music: General Considerations	44
VI.	The Literal Setting of Vocal Music	53
VII.	The Dramatic Setting of Vocal Music	62
VIII.	The Dilemma of Opera	87
IX.	Repetition and Variation	100
X.	Balance and Contrast ⋆	114
XI.	Theme and Variations	127
XII.	ABA Form and the Rondo	135
XIII.	The Fugue	149
XIV.	Sonata Form	161
XV.	The Musical Development of Symbols: Whitman	178
XVI.	The Poetry of Conrad Aiken	195
XVII.	Fiction and the Leitmotiv	208
XVIII.	Literary Types in Music	219
XIX.	Program Music: a Short Guide to the Battlefield	229
XX.	Descriptive Music	245
XXI.	Narrative Music	257
XXII.	Conclusion	268
	Notes	272
	Index	279

CHAPTER I

Science and Art

THERE is a great deal of loose talk about the relationships between science and art—so much, in fact that an unwary listener is likely to find himself considering them as mutually exclusive and furiously championing one or the other without having any clear idea of what either actually is. And yet, in spite of borderline cases and special problems which furnish endless subjects for academic discussion, the main distinction is simple and clear enough. Furthermore, when that distinction has been grasped, the old quarrel between science and art disappears and we find that they are not two different fields of subject matter, but two points of view, both of which are necessary for any balanced outlook on the world.

True science is concerned first of all with the concrete fact which can be isolated and verified. The scientist's first problem is to isolate the phenomenon which he wishes to study. Thus the effect of gravity could not be adequately investigated as long as it was complicated by air resistance; thistledown and cannon-balls seemed to follow utterly different laws until experiments were made in a vacuum. Then it became obvious that the problem had been primarily the isolation of the effect of gravity from other—and at this point irrelevant—considerations. Once the effect of gravity had been clarified, it became possible to discount it and study separately the phenomena of air-resistance. Similarly, the scientist doing animal experimentation finds it necessary to use *controls*—animals of the same stock as the subjects of his experiment, kept in adjoining cages, and treated identically in all respects except for the one thing which is the subject of investigation. Thus if the only difference in the treatment of the experimental group and that of the control group is one of diet, the investigator can know that whatever differences develop between the two groups of animals are due to the difference of diet. In the same way, diet may be kept identical for

1

both groups, and temperature, light, oxygen supply, or any one of an almost infinite number of variables may be isolated for study.

Once the scientist has collected enough isolated and verifiable facts, he can put them together into abstract, frequently mathematical statements. The physicist investigating gravity eventually discovers that the force itself varies from place to place, and he has to isolate and study this variation, but finally he reaches the point where he can make the general statement that $s = \frac{1}{2}gt^2$, and this abstraction holds true for all bodies falling under the influence of gravity alone. When this generalized statement has been sufficiently checked both by experiment and by logic, the process by which it was discovered may be reversed. The formula was *induced* from a great many individual cases, but as soon as it is accepted we may *deduce* the individual case from the formula. Our original physicist measured the distance fallen and the time taken, arrived at a value for the gravitational constant, and made his formula. We may take his formula and gravitational constant for granted, measure the time which it takes an object to fall, and hence compute the distance which it has fallen.

In many types of science the methods are not so clearly visible as in this example, but nevertheless the processes of isolating a phenomenon, determining the individual fact, inducing the general principle, and on occasion deducing the individual fact from the established principle are the basic processes of all scientific thought. Once the variables have been isolated and understood, they may be combined almost indefinitely: the expert in ballistics deals with the combustion of explosives, gas pressures, falling bodies, air resistance (including the wind-drift of air in motion), the rotation of the earth, etc., but his principles are those already established by separate sciences and his methods of combining them are the same methods.

This scientific approach to the universe has tremendous values—and the construction of gadgets which enable us to ride faster, talk further and louder, undersell our competitors, and kill our enemies is one of the less important of these. We all need the ability to view things disinterestedly, whether these things be falling bodies or political philosophies; and whenever we succeed in leaving our own tastes, prejudices, sensations, creeds—all those things which make us John Doe as distinguished from Richard Roe—out of consideration, we are thinking scientifically.

This type of disinterested analysis, however, has a great shortcoming which is the necessary consequence of its advantages. It does not, and by its very nature cannot, present complete human experiences. Outside of the physics laboratory, no one ever saw an object fall in either a literal vacuum or the figurative vacuum of disinterestedness. What does happen is that an individual (with his basic stock of common human nature and his additional group of personal peculiarities) sees or imagines that he sees, at some specific time and place, some specific object (towards which he necessarily has certain specific attitudes and relationships) fall—for certain reasons towards which he cannot remain indifferent. This complex phenomenon may be called *human experience*, for lack of a better term, and it is obviously very different from the physicist's law of falling bodies. Furthermore, its particularity is such that it is never twice alike. We have only to consider Satan's fall:

> Him the Almighty Power
> Hurld headlong flaming from th' Ethereal Skie
> With hideous ruine and combustion down
> To bottomless perdition [1] . . . .

and

> from my neck so free
> The Albatross fell off, and sank
> Like lead into the sea,[2]

and

> Of no distemper, of no blast he died,
> But fell like autumn fruit that mellow'd long,—
> Even wondered at because he dropp'd no sooner,[3]

and

> An Ace of Hearts steps forth: the King unseen
> Lurked in her hand and mourned his captive Queen.
> He springs to vengeance with an eager pace,
> And falls like thunder on the prostrate Ace,[4]

in order to see that the formula of science is the only thing in which falling bodies are alike, and that this is true precisely because the abstraction of science censors the human experience. Art, on the other hand, is the unique means by which such experience can be communicated: hence it is the function of art to present that aspect of things which science rigorously rejects. As long as the zoölogist remains purely scientific we can discern no difference in tone between his description of the nightingale and his account of the skunk; but his approach to either one will differ tremendously from the artist's.

How does the artist go about the task of communicating human experience? Once again we must make the reservation that many points are debatable, even to the basic idea of communication. But for our purposes the essentials of the process are reasonably clear. The artist begins with an experience of his own—anything from Wordsworth's view of a field of daffodils or Leonardo's perception of a beautiful woman to Dante's feeling of the essential unity of all knowledge and history into a higher theological and ethical principle, or Shakespeare's reading of a story of ambition and murder among the Scottish nobility. In his own mind he then works over the experience, organizing it in such a way that it can be made viable and be incorporated into some physical medium—words, tones, lines, colors, masses of wood or stone. When this physical medium has come into existence, it is what we ordinarily call the work of art, but the artistic process is only half achieved. It is now the task of the recipient to reverse the process of the artist: he takes the "work of art," perceives its structure, relationships, and "meanings," and comes finally to an experience of his own which is as nearly as possible the same as the experience of the artist. The process may be represented by the following diagram:

artist

Experience [1]   organization   work of art   organization   experience [2]

recipient

The pre-electric phonograph offers an almost exact analogy. A sound—say a sustained middle C on a violin—is the original experience. The vibrations of air which constitute this sound are evanescent, but they can be converted into motions of a more substantial object, a stylus. Motion, however, is still transitory, and it is necessary to record this motion in a permanent physical form—a disc of wax which is the parallel of the work of art. At this point the manufacturer, or artist, has completed his half of the process. The recipient now makes use of a device which translates the physical characteristics of the wax disc into motions of another stylus, and these motions are in turn converted back into atmospheric vibrations which give approximately the sensation of the original sound. Approximately only, because some of the higher overtones will be lost and some mechanical noises such as needle-scratch will necessarily be added. Here again the parallel will hold: no one can ever receive from a work of art an experience absolutely identical with the one which inspired it: some of the subtleties and private references of the original experience will necessarily be lost, and some other elements will necessarily be added by the general background and character of the recipient. Nevertheless, just as a good recording gives a reasonably accurate reproduction of the original sound, a good work of art gives a reasonably accurate duplicate of the artist's original experience.

All communication, of course, follows this same general pattern. However, we call it art only when the experiences communicated are human experiences which we feel to have some permanent value and when they are of such a nature that their communication requires particular ability and is not a matter of everyday occurrence.

We are now in a position to return to the statement that science and art are two different points of view rather than two types of subject matter. A Beethoven symphony could be represented by a series of curve-tracings on smoked paper, and any mathematician who felt so inclined could, if he lived long enough, publish it as a shelf of volumes giving the formulas for these curves. If he did this, however, he would be presenting a scientific study of the work of art—an utterly impersonal study which would conscientiously ignore that human experience which Beethoven sought to communicate to his audience. The curve tracings would similarly ignore the artistic point of the music; yet a line drawing can present a series of curves which constitute a work of art. The difference is clear and simple: the curves of the drawing embody in a physical form the experience of its creator, but the curve-tracings of the symphony, although they can tell us a great deal, scientifically, about acoustics, are not comprehensible in themselves in terms of the experience of *sound* which the composer set out to present.

Perhaps the most widespread fallacy about art is the idea that it is merely an irresponsible wallowing in unrestrained emotion. This misconception probably arises from the fact that we have not yet left behind the romantic era, in which the emotional element was certainly stronger than any other single part of the complex of human experience, and that the more sentimental and poorer works of this movement took, because of their very defects, a strong hold on the popular imagination. Aristotle remarks that the plot which rewards the good and punishes the bad "is accounted the best because of the weakness of the spectators;" [5] the same thing may be said of sentimentality in the arts in general. In the greatest art feeling and emotion are essential, but so are thought, understanding, imagination, and many other sterner qualities.

The similar misconception about science likewise takes the most obvious and easily accessible part and tries to make it the whole thing. Thus, with the help of absurd advertising, we have come all too often to think of the scientist as a man in a white coat mysteriously looking through a double-barreled spectroscope at a smear of lipstick to show how pure it is. True science is something quite different—a pursuit of knowledge for its own sake with a passion which, by refusing to be suppressed, sometimes creeps into the scientific treatise and communicates the experience (as well as the objective discoveries) of the searcher for scientific truth to such an extent that his treatise becomes a work of literature.

This book will be devoted almost entirely to a discussion of the relationships of two of the arts, but this consideration of the nature of art in general and its differences from science should be of assistance in clarifying the nature of the material and phenomena under discussion.

CHAPTER II

The Fine Arts

IT IS customary to divide the arts into two somewhat arbitrary classes designated as the fine arts and the useful arts. According to this scheme the fine arts are painting, sculpture, architecture, music, and literature (and, according to some authorities, the dance). Broadly speaking, the fine arts are an end in themselves, and aim at nothing beyond that communication of experience already referred to as the province of art. It is obvious that architecture is least able to come strictly under this classification, but any of the other fine arts may occasionally depart from it: a march may be intended primarily as a means of keeping soldiers in step, or a statuette may be designed to serve as a paperweight or to be duplicated and mounted as book-ends. In spite of these exceptions, however, we call these arts fine arts as long as they are of sufficient importance and have sufficient aesthetic appeal to be called arts at all. Hence we do not say that designing a pigpen and writing a society column in a newspaper are useful rather than fine arts—we say, rightly enough, that they are not arts of any kind.

The useful arts are practised with some consideration for aesthetic appeal, but their primary function is the production of objects which serve some physical purpose. Ceramics, basket-weaving, wrought-iron work may serve as examples of this class of art. At their best the useful arts may almost attain the status of the fine arts; at their lowest they are mere handicrafts. They need concern us no further, for, in spite of certain recent theories that the music of the future will be a useful rather than a fine art, and in spite of such uses as the sung advertisement on the radio and the background music of a good many films—both of which are handicraft or unhandycraft as the case may be—whatever we ordinarily think of as music is a fine art. Similarly, when we speak of literature we exclude the multifarious uses of language—advertisements, gossip, recipes, many books (including this one)—which cannot come under the classification of fine art.

7

The five generally accepted fine arts can be classified in various ways, but the easiest and most obvious distinction is that based on the senses by which they are perceived. Painting, sculpture, and architecture must be seen; music and literature are intended to be heard. Arts appealing to the senses of smell, touch, and taste have been more or less seriously suggested, and at least one perfume-concert has actually been given [1]—not to speak of any number of elaborate dinners. Nevertheless, the fine arts are confined to the visible and the audible for their media of presentation.

Before going further with this classification, it may be necessary to justify the statement that literature is intended to be heard. Since the great majority of our reading is done without the production of any physical sound, many persons are inclined to think offhand of literature as something presented to the eye. A moment's reflection will dispel this idea. No one mistakes the printed notes on a sheet of music for *music*: they are simply symbols which tell a performer what sounds he is to produce, and the sounds themselves are the music. Precisely the same thing holds true for literature and no illiterate would ever be guilty of this confusion. In fact, the only reason that we do not make the same error with respect to music is that we are largely musical illiterates: the symbols on a musical score mean little or nothing to us until they are translated into the sounds for which they stand. We are so accustomed to translating printed words into sounds effortlessly and without having physically to produce those sounds that we sometimes tend to forget their existence.

A few reminders will easily show their importance. The lines of this book are of equal length on the page, but those of *Paradise Lost* are not; yet those lines of blank verse are structural units to the ear, whereas these lines are mere physical accidents devoid of structural significance. Does *Achilles* rhyme with *pastilles?* If the eye were the judge it would. And, in spite of the eye, *queue* rhymes with *you.* In fact, when we read we mentally hear sounds to such an extent that we instantly spot a halting line of poetry or a false rhyme. We even go further, as psychological experiments have shown, and make slight movements towards pronouncing the words which we see, and these movements are an aid in imagining the sounds. To demonstrate this fact one need only hold his mouth as wide open as possible while silently reading the next sentence. He will inevitably get the impression of a strange, yawning kind of enunciation. We are thus justified in the original statement that literature is an art presented to the ear rather than to the eye.

The visual arts of painting and sculpture, while differing markedly in media and processes, are much the same in general principle. Both may or may not employ color. (The term "painting," as used here, should be understood to include drawing, etching, the woodcut, etc.) In general we tend to think of sculpture as form independent of color, but history will not tolerate such a view: the colored bust of Queen Nefertiti is widely known, and there is good reason to believe that many of the Greek statues were originally painted. In principle, then, the primary difference between painting and sculpture is that the former is in two dimensions and the latter in three. Even this distinction tends to break down in borderline cases, for some paintings in which the pigments are laid on very heavily may actually have a greater dimension of depth than some sculpture in very low relief. Also, it is interesting to note that such two-dimensional forms as the etching and the woodcut are actually made in three dimensions and then printed in a two-dimensional form.

Architecture again is somewhat of an anomaly. It is clearly a three-dimensional visual art, but the necessity of arranging great masses of material in physically stable equilibrium allows it far less freedom than the other visual arts have. The fact that a building is designed for some non-artistic purpose imposes further limitations, and the fact that architecture tends to be far more regular and symmetrical than the other arts is probably due to this combination of functional and mechanical limitations. Frequently the other visual arts, in the form of frescoes, friezes, gargoyles, stained glass, etc., are combined with the basic architectural idea to give an effect of greater richness and variety than the purely architectural work allows.

Architecture also has certain peculiarities which have led some critics to consider it an art parallel to music. Thus the nineteenth-century German critics were inordinately fond of the dictum that "Architecture is frozen music," and of its converse that "Music is moving architecture." Others, with less justice, have remarked that architecture resembles music in that both surround and encompass the spectator instead of being experienced entirely from the outside. And, finally, architecture differs from all the other arts in that it is intended to be seen from many different points of view (as opposed to all paintings and many statues) and that its component parts can be contemplated in almost any order (as opposed to literature and music). One must "enter" a poem or a symphony at one point only and go through it in one definite sequence of parts, but one can approach a cathedral from any point of the compass, enter it through any door, and visit its interior parts in any order without appreciably affecting the artistic impression derived from the building as a whole.

The most conspicuous difference between the visual arts and the auditory arts is that the former are spatial and the latter are temporal. Here again certain reservations must be made, but the general effect of these reservations is only to emphasize the difference. Moving pictures may seem, at first, to present a visual art developing in time as well as in space, but the film is simply a photographed play, and the play is a literary form presented by action rather than by narration. The devotees of the color-organ have envisioned an art of mobile color,[2] but have never really attained it, and most of their work has been done in conjunction with music. The closest approach to a mobile (and hence temporal) visual art is undoubtedly the dance, but this form is entirely dependent on music and by its very dependence seems to underline the fact that, whatever the future of the arts may hold, no temporal form of visual art does actually exist in anything resembling a pure state.

Generally speaking, then, the visual arts are static and have their extension, development, and relationships in space. The auditory arts are dynamic and have their extension, development, and relationships in time. Modern high-speed photography can reproduce a painting or a statue with an exposure of one millionth of a second, because the entire work is present at any infinitesimal point of time. The significance here is independent of time, for it is entirely a matter of spatial relationships. Thus any given instant presents the entire work, but any given square inch of a painting or cubic inch of a statue would be devoid of meaning. The auditory arts reverse this principle: the element of space is meaningless when applied to them, for they can theoretically exist in any point of space whatsoever. On the other hand, an instantaneous exposure (or even one of sufficient duration to include a full word of the poem or beat of the sonata) is as meaningless as the square inch of the painting. This is obviously due to the fact that the literary or musical work develops in time rather than in space.

This basic difference between the visual (spatial) and the auditory (temporal) arts automatically produces a difference in the mental equipment necessary for their comprehension. The recipient of the painter's experience must have a sharp sense of spatial relationships and, it may be, of color. Except for architecture, in which the component parts cannot be simultaneously viewed, the visual arts require practically no exercise of memory except in such pursuits as the tracing of an artist's development or the history of a school, and these are properly questions of scholarship rather than of aesthetic perception. The reader of books and the hearer of music, on the other hand, must have a very retentive memory. One who forgets Hamlet's conversation with his father's ghost cannot possibly make sense of the rest of the play. Similarly, the hearer who does not retain the subject of a fugue, or who forgets a theme used as the basis for a set of variations, has no chance of following the composer's intentions. Sometimes the demand for memory in music covers almost as long a span as it does in literature: the opening of the last movement of Beethoven's *Ninth Symphony* is merely an incongruous hodge-podge unless one clearly remembers the openings of the first three movements.

Music and literature, then, are alike in that they are arts presented through the sense of hearing, having their development in time, and hence requiring a good memory for their comprehension. Their many other relationships will be discussed in detail in the chapters which are to follow, but their basic difference should be noted here, with the understanding that it must later be modified by certain reservations and exceptions. Broadly speaking, music is an art of sound in and for itself, of sound *qua* sound. Its tones have intricate relationships among themselves, but no relationship to anything outside the musical composition. As Schopenhauer pointed out,[1] they inhabit and form a universe of their own which has only remote relationships, by analogy, to the general universe in which we live.

Literature, on the other hand, is an art employing *sounds to which external significance has been arbitrarily attached*. This question of the meanings of words is an intricate one, as recent studies in semantics have shown, but the distinction between the "meaning" of the word and the absence of "meaning" of the musical tone is simple enough. A glance at the same words in different languages is sufficient to show that there is no reason, in the nature of things, why a certain combination of speech-sounds should be associated with any particular external object or concept. Even such an imitative word as *whisper* is far from inevitable: the French say *chuchoter*, the Germans *flüstern*, the Italians *bisbigliare*, the Spaniards *cuchichear;* and in English *vesper* would be as satisfactory an imitation as *whisper*. But the great majority of words are not imitative, for only concepts of sound can be directly imitated by words.

In practice, then, the association of a certain sound (and of the alphabetical symbols used to represent it) with a certain concept is no more than an arbitrary association of ideas arising from the fact that speakers of the same language have always heard these collections of sounds used in connection with certain objects or concepts. Communication of ideas is made possible only by the fact that these associations are identical, or at least very similar, for speakers of the same language. The possibility of different associations and their disastrous consequences for communication are clearly evident when an American in England uses such words as *bug* and *bum*. In general, however, our everyday speech and reading involve such simple concepts and such fixed associations between sound and meaning that we are not conscious of the intricate mental processes necessary to connect a set of sounds with its proper meaning (when often, as in the case of *I*, *aye*, and *eye*, or of the one word *flat*, several different meanings may be possible) and to interrelate these individual meanings into a statement, command, or logical unity of any other type.

In so far as the poet is concerned with such technical matters as meter, rhyme, assonance, and alliteration, he affords a close parallel to the composer; but the fact that his sets of sounds do not stop with auditory sensations, but have fixed external significations, makes his problem in many respects totally different. We shall see later that the *Leitmotiv* can be considered as a sort of musical word, but as compared with the use of words in literature its most elaborate and successful employments hardly go beyond baby-talk. On the other hand, those writers who have experimented with a "pure" poetry of sound alone, without meaning, have invariably produced more or less interesting stunts rather than poems. One of the most successful attempts in this vein is not a serious poem, but a brilliant parody of the swooning-with-ecstasy sort of magazine verse. J. C. Squire's *The Exquisite Sonnet* [4] will serve to show both the possibilities and limitations of sound alone in poetry; also, it will be a useful reference for some later discussions.

> No purple mars the chalice; not a bird
>   Shrills o'er the solemn silence of thy fame.
>   No echo of the mist that knows no name
> Dims the fierce darkness of the odorous word.
> 5 The shadowy sails of all the world are stirred,
>   The pomps of hell go down in utter flame,

And never a magic master stands to shame
The hollow of the hills the Titans heard.

O move not, cease not, heart! Time's acolyte
10   Frustrates forlorn the windows of the west
And beats the blinding of our bitter tears,
Immune in isolation; whilst the night
Smites with her stark immortal palimpsest
The green arcades of immemorial years!

The elaborate patterns of sound in this parody are interesting and effective in themselves, not only in the meter and rhyme demanded by the form of the Italian sonnet, but in extra patterns of alliteration and assonance as well. But the point which concerns us at the moment is not the use of sound, but the powerlessness of sound alone, even in a nonsense poem. Taken as a whole, of course, the sonnet means nothing whatsoever, and even single phrases are often composed of skillful and —at a first reading—elusive nonsense. "O move not, cease not, heart" —what *does* he want it to do? How can one "dim the darkness," however fierce it may be? Yet this is all very far from a pure verbal music. It makes good grammatical sense, which is simply another way of saying that the meanings of words as actions, names, attributes, connectives, etc., are rigorously observed. Furthermore, an ingenuous use of the *meaning* of negatives enables the author to have his cake and eat it too, so far as the suggestions of his lines are concerned. It has been observed that literature is the only art which can present a negative idea. A painter can easily enough produce a chalice from which purple is entirely absent, but he can never communicate the idea carried by the words "no purple." This trick of the negative *meaning* enables Squire at the same time to present the suggestion of purple, with all its wealth of associations, simply by denying its presence, and to go on to the equally effective (and contradictory) picture of the pure, spotless chalice. This same trick is employed in "not a bird," "no echo," and "never a magic master."

Furthermore, the single words are chosen partly because they are beautiful in sound, but also because they are rich in poetic associations which can here be exploited without being controlled. In fact, it is nearly impossible to distinguish the sound of a word, as sound, from the associations which it evokes. If a person is asked to list the ten most beautiful words (as pure sound) which he can think of, it will almost invariably develop that his choices are also beautiful in their associations. Someone has pointed out that an initial *v*, as in *violin*, *violet, vernal,* is a very pleasing sound, and that *ermine* is unquestionably a beautiful word. Yet it takes a strong effort of the imagination to divorce sound and meaning sufficiently to appreciate the beauty of *vermin.* In addition to lulling the logical faculty to sleep by beautiful patterns of sound, Squire's nonsense ingeniously seems to mean something by giving free play to the vague associations of his carefully selected words. There is a chain of religious suggestion running through such a series as "chalice . . . word . . . hell . . . magic . . . acolyte . . . windows of the west . . . immortal." Another such chain, interlocking with this one, suggests a definite sequence of light and, by inference, time: "mist . . . dim . . . darkness . . . shadowy . . . flame . . . windows of the west . . . night." Numerous other series of suggestions exist in the parody, and it is a fascinating pursuit to work them out. Enough has been said, however, to establish our present point: language consists of sounds endowed with associations and meanings, and even in deliberate nonsense it is impossible to escape the external associations which are always present in the sounds of speech.

As we shall see later, the composer has at his command a far greater variety of sounds than the poet, and far greater freedom in his arrangement and combination of them, but as a rule his sounds convey nothing which is not a part of the audible world. The poet invariably deals with sounds which do convey something beyond themselves, and this fact, while greatly limiting his achievements in the realm of pure sound, opens up to him other possibilities which are closed to the composer.

CHAPTER III

Rhythm and Pitch

WE HAVE seen that both music and literature are presented to the intellect and the emotions by means of sound, the principal difference being that musical sound is used only for itself and the sounds of literature have external significance. We must now consider the characteristics of this audible raw material by means of which it can be organized into coherent works of art. For this purpose we must keep both arts in mind in order to see to what extent they agree in their treatment of the sounds of which they are composed. The topics to be considered, then, will be rhythm, pitch, and timbre (or tone-color). It will also be convenient to include the possibilities of simultaneous sound, in the form of harmony and counterpoint, though this phenomenon is not strictly parallel with the other three.

RHYTHM is universally recognized, but almost incapable of complete definition. The term is applied primarily to relationships of movement of either sounds or physical bodies, but it is also extended to include the static relationships of the visual arts. Since this latter use of the word is likely to lead to confusion, in the following discussion only the rhythmic characteristics of bodies or sounds in motion will be taken into account.

In its larger forms rhythm may be defined as any organized and intelligible relationship between the individual items of a series of sounds or motions, such relationship being organized with respect to emphasis and duration. No repetition of a set pattern is implied: the actions of a good tennis player are rhythmical in that they form a smooth pattern of movement, effort, and relaxation, but the intervals of time between strokes, the number of steps between strokes, and the duration of the strokes themselves fall into no fixed or repeated pattern. The same thing may be said of good prose. It has a certain "swing" to its movement which distinguishes it from bad prose, but the attempts to analyze prose rhythms and reduce them to certain identifiable patterns are as unconvincing as they are laborious. One normally thinks of music as having a recurring beat and hence being capable of division into bars, but this impression is largely an accident arising from the nature of the music which we most frequently hear and, to some extent, from the mechanics of musical notation. The music of our dance-bands and symphony orchestras *is* very largely metrical, but the earlier ecclesiastical music of the Christians, Hindus, and Mohammedans is "unmeasured," taking its rhythm from the prose texts for which it was designed. Gregorian chant is a good illustration: for "plain-song is analogous to prose, while measured music, with its definite subdivisions of time, is analogous to poetry, with its definite subdivisions of metre." [1]

For some centuries music ceased to be composed in prose rhythms, but now—as often happens—the very new is going back to the very old. Modern composers have protested vigorously against "the tyranny of the bar-line," and though they have kept the mechanical line, for the most part, in order to facilitate the performance of concerted music, they have come more and more to ignore it in their rhythms. A sufficient, though by no means extreme example may be found in the horn theme which appears early in Richard Strauss' *Till Eulenspiegel*:

The thrice-repeated phrase has seven beats, but it is written in what is ostensibly 6/8 time. Hence each repetition begins one beat later in the bar, and if the theoretical accents of the time were observed, the phrase would have a different rhythm at each recurrence. Actually, though, the rhythm of the phrase is the same each time, and the only real purpose which the bar-lines serve in this passage is to enable the conductor to beat time and keep the orchestra together. This horn passage is similar to good prose split into ten-syllable lines and printed as blank verse, but remaining as prose to the ear.

Little can be said about rhythm in general except that it is or is not present or effective. Most familiar music and poetry, however, are designed on the basis of meter—a more or less regularly repeating rhythmic pattern; and our principal problem is to determine the relationship between the use of meter in poetry and its rôle in music.

Both musical and poetic meters are based on the same general principle: a short, easily recognized pattern of time and accent is chosen for the basic unit and is then constantly repeated with sufficient variation to prevent monotony, but with sufficient uniformity to be easily perceived. Classical Greek and Latin poetry used a time scheme depending on whether the vowel of a syllable was long or short. Since a long vowel occupied twice the time of a short one, all classical meters fall into patterns which can be represented by quarter and eighth notes, and the principal method of variation is the substitution of two shorts for one long or the reverse. Since the methods of scansion used for poetry in the modern European languages were adapted from classical scholarship, it is customary to use the marks for "long" and "short"; but it must be understood that they do not necessarily have any relationship to the length of vowels. In fact, no less an authority than Saintsbury [2] admits that no one is quite certain just what differentiates the types of syllables in English poetry: the generally accepted theory says that it is entirely a matter of accent (or stress), but champions have arisen and contended for vowel length, equivalent time for the foot as a unit, and even pitch as the deciding factor. However that may be, everyone will agree that the line which (according to Dr. Johnson) is as perfect an iambic pentameter as can be written,

$$\smile \; - / \smile \quad - / \smile \quad - / \smile - / \smile \quad -$$

I lay my knife and fork across my plate,

has a clear pattern which is adequately represented by the marks above the line. We need not be dogmatic as to what constitutes the exact difference between the syllables marked _ and those marked ◡, for we will all agree that they *are* different. Perhaps accent, time, and pitch all play a part, but since accent is unquestionably an important element of the difference, we may as well refer to the syllables marked _ as "stressed" syllables, and to the others as "unstressed."

On this basis, the line clearly breaks up into a basic unit of an unstressed followed by a stressed syllable, and this pattern is repeated five times with perfect regularity. The repeated rhythm of the "foot" in poetry bears a very clear and close relationship to the repeated rhythm of the musical "bar" or "measure." So evident is this relationship that some critics, notably Sidney Lanier,[3] have written at length to prove that English verse is simply language written in musical time. Attractive as this theory is, there can be no doubt that its schematic notations of English verse, while mechanically accurate, frequently falsify the actual feeling of the rhythm. A more detailed consideration of the different types of feet and bars will show why this must necessarily be true.

There are four, and only four, types of feet which can be used in extended passages of English poetry (and except for French, which, lacking syllabic stress, cannot be said to have feet at all, these remarks will apply with equal accuracy to the poetry of most of the modern European languages). The foot consists of one stressed syllable and of either one or two consecutive unstressed syllables; and the stressed syllable may either begin or end the metrical unit. Thus the mathematical possibilities are:

⌣ — iamb	trochee — ⌣
⌣ ⌣ — anapest	dactyl — ⌣ ⌣

Some feet not coming under these rules, such as the spondee (˗ ˗), the pyrrhic (⌣ ⌣), and the amphibrach (⌣ ˗ ⌣) may occasionally occur, but for obvious reasons they cannot be basic units: even if spondees or pyrrhics could be strung together the absence of different types of syllables would destroy all possibility of rhythm, and consecutive amphibrachs necessarily break down into either dactyls or anapests.

In its simplest schematic form, the musical bar is named by means of a numerator which tells how many notes it has and a denominator which tells what kind of notes they are. Thus 3/4 (waltz) time consists of three quarter-notes to the bar. But we do not distinguish between anapestic and dactylic waltz time, because 3/4 time always (except for variations felt as working *against* its fundamental rhythm) has the accent on the first beat of the bar, and is hence necessarily dactylic. Similarly, 2/4 time is necessarily trochaic. To make the principle general, since the first beat of any musical bar normally receives the strongest accent, only the types of poetic feet beginning with the accented syllable (those in the second column of the listing above) will be available as basic musical beats, unless duration is substituted for accent.

Theoretically it is quite possible to force iambic poetry into a scheme of musical notation of 2/4 time, but to do this ignores the very real distinction between iambic and trochaic verse. Superficially we have only an alternation between stressed and unstressed syllables, and it might seem that to debate which comes first is as pointless as to contend for the priority of the hen or the egg. The fact remains, however, that the effect of iambic meter is quite different from that of trochaic, as an example will readily prove. The opening lines of Tennyson's *Morte D'Arthur* will serve well enough, since they form a very regular alternation of stresses:

> So all day long the noise of battle rolled
> Among the mountains by the winter sea,
> Until King Arthur's table, man by man,
> Had fallen in Lyonness about their lord,
> King Arthur; then, because his wound was deep,
> The bold Sir Bedivere uplifted him,
> Sir Bedivere, the last of all his knights,
> And bore him to a chapel nigh the field,
> A broken chancel with a broken cross,
> That stood on a dark strait of barren land.

Suppose, now, that we make a simple transposition of these lines into a trochaic form. (I have played the rôle of Devil's Advocate to the extent of choosing a passage in which this can be done without the ludicrous effect of dividing words at the end of lines.)

> . . . All day long the noise of battle
> Rolled among the mountains by the winter
> Sea, until King Arthur's table, man by
> Man, had fallen in Lyonness about their
> Lord, King Arthur; then, because his wound was
> Deep, the bold Sir Bedivere uplifted
> Him, Sir Bedivere, the last of all his
> Knights, and bore him to a chapel nigh the
> Field, a broken chancel with a broken
> Cross, that stood on a dark strait of barren
> Land.

As the reviewer said of Wordsworth's poetry, "This will never do." Yet this effect is precisely what is produced by the attempts to indicate iambic meters by means of musical notation (and by Mr. Archibald MacLeish in *Panic*, where he contended in a preface that the meters of English are really trochaic, and demonstrated the fact by printing the primarily iambic lines of his poem in a manner suggestive of our second version of Tennyson). Why it will not do is a difficult question. Probably the answer is that the rhythm keeps the line in mind as a metrical unit (not too subtly, in the passage from Tennyson), and that enough phrases coincide with the rhythm of the line to keep constantly reminding us that the unstressed syllable comes first—that the meter, no matter how it may be printed, is actually iambic.

This difference between "rising" meters (those beginning with an unstressed syllable) and "falling" meters (beginning with a stressed one), is the great stumbling block of all theories which seek to identify poetic meters with musical time-signatures. Dactylic meters are much more docile in this respect, but even here there is dissension as to whether the pattern is one of equivalent syllables with a difference of stress only, or whether there is a difference of duration as well. Thus the inevitable illustration (the first line of Longfellow's *Evangeline*) might be represented in either of two ways:

This is the forest primeval; the murmuring pines and the hemlocks . . .

Likewise, the advocates of vowel-length as a basis for English metrics make trochaic rhythms into 3/4 time, with a half-note for the stressed syllable and a quarter for the unstressed one.

These attempts to adapt English versification to musical notation are illuminating because of the problems which they raise rather than because of any questions which they may answer. The problems of rhythmic relationships between poetry and music are vital ones, on the creative side, only for the composer of vocal music, who must decide whether to force his musical idea into the rhythm of the poem (when, as is usually the case, the two are different), or to force the verbal rhythm into his musical pattern. Broadly speaking, the Elizabethan composers respected their poets far more than have recent composers, and for the last three centuries the tendency has been to see to the music and let the poem take its chances. Strangely enough, the composers of light and comic music have abided by the rhythms of their librettists far more closely than have their more pretentious colleagues: in any of the rapid "patter" songs of the Gilbert and Sullivan operas the verbal and musical rhythms will be found to be practically identical. But perhaps this fact is not so strange when we remember that few other songs move at the same speed as spoken language, and also that jingles are far easier to handle, both in verse and in music, than are more imposing rhythmical structures.

Up to this point rhythms have been discussed on the assumption that, once a pattern is established, they conform to it rigorously. Fortunately this assumption is false, for nothing is more tedious than a series of rhythmically identical feet or bars. Since the variations possible in verse are far fewer than those at the disposal of the composer, perhaps they should be considered first.

Probably the most frequent irregularity is the dropping of an accent required by the theoretical scheme of scansion. Thus pentameters tend to have only four real accents to the line: in other words, about one fifth of the accents in the scheme fall on words which are actually unstressed. The omission of these stresses is not sufficient to interfere with the general pattern, but since such an omission may occur not at all or for any one (or more) of the five accents of a pentameter, we immediately have at least six possible effects from this device alone. In Squire's *Exquisite Sonnet*, for example, line 1 drops (or greatly subdues) the fourth stress, *not;* line 2 likewise drops the fourth, *of;* line 3 drops the second, *of;* line 4 drops the third, *of;* and line 5 keeps all five stresses. The fact that three out of four dropped stresses fall on the word *of* is accidental, but the large number of unimportant (but grammatically necessary) prepositions, conjunctions, and generally unimpressive words does explain this tendency to omit stresses. Another possibility of variation—one used with particular effectiveness by Milton, who likes to hold over the climactic word of a periodic sentence until the beginning of a line—lies in the substitution of a trochee for an iamb, particularly in the first foot of a line. This amounts to no more than a reversal of accent for one foot, and makes a pleasant ripple in the smooth flow of the meter. Squire's sonnet has examples of this reversal in lines 2, 4, 10, and 13. Still another possibility lies in the addition of extra unstressed syllables, slightly hurrying the line in which they occur. Examples are to be found in the fifth foot of line 4 ("od*orous* word"), the second foot of line 5 ("sha*dowy* sails"), and the second foot of line 7 ("nev*er a* magic").

The poet can also drop a syllable entirely (making an effect corresponding to a rest in music). Though this privilege is sparingly used, it is more common than might be expected. The only requirement is that the pause be sufficiently obvious for the reader to make it at the proper place instead of trying to go on immediately and then becoming involved in a metrical impossibility. The concluding "Indian Summer" section of William Ellery Leonard's *Two Lives* supplies two excellent instances:

> The shriveled stalks of goldenrod are sere,
> And crisp and white their flashing old racemes.

(. . . forever . . . forever . . . forever . . .)
This is the lonely season of the year
This is the season of our lonely dreams.

.   .   .
The low haze
Dims the scarped bluffs above the inland sea,
Whose wide and slaty waters in cold glaze
Await yon full-moon of the night-to-be.
(. . . far . . . and far . . . and far . . .)
These are the solemn horizons of man's ways,
These the horizons of solemn thought to me.

Both the parenthetical lines depend on rests for their rhythm—a rhythm which, in the context of the entire poem, is hauntingly effective. In the first of these lines two syllables are dropped out: all that is required to restore complete regularity (and wreck the line poetically) is the insertion of two *and*'s. The second example is similar in principle, but since the reader has already been prepared for the effect, it can be more daring. It actually retains only five of the theoretical ten syllables, and we would have to scan it something like this:

$$(\smile) - (\smile -) \smile - (\smile -) \smile -$$

The methods described above do not exhaust the possibilities of variation in poetic rhythm, but they do cover the principal ones. There is also, of course, infinite variety to be gained by varying the position of the natural pauses (not rests, since no syllable is omitted) within the line. The really astonishing thing about poetic rhythm is the wide variety of effects which can be produced by means of these comparatively slight liberties with rigid patterns. Perhaps the most perfect example of how far from his scheme a poet can go without upsetting his audience is to be found in Milton,[4] where Samson speaks derisively of the difference between the prophecies about him and his own achievement:

Ask for this great Deliverer now, and find him
Eyeless in Gaza at the mill with slaves,
Himself in bonds under Philistian yoke.

The second line owes a good deal of its memorable character to the boldness of its rhythm. At first sight it seems to be perfectly regular except for the trochee in the first foot:

$$- \smile \; / \; \smile - \; / \; \smile \; \asymp \; / \; \smile - \; / \; \smile -$$

Further inspection, however, reveals the fact that ordinary scansion may (as may musical notation) represent the mechanics accurately and at the same time belie the real rhythm. The logical structure of the line necessarily breaks it into four parts, and no two of these are metrically alike. Thus the line must be rhythmically represented as a tetrameter consisting of a trochee, an amphibrach, an anapest, and an iamb:

$$\_\, \smile \;/\; \smile \_ \smile \;/\; \smile \smile \_ \;/\; \smile \_$$

Yet this line runs smoothly into a passage of comparatively regular iambic pentameter and its irregularity attracts only favorable attention.

As a final example of how much may depend on the rhythm of poetry we may take Masefield's familiar *Sea Fever*. Probably few lovers of the poem have ever consciously realized that almost the entire effect depends on contrasting rhythms. In general, the poem presents the sea under two aspects: first, as a symbol of freedom and action; second, as a symbol of peace and mystery. Each stanza tends towards the first aspect in the two opening lines, and turns to give expression to the second in its two remaining lines. The contrast is beautifully worked out in the rhythms. The first half of each stanza has numerous unstressed syllables which give an impression of lightness and speed, but the concluding half of each stanza, by using consecutive stressed syllables (italicized in my excerpt), gives the opposite effect of slowness, majesty, and almost awe. The first stanza will illustrate as well as any:

> I must go down to the seas again, to the lonely sea and the sky,
> And all I ask is a tall ship and a star to steer her by,
> And the *wheel's kick* and the *wind's song* and the *white sail's shak*ing,
> And a *grey mist* on the *sea's face* and a *grey dawn break*ing.*

It is possible to test the effectiveness of the rhythm here by altering it to the rapid pattern of the first lines without too seriously changing the meaning or connotations of its words. If we read the last line, "And a greyish mist on the ocean's face and a greyish morning breaking," we will have a scansion which fits perfectly into the scheme of the stanza, but the particular effect which really makes the poem will have disappeared.

Perhaps the best proof that ordinary poetic rhythm is different from musical rhythm lies in the fact that occasionally poetry is definitely modeled on musical rhythms, and any poem of this type immediately strikes a reader as something quite novel. Browning wrote

* From John Masefield, *Poems*. By permission of The Macmillan Company, publishers.

one of his *Cavalier Tunes* to a standard drum-beat used for marching,
and the effect is most striking:

> Kentish Sir Byng stood for his King,
> Bidding the crop-headed Parliament swing;
> And, pressing a troop unable to stoop
> And see the rogues flourish and honest folk droop,
> Marched them along, fifty-score strong,
> Great-hearted gentlemen, singing this song.

By allowing for a considerable use of omitted syllables we can force
this two-line repeated pattern into a scheme of ordinary scansion:

$$— \smile \smile \;/\; — (\smile \smile) — \smile \smile \;/\; — (\smile \smile)$$
$$— \smile \smile \;/\; — \smile \smile \;/\; — \smile \smile \;/\; — (\smile \smile)$$

Much more convincing, however, is a score such as might be given to
the snare drummer.

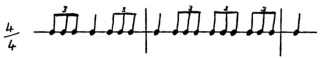

Considering both the theme of the poem and Browning's general interest in music, there can be no doubt that he was deliberately adopting
the drum-beat as the pattern of his rhythm.

Several poems have been written in straight 4/4 (march) time,
and the most blatantly obvious of these will furnish the clearest
example. When Vachel Lindsay first published *The Congo* it had a
popular success almost comparable to that of Ravel's *Bolero*. (An easy
but superficially tricky rhythm is one of the surest means of gaining
such a success.) Critics then spoke of Lindsay as having broken new
paths by employing "jazz rhythms" in poetry, and this misconception
has been frequently echoed up to the present time. In so far as jazz has
different rhythms from any other music, it differs in its more extensive
use of syncopation. There is nothing of this sort to be found in *The
Congo*, however; its rhythms are not those of the fox-trot, but rather
the pounding, regular beat of the Sousa march. The first few lines will
show the method:

> 1 Fat black bucks in a wine-barrel room,
> 2 Barrel-house kings, with feet unstable,
> 3 Sagged and reeled and pounded on the table,
> 4 Pounded on the table,

5   Beat an empty barrel with the handle of a broom,
6   Hard as they were able,
7   Boom, boom, BOOM,
8   With a silk umbrella and the handle of a broom,
9   Boomlay, boomlay, boomlay, BOOM.*

This is march time of the most obvious kind. Though it almost defies
conventional scansion, it falls very readily into musical notation requiring no more freedom than is demanded by the use of rests and the

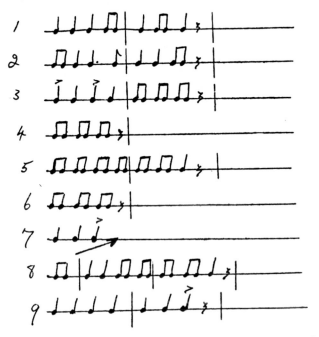

choice between quarter and eighth notes. This rhythm is so clear that
when I once tried the experiment of handing the following score, without comment, to a friend (whom I knew to be familiar with the poem),
he began to tap it out on the table, and, when he finished the fifth line,
exclaimed, "The Congo!"

* From Vachel Lindsay, *Collected Poems.* By permission of The Macmillan Company, publishers.

Only one or two points may be open to question in this scheme, and the questions arise, not because there is any doubt as to the real nature of the rhythm, but because the poet, not having any device for indicating rhythm strictly, must leave some things to the choice of the reader. Thus some readers will so fall into the regular beat that they will drawl out the last two syllables of *unstable* and the words *table* and *able* into two quarter notes instead of my two eighths followed by a quarter rest. There is also a choice in the last two beats of the first bar of lines 2 and 3, for in either case we may read with a dotted quarter and an eighth (as I have done, following the indication of the comma, in line 2) or with two regular quarters (as I have done in line 3). These, however, are matters of individual interpretation, and do not affect in any way the fundamental rhythm of the poem.

Vachel Lindsay exploited his "discovery" in a number of poems whose popularity has unfortunately obscured his more valuable achievements. As a matter of fact, however, the new thing in such poems as *The Congo* and *General William Booth Enters into Heaven* is not the rhythmical device itself, but the obviousness of its application. At about the same time Chesterton wrote *Lepanto* in a similar but more restrained rhythm. Three passages will serve to illustrate it:

> White founts falling in the Courts of the sun,
> And the Soldan of Byzantium is smiling as they run;
> There is laughter like the fountains in that face of all men feared,
> It stirs the forest darkness, the darkness of his beard;
> It curls the blood-red crescent, the crescent of his lips;
> For the inmost sea of all the earth is shaken with his ships.

> In that enormous silence, tiny and unafraid,
> Comes up along a winding road the noise of the Crusade.
> Strong gongs groaning as the guns boom far,
> Don John of Austria is going to the war. . . .

> Don John laughing in the brave beard curled,
> Spurning of his stirrups like the thrones of all the world,
> Holding his head up for a flag of all the free.
> Love-light of Spain—hurrah!
> Death-light of Africa!
> Don John of Austria
> Is riding to the sea. . . .

In two expressions we see greater flexibility than we found in Lindsay: "for the" (just before the first omission) makes two sixteenth notes following the eighth rest of the preceding semicolon; and "tiny and" (in the line immediately following) is clearly an eighth-note triplet. But before *Lepanto* there was George Meredith's *Love in the Valley*:

> Lovely are the curves of the white owl sweeping
> Wavy in the dusk lit by one large star.
> Lone on the fir-branch, his rattle-note unvaried,
> Brooding o'er the gloom, spins the brown evejar.
> Darker grows the valley, more and more forgetting;
> So were it with me if forgetting could be willed. . . .

And before Meredith, Coleridge had written *Christabel* as a conscious metrical experiment which he explained in a preface: "I have only to add, that the metre of the Christabel is not, properly speaking, irregular, though it may seem so from its being founded on a new principle: namely, that of counting in each line the accents, not the syllables. Though the latter may vary from seven [actually four] to twelve, yet in each line the accents will be found to be only four." The first stanza shows this variety, as well as the fact that sometimes one of the four stresses may be, as in the last line, a rest:

> 'Tis the middle of night by the castle clock,
> And the owls have awakened the crowing cock,
> Tu—whit!—Tu—whoo!
> And hark, again! the crowing cock,
> How drowsily it crew.

This, again, is 4/4 time, one bar to the line, though it has a strong tendency to fall into regular iambs and anapests. It has seemed worth while to trace this form of verse backward in some detail, both in order to show that it is not a new discovery and to substantiate, by quotations, the statement that musical time gives verse a different effect from that produced by ordinary methods of scansion. And before leaving the subject, it is interesting to note that Coleridge's "new principle" of four accents and an indeterminate number of unaccented syllables to the line is the regular formula of Anglo-Saxon and early Germanic poetry generally—and the latest analysis [5] of this metrical system shows that it is founded on musical time.

Passing on to the metrics of music, we immediately note that musical rhythms are infinitely more varied and flexible than are those of verse. There are three reasons why this should be true. In the first place, the musician has a far greater range in the speed of performance. The poet is limited here by the fact that he cannot normally give any indications whatsoever as to tempo, and the differences in the speed with which different persons read or speak are not really great; probably the fastest is not more than twice the speed of the slowest. But in music the differences are far greater and are subject to change by the composer. To take a convenient, but not extreme example, Beethoven's metronome indications for his *Ninth Symphony* indicate that the opening bars of the second movement go at the rate of 116 to the minute, whereas those of the third movement run only 15 to the minute—a ratio of nearly 8 to 1. Also, within the same tempo, the musician can subdivide to a far greater extent than can the poet because the mechanics of instrumental performance allow far greater agility than do those of speech. In the poems in 4/4 time we found syllables corresponding to quarter, eighth, and occasional sixteenth notes, but half notes, wholes, or breves would produce an intolerable drawl, and thirty-seconds, sixty-fourths, and shorter notes would be impossible problems both in enunciation and in comprehension. On the same principle, irregular groupings like Chopin's notes in sevens and thirteens are beyond the reach of the poet, who can attain, at most, an occasional triplet.

We can easily see what this matter of variable and controllable speed means to the composer if we consider the possible rhythmic effects which an instrument playing only one note at a time—say a flute—can produce within a single bar of 4/4 time in moderate tempo. An exact mathematical computation of possibilities would be an involved task, but it is simple to arrive at some general idea. Considering only note values proceeding in regular divisions by two—wholes, halves, quarters, etc., on down to 128ths—we see immediately that one sixty-fourth could always be substituted for any two consecutive 128ths, and vice versa, and that this principle will apply all along the line, with staggering possibilities. But there are also the irregular groupings of three instead of two, two instead of three, five instead of one, etc.; and they have equal possibilities of substitution at any point or points. If we could arrive at any figure for the number of rhythmic combinations of *notes*, we could then square that figure in order to arrive at the total possibilities, for rests can always be substituted for any note or notes in any of these combinations. Without laboring the point further, we may as well make a conservative guess that any reasonably competent flautist could play at least ten thousand rhythmic patterns within a single bar of 4/4 time. And the poet's choices within an iambic foot, including substitutions of other feet, will not be more than about ten!

The composer also derives an advantage from the fact that his bars can be considerably more extended and complex than the poet's feet.

(The poet's line, as a rhythmic unit, is of course parallel to the musical *phrase*, and if we consider lines and phrases instead of feet and bars, the same difficulty remains.) The normal foot has one accent only, and though poetry makes some use of half-accents (I have been told that they are an integral part of Persian scansion), their use is sporadic. In music they are essential: the secondary accent on the third beat of 4/4 time and on the fourth beat of 6/8 time allows possibilities entirely unknown to the poet and enables the musician to make a highly complex and interesting structure out of his basic rhythmical unit.

Music also allows conflicting rhythms to a far greater extent than poetry. The most that the poet can do is to have two rhythms present in the mind simultaneously—the theoretical beat of his meter and the particular variation of that beat which is being heard or read at any particular moment. But the composer is limited in this respect only by the number of his voices or instruments and by the psychological point at which the complication of rhythms would become simply no rhythm at all. He has not only the possibilities of combinations of wholes, halves, quarters, etc., but also the incommensurable and highly interesting conflicts of two against three, three against four, four against five, etc. We have guessed that a solo instrument can easily produce ten thousand metrical versions of a bar of 4/4 time, but when we add the possibilities of indefinite numbers of instruments, each with a different rhythm, and of all the times other than 4/4, we see that the number of rhythmic effects possible within a single musical bar will run into astronomical figures.

PITCH, though an essential element of music, is of comparatively little importance in literature. The writer has no control over the pitch-relationships employed by his readers, and the only control of any sort is exercised by the general inflections of the spoken language. Some of these, like the ascending pitch at the end of a question, are well established and easily recognizable, but not many are so definite. A few writers, notably Sidney Lanier, have made much of the "tunes" of English speech and have asserted that there are a great many standardized and recognizable patterns of pitch. Probably the truth lies somewhere between the doubtless exaggerated claims of Lanier and the flat denial, made by some other authorities, that pitch relationships enter into English literature in any way. Without attempting any final settlement of this dispute, we may point out two important factors which enter into it.

The first of these has to do with the nature of the expressions which unquestionably do tend to fall into clear patterns of pitch. They are largely the trivial expressions of everyday casual conversation—"How do you do?", "Good morning," "Thank you," "You're welcome," "Not at all"—phrases which have become absolutely conventionalized and hence have shown a tendency to fall into stereotyped pitch relationships as well as rhythms and uses. It has been pointed out that we can recognize them by their intonations alone, and that is true; but we must remember that their uses are so obvious that we could almost equally well guess them (in context) without hearing them at all. Phrases of this type cannot get the writer very far on the road to Parnassus, and the less platitudinous his expressions are, the less he can count on his readers to agree with him in their use of pitch. In Portia's speech, "The quality of mercy is not strained . . ." the word *strained* ("constrained, forced") clearly requires a scornful emphasis, in echo of Shylock's reply when told that he must be merciful: "On what compulsion must I? Tell me that." But I have heard this peculiar emphasis very successfully given by two different actresses, one considerably raising the pitch on the word *strained,* and the other considerably lowering it. Studies in the pitch relationships employed by readers of poetry have shown certain general tendencies of agreement, but a great many striking differences.

The second point is that even when patterns of pitch in speech agree perfectly in their direction, they do not agree in their intervals. Women tend to employ larger intervals of pitch in their speech than do men, and an excited person uses larger intervals than a calm one. In the intervals of speech there are such national, regional, sexual, emotional, and individual differences that even the most obvious patterns agree only crudely. Since the claims for a prominent rôle of pitch in literature are almost always based on musical analogies, we are justified in comparing the writer's control over the pitches used by his performers with the composer's. And what composer would not desert his baton for a butcher knife if he had a performer who, given an ascending leap of an octave, might jump 9.7 degrees of the scale if he were excited, but only 6.43 degrees if he happened to be bored? Yet no one claims that the pitch relationships of speech are any more consistent than such a performer.

All things considered, we may conclude that pitch may be an effective element in a given performance of a piece of literature, but that it is not an essential literary element, that it is entirely outside of the author's control, and that it belongs to a particular rendition of a work rather than to the work considered as a permanent thing.

CHAPTER IV

Timbre, Harmony, and Counterpoint

TIMBRE is the next element to be considered. It is also called tone-quality or tone-color, but there is really no good English word for it. It may be defined as that characteristic by which one instrument produces a tone differing from that of a different instrument, even though they play the same note at the same degree of loudness. Less technically, it is the quality by which we can instantly tell the sound of a 'cello from that of a trumpet.

From the physicist's point of view, timbre is a mathematical relationship of overtones. When anything (say a musical string) vibrates, it vibrates not only as a whole, but also in segments (halves, thirds, fourths, etc.), and each of these produces its own overtone, or partial. The string produces, then, not a single tone of one pitch only, but a series of tones. If the lowest of these (the fundamental in musical terminology, and the first partial in physical) is C, the next will be c (musically the first overtone; but physically the second partial), and the series will go on with g, c′, e′, g′, b′♭ (approximately), c″, d″, e″, etc. In the higher parts of this series many of the partials (like the approximate b′♭ referred to above, which is actually lower than b′♭) will not lie on our musical scale. The pitches of this *harmonic series* will be. present in any musical tone, but the quality of that tone is determined by the relative strengths of these pitches. Physical analysis can explain the differences between the tone of a fine violin and that of a poor one in terms of the strength of the various partials.

The difference between a tone and a noise is capable of clear definition. A tone produces a series of regular atmospheric vibrations in the form of a highly complex, but consistently repeating wave. A noise produces disturbances which do not have this periodic character, and since the pitch of a sound is determined by the number of these cycles per second, it may be said that in general a tone has a definite pitch, while a noise does not. We can observe this distinction in music: most

31

instruments produce sounds of a definite pitch, but a few percussion instruments, such as cymbals, triangles, snare drums, and bass drums merely produce noises. Kettledrums produce a definite pitch, and hence require tuning; a bass drum requires no tuning, and will come as near to harmonizing with one tone as with another. The singer, having to employ definite pitches, will illustrate the point for speech. All the vowels and some consonants, such as *m* and *n*, will clearly have pitch, but such consonants as *s* will be merely pitchless noises. And singing is merely a form of speech which is performed on a definite system of pitch and time values.

By far the greater part of music employs tones almost exclusively, and the attempts to create artistic sound-effects relying heavily on noise have been very largely confined to imitation of already familiar noises—battles, galloping horses, thunder-storms, etc. In speech we cannot discard noises so readily, for almost every word contains both tone and noise. Here again we find that the poet's chief preoccupation with noises lies in avoiding offensive collections of them (like "Forgive us our trespasses, as we forgive those who trespass against us"), or in imitating familiar sounds. Thus we see that, though literature necessarily contains a great number of noises, it relies largely on the timbre of its tones for those beauties of sound not obtained by rhythm.

Timbre is a very important element in music—so important that many transcriptions of compositions for instruments other than those for which they were originally composed are almost travesties. Especially during the last century have composers, with a decline of interest in the structural features of music and an increasing desire for programmatic suggestion, relied on timbre. Debussy's *Afternoon of a Faun* is a good example, for it would clearly lose much of its effect if transcribed for the piano or for a string quartet.

But however we might inveigh against the tasteless blockhead who would make such a transcription, we would still recognize it. This fact leads to the paradox that timbre is actually more important in literature than in music. In speech we distinguish one tone from another entirely by its timbre. We instantly distinguish between such words as *sit, set, sat, sot, sate, soot, suit, seat,* and *site*; yet these words differ from one another only in the timbre of the vowel. In other words, if we change the timbres in speech we immediately get either different words or gibberish. Experimental physicists have even constructed sets of organ pipes which can be so combined as to produce perfectly any of the vowels. The elaborate mathematics of partials and their combinations to produce recognizable timbres is not only a physical explanation of many of the beauties of poetry; it is an explanation of the intelligibility of everyday speech.

The fact that recognition of timbres makes speech intelligible leads to another difference between their use in music and in literature. In music the same timbre is usually employed consecutively for some time. We call it a rapid shifting when Beethoven indulges in his favorite devices of tossing a phrase back and forth between strings and wood-winds, or taking the same phrase consecutively with different members of the woodwind choir. Even here, however, the entire phrase is given in one timbre before a change is made. One can hardly imagine an arpeggio of sixteenth-notes in which each note would be played by a different instrument. Yet that is precisely what happens in poetry: every sound of speech is a different timbre, and hence we have not only a conspicuous change with the vowel of each syllable, but also the timbres and auxiliary noises of its accompanying consonants. This fact springs from the very nature of language, and the poet has no control over it. The best that he can do is to repeat a few timbres sufficiently often and in sufficiently emphatic positions to give a certain coloring to the passage as a whole, or else to provide for regular sequences and gradations of his conspicuous timbres.

The first of these methods is particularly useful for imitative effects. An old stand-by for a somnolent effect is Tennyson's

> The moan of doves in immemorial elms,
> And murmuring of innumerable bees,[1]

and a poetically better, because less obvious one, is Spenser's description of the Cave of Morpheus:[2]

> And more, to lulle him in his slumber soft,
> A trickling streame from high rocke tumbling downe
> And ever-drizeling raine upon the loft,
> Mixt with a murmuring winde, much like the sowne
> Of swarming bees, did cast him in a swowne. . . .

For the opposite effects of harshness we may consider Miss Millay's

> Bizarrely with the jazzing music blended,[3]

and Tennyson's more extended description of the sound of mail-clad Sir Bedivere carrying his wounded king down to the lake by a narrow path along a cliff. This passage is particularly interesting in the sudden change from the harsh imitative sounds describing the trip itself to the peaceful passage, dominated by liquids and nasals, representing the arrival at the shore:

> Dry clashed his harness in the icy caves
> And barren chasms, and all to left and right
> The bare black cliff clanged round him, as he based
> His feet on slippery juts of crag that rang
> Sharp-smitten with the dint of armèd heels—
> And on a sudden, lo! the level lake,
> And the long glories of the winter moon.[4]

It will be noticed that these passages rely heavily on the natural imitative faculty of language, for many of their most effective sounds are contained in words like *murmur, moan, clash, clang, rang,* which are already imitative formations. Frequently in passages of this type the real problem is only that of finding other words to reinforce the effect of the obvious onomatopoetic words that lie ready to hand.

In this connection the poet's attempts to imitate musical timbres are particularly interesting. Imitative words, often invented for the purpose, are useful, especially for suggestion of the noise instruments. A good example is Detlev von Liliencron's *Die Musik kommt,*[5] which describes the progress of a military band through a little German village. We have first the approaching sound, then an account of the marching men, each with the attributes and bearing proper to his military rank. The children peer out at them from doors and windows, and finally the sound dies away in the distance and peace is restored.

> Klingling, tschingtsching und Paukenkrach,
> Noch aus der Ferne tönt es schwach,
> Ganz leise bumbumbumbum tsching,
> Zog da ein bunter Schmetterling,
> Tschingtsching, bum, um die Ecke? *

For comic purposes like this such imitation can be quite effective, but it is obviously unsuited for more serious poetry. The poet who wishes seriously to suggest musical timbres can make little use of purely imitative devices; hence he has to rely on general patterns arranged about certain dominating timbres. De Vigny's

> J'aime le son du cor, le soir au fond du bois[6]

> * Klingling, chingching and kettledrums,
>   Still from the distance softly comes,
>   Quite faintly, boom-boom-boom-boom ching—
>   Did a gay butterfly take wing,
>   Chingching, boom, round the corner?

sustains the horn-effect very well for at least this one line, and the first stanza of Paul Verlaine's *Chanson d'automne* [7] is a more extended example, this time imitating the violin:

> Les sanglots longs
> Des violons
>   De l'automne
> Blessent mon coeur
> D'une langueur
>   Monotone.

I have refrained from attempting a translation of these last two excerpts because of their very nature: the point of the passages lies in skillfully arranged patterns of sound which defy translation—an obvious distinction between this type of poetic use of timbre and the imitative words of Liliencron's poem, which invite it. Even here, however, the effect of verbal timbre is strongly reinforced by verbal suggestion: each of these passages names the instrument which it is imitating, and, with the instrument in mind, a reader finds the imitation convincing. Yet it is quite possible that, if a similar association were set up by the name of a different instrument—say the horn for Verlaine's stanza—one might find the imitation equally effective for that instrument. Obviously the only thing that actually produces the timbre of a horn is a horn, and suggestion is necessary to make up for the inadequacies of imitation.

The limitations of this imitative use of timbre in literature are obvious. The demands of vocabulary make it extremely difficult to sustain imitative passages; hence they must necessarily be brief. Even at that, many of them are too long, for the device smacks strongly of artifice unless it is greatly restrained, and literary taste is generally satisfied with suggestion rather than imitation. At this point music offers an exact parallel. The wide range of pitch, rhythm, and timbre available to the composer makes it far easier for him to imitate familiar sounds, but this fact does not remove the questionableness of the procedure. There are, of course, good precedents for even the most literal musical imitations—the cock-crow in Bach's *St. Matthew Passion,* and the nightingale, quail, and cuckoo in Beethoven's *Pastoral Symphony* are perhaps the most famous. Yet, even though these are slight and incidental, many critics find them objectionable and unworthy of a place in the works in which they occur. The great advantage of music lies not in its greater capacity for realistic imitation, but in its ability to suggest by purely musical means. Both timbre and rhythm enter into such effects as the undercurrent of the running brook throughout the second movement of Beethoven's *Pastoral Symphony* and the surging seas of Mendelssohn's *Hebrides Overture*. This whole question, however, is properly a part of the problem of "program music," under which heading it will be considered in some detail later.

Far more important than imitative timbres in literature is the selection of non-imitative timbres for their value as sound. Under the general method of accumulating similar sounds come such devices as alliteration and assonance. The former of these is more generally familiar, though not more conspicuous, than the latter. The Squire sonnet furnishes numerous examples of both—in fact, pleasing combinations of sound are one of its chief devices for lulling the reader's attention to such a degree that the absence of meaning may easily escape his notice. A few examples will suffice, for others can be easily enough found in almost any poetry:

> *N*o echo of the *m*ist that *k*nows *n*o *n*ame
> (Nasal alliteration, line 3)
> And *n*ever a *m*agic *m*a*st*er *st*ands to *sh*ame
> (Cross-alliteration of nasals and
> sibilants, line 7)
> The *h*ollow of the *h*ills the Titans *h*eard
> (line 8)
> *F*rustrates *f*orlorn the *w*indows of the *w*est
> And *b*eats the *b*linding of our *b*itter tears
> (lines 10–11).

But assonance plays as great a part as alliteration. It may be defined as an agreement of vowels without the agreement of consonants necessary to produce rhyme: *wheat* and *seal* show assonance, but in order to produce rhyme we must make the consonants following the accented vowels identical, as in *wheat* and *seat*. Thus we have good examples of assonance in

> Dims the fierce darkness of the odorous word.
> The shadowy sails of all the world are st*i*rred,
> (lines 4–5)

and, even more strikingly, in the long *i*'s of

> And beats the bl*i*nding of our bitter tears,
> Immune in *i*solation, wh*i*lst the n*i*ght
> Sm*i*tes. . . .
> (lines 11–13)

It will be noticed that in each of these examples there is a cross-pattern of rhyme and assonance, the same vowel entering into both, and this fact gives an added pleasure of sound.

Assonance and alliteration, like imitation, must be kept strictly under control or they will degenerate into mere artifice. Swinburne is notorious for the fatal facility with which he handled such devices—a facility which frequently led him to use strikingly beautiful language as a means of saying nothing in particular.

Probably the most difficult, most effective, and least obvious literary use of timbre lies in the employment of sequences of vowels (sometimes including assonances) which are particularly attractive. The effect of such sequences cannot be entirely explained, but it seems to be due, in part at least, to definite progressions of vowels from the point of view of phonetics. Of this type is the magnificent passage from *Ecclesiastes*,

> Or ever the silver cord be loosed, or the golden bowl be broken. . . .[8]

If one simply pronounces in order the accented vowels of that sequence he will find that they produce a pleasant effect. Similar, but less elaborate, is Coleridge's

> Ancestral voices prophesying war.[9]

Unfortunately for our purposes, one of the most impressive vowel sequences in English verse happens to be in an unquotable limerick having to do with an aged courtezan of Baroda.

Rhyme is so familiar as to require no more than passing comment. It is a specifically literary use of timbre, and is really only an extended form of assonance. Like assonance and alliteration, it works hand in hand with rhythm, and no accurate definition of rhyme can omit the question of stress.

None of these literary uses of timbre is an essential of the writer's art. Timbre itself, of course, must be present in any use of words, since a word, acoustically considered, is nothing more than a definite sequence of timbres; but such devices as imitation, alliteration, assonance, and rhyme are all accessories available for the writer who chooses to use them rather than inevitable parts of the writer's—or even the poet's—art. It is certainly possible to find good poetry in which there is no more alliteration or assonance than can be explained on the basis of pure chance. Rhyme is so conspicuous that accidental occurrences of rhymed words seem faulty; hence the poet is forced to make a deliberate choice either to seek it (usually according to some set and repeating pattern) or rigorously to reject it. But since rhythm is alone powerful enough to organize verse into a pleasing structure, the poet does not feel compelled to employ rhyme. The large body of excellent blank verse goes far towards supporting Milton's uncharitable view in his preface to *Paradise Lost*:

> . . . Rime being no necessary Adjunct or true Ornament of Poem or good Verse, in longer Works especially, but the Invention of a barbarous Age, to set off wretched matter and lame Meeter, . . . a thing of itselfe, to all judicious eares, triveal and of no true musical delight; which consists only in apt Numbers, fit quantity of Syllables, and the sense variously drawn out from one Verse into another.

The contention that the ear's proper pleasure in verse is derived entirely from rhythm is particularly interesting. French poetry cannot have blank verse because the language does not have syllabic stress: there can be no iambic pentameter, for example, because there can be no iambs; and in French poetry a line can be completely characterized simply by stating how many syllables it contains. Hence the line as a metrical unit alone can hardly exist, and rhyme takes the place of metrics as the essential organizing force in French poetry.

The devices of alliteration, assonance, and rhyme have no parallels in music because music does not have those constant and rapid shifts of timbre which make them possible in language. The term *rhyme* is sometimes used in a musical connection, but this use is an illegitimate extension of the literary term, and is applied to a phenomenon of rhythm.

One other characteristic of the literary use of timbre must be noted. The human voice itself is a wind instrument of the reed family, and each voice has its own recognizable timbre—just as, less obviously, each piano or violin has its individual sound. But when a poem is read, we have two aspects of timbre to consider: the quality of the voice itself, and the quality of the particular speech-sound which is being pronounced at any given time. With a remarkable power of analysis, the ear keeps these two aspects distinct. If we can recognize a friend's voice when he says "oh," we can also identify it when he says "ah." At the same time, we recognize "oh" as the "same" sound, no matter who says it. It is possible that poets writing for a particular person—d'Annunzio writing plays for Duse, for example—may take into account the timbre of the individual voice; but in general the poet cannot select his reader's voice, and hence he is concerned only with timbres in their function as the distinguishing sounds of language.

HARMONY AND COUNTERPOINT, while not strictly parallel with rhythm, pitch, and timbre, may well be considered here. For our

present purposes they need not be distinguished, since both are the results of simultaneously produced tones. They have fascinated many
poets, and numerous devices have been tried in attempts to find some
literary equivalent, but invariably the problem of simultaneity has
proved an insuperable barrier. We shall not find it necessary to consider harmony and counterpoint separately unless we find that literature has some way of producing two things at the same time, for it is
clearly unnecessary to look for the species in literature if the genus
itself does not exist.

There are certain words which must be carefully watched in any
discussion of this nature, and *harmony* is one of them. The word has a
long and honorable history as it is sometimes applied to poetry, and if
this sense be clearly understood there can be no harm in referring to the
"harmony" or "harmonies" of a poet's versification. The great danger
lies in the ease with which unconscious puns are made: if poems can
be said to have harmony, and the same statement can be made about
musical compositions, there is more than a remote danger of un-
critically jumping to the conclusion that poetry and music have harmony as one of their common attributes. The fact is that when we
speak of harmony in poetry we refer only to general pleasantness of
sound, whereas when we apply the term musically we refer to the pitch-
relationships of simultaneously produced tones. In the discussion of
the rôle played by pitch in literature, the term *melody* (as applied to
poetry) was studiously avoided for the same reason. When we consider
that the "melody" of a poem and its "harmony" mean the same thing,
we realize that when these words are applied to poetry they mean
something quite different from their musical significance. In order to
avoid any mere confusion of words, I shall use terms like *harmony* and
melody only in their strict musical sense.

The general basis of harmony and counterpoint—the simultaneous
presentation of two or more tones—presents such mechanical difficulties
as to be practically impossible in literature. It is, of course, a matter
of frequent occurrence for two or more persons to talk at the same
time, and at a party where there are several conversations going on at
once it is perfectly possible to station oneself between two groups and
follow two conversations simultaneously. Likewise, of course, one can
read a book and follow a conversation at the same time—provided
neither the book nor the conversation has enough to it to be really
worth following at all. These possibilities of grasping two streams of
language at once are clear enough, but they no more give an equivalent

of counterpoint than would opening the doors of two practice rooms in a conservatory and standing between them. If any artistic purpose is to be served, the parts must be at the same time separate—almost independent—and yet related. There must be some unifying idea behind them, and this requirement rules out the chance occurrence of simultaneous speech.

The drama offers obvious possibilities for contrapuntal technique, but they have never been exploited. Occasionally a comic playwright will allow two characters to speak at the same time for a sentence or so, but the idea seems to have gone no further than that. Contrapuntal singing frequently involves contrapuntal texts, but as a rule in passages of this type the words are either indistinguishable or irrelevant.

There have been a few attempts at poems of a literarily contrapuntal nature. Sacheverell Sitwell has written one entitled *On Hearing Four Bands Play at Once in a Public Square* [10] which is printed in four parallel columns, apparently with the intention that these columns are to be read simultaneously. One might as well compose a contrapuntal duet for trumpet and oboe, to be played by a single performer—the thing is physically impossible. And the same statement applies to any work in which one is required to read two sequences of words at the same time.

Most of the writers who have been haunted by a desire for counterpoint—and there are more of them than one might think—have seen from the beginning the impossibility of an exact literary parallel, and consequently have sought some device that might be a rough sort of equivalent. The commonest attempt at a solution has involved the idea of rapid shifts of attention from one thing to another. Conrad Aiken, who has concerned himself long and fruitfully with the problem of adapting musical effects and devices for literary use, once wrote a rather detailed discussion of his "hankering" for counterpoint and the methods by which he sought to secure it in poetry. [11] Omitting such devices as balance and contrast, which are obviously different from counterpoint, his chief solution lies in this alternation of figures, moods, etc. One of Aiken's poems, [12] originally published with the title *A Counterpoint*, is a good illustration of the method in its simplest form. It deals with two persons, an old man and a young woman, living in separate apartments, one above the other, and though structurally there is simply a rapid alternation between them as they "pursue their separate dreams," a constant interrelation between the two sets of independent thoughts is kept up. If such an alternation is counterpoint, however, the device was at its height in literature before it was even known in music. The skaldic poets of Iceland were in the habit of alternating the phrases of two different sentences, so that both ran simultaneously. In the following verse,[13] composed by King Harald at the Battle of Stamford Bridge, the part in parentheses is one sentence, and the rest is another:

> Kriúpum vér firir vópna
> (valtæigs) brokon æighi
> (svá bauð Hilldr) at hialdri
> (haldorð) í bugh skialdar.*

If the rapid alternation of literary materials could really be called counterpoint, we should have to concede that the art of literary counterpoint has been in a decline for the past thousand years.

The contention that such devices constitute true counterpoint has frequently been supported by the statement that, in the case of any literary treatment of two more or less distinct plots or viewpoints, both are simultaneously present in the reader's mind, even though they must necessarily be presented separately. According to this theory, any Italian sonnet is necessarily contrapuntal, for the sestet is different in content and approach from the octave, and yet is modified by the effect which the octave has already created. The same thing would be even more obviously true of the common type of adventure story in which the principal characters are separated: one chapter leaves the hero tied down on a pile of dynamite with only an inch more of fuse to burn before it explodes; and the next chapter leaves the heroine (three hundred miles away) treed by a pack of wolves and so faint from hunger that she will fall unless the hero can get there during the next fifteen minutes. Certainly in all literature what is being said is strongly affected by what has been said earlier. We have already pointed out that for this reason any reader must have an adequate memory. But precisely the same conditions prevail in music: the second theme of a movement in sonata form is dependent for a good deal of its effect on the principal theme which precedes it. Yet in music, where true and

---

* Creep we before of weapons
  (of hawk-land) the clash not
  (so bade the goddess) in battle
  (true of word) into the shelter of a shield.

I have translated this very literally in order to keep the wording of the original and demonstrate the interweaving of sentences. Noting that "the goddess of hawk-land" is an elaborate figure of speech for "fair lady," and rearranging into idiomatic English, we get: "In battle we do not creep behind our shields before the clash of weapons— (the fair lady, true of word, gave me this order)."

literal counterpoint exists, we can easily see that both the nature and the effect of this modification by memory are utterly different from those of counterpoint. In literature they are equally different, and any attempt to identify them with each other is simply a confusion of terms resulting from a desperate attempt to force the musical analogy.

There are, however, literary devices by which two different things can be presented with a sort of simultaneity. The simplest of these is the genuine pun. Stephen Leacock tells of standing with a friend in an old-fashioned saloon with a free-lunch counter. A drunk picked up a sandwich, bit into it once, and then furiously slammed it against the mirror over the bar. Whereupon Leacock's friend remarked quietly, "There's food for reflection." By means of puns on two of the words, this remark actually succeeds in saying two utterly different things at the same time. But it is a serious mistake to think of the pun as only a form of jesting. It is also the basis for a great deal of serious literature, particularly in the school of "metaphysical wit" which had its finest representative in John Donne and has been sedulously revived by both poets and critics in recent years. A simple example from Milton will show the possibilities. The captive Samson, in giving his past history to the Chorus, says:

> . . . the next I took to Wife
> (O that I never had! fond wish too late)
> Was in the Vale of Sorec, Dalila,
> That specious Monster, my accomplisht snare.[14]

The word *accomplisht* here says two things simultaneously as clearly as does the jest of Leacock's friend: (1) Delilah is wily, clever, sly; (2) she has already achieved her deceitful end, and Samson's downfall is a *fait accompli*.

If we are looking for literary counterpoint this comes close enough to be a very honorable miss, but it is certainly not a clean hit. What we have here is the presentation of *one* thing which has two aspects—somewhat like a sustained note that, by enharmonic change, is simultaneously G-sharp in one key and A-flat in another. We do not have *two* verbal symbols presented together. The same objection holds for the associations of a word, as distinct from its controlled meanings. In this respect one might be tempted to say that a word can easily have a literal meaning plus a sustaining background of suggestions, and hence can be something analogous to a chord. The uncontrolled associations of words in Squire's sonnet take full advantage of this possibility. Thus, in the first line, *purple* suggests (1) a sensuous impression, (2) royalty, and the associated ideas of magnificence and luxury, and (3) blood (specifically, the blood of Christ as a retrospective meaning after the word *chalice*); and *chalice* suggests (1) the Grail and the communion service, (2) a general idea of precious metals and gems, and (3) a flower. But again we have, not two things, but one word with different relationships.

The stage does offer one possibility of genuine counterpoint, not in simultaneous speech (which we have already rejected) but in action. In many Elizabethan dramas a clearly defined sub-plot alternates with the principal plot, and in the alternation of plots such plays are parallels to the adventure-story already considered. But occasionally we find a scene in which both plots are carried on at the same time. In this case the speeches—even the words—will come one at a time, but they will have very different effects for different characters. If we are confined to a reading of the play these effects will merely parallel the simultaneous meanings of single words. But on the stage the facial expressions, gestures, and general conduct of the actors can very easily give two contrapuntal lines of action. During the scene in which the murder of Duncan is revealed a good performance indicates Macbeth's consciousness of the suspicion directed against him—a consciousness which leads him to overshoot the mark in self-exculpation. It also shows Lady Macbeth's cool awareness of what is going on, her attempts to check her husband, and finally her decision to distract attention by fainting. And along with this we have the collective action of Macduff, Lennox, Banquo, and the other Scottish nobles; they know that this is no time or place for an accusation of murder against Macbeth, but they watch him narrowly and exchange such significant glances that their thoughts are clear to the murderers as well as to the audience.

Nevertheless, the impossibility of true counterpoint in literature still stands. If we take the purely literary element in this scene—the speeches, as they are printed in the book—we find one thing at a time with only such contrapuntal implications as have already been considered. From this point of view the plural significance depends entirely on memory and the different possible relationships of the single word or sentence. It is only by introducing the non-literary medium of physical activity that we can produce different and contrapuntal effects simultaneously.

CHAPTER V

Vocal Music: General Considerations

HAVING examined the elements out of which poetry and music are constructed, we can now go on with better understanding to an examination of the relationships between the two as they occur in complete works (instead of artificially isolated feet, bars, timbres, and pitches) and in the actual practice of writers and composers. The simplest relationship with which to begin the investigation is the obvious one of vocal music.

Any piece of vocal music, from nursery rhyme to *Missa Solemnis,* is of the same general nature, for it is simply a simultaneous presentation of a literary work and a musical work. These two works can always be separated at will and examined separately by merely reading the text or by substituting instruments for voices—or, if we wish to disturb even the timbre as little as possible, by letting the singer simply sing some pure vowel. If both the music and the text lose by such a divorce it is clear that a genuinely artistic combination has been effected, for in the work of art the whole is always paradoxically greater than the sum of the parts. If both gain by the separation, their union was obviously a misalliance in the first place. If the separation makes no difference, the chances are that neither element by itself matters. And, finally, if one gains or remains unaffected by the divorce and the other loses, it becomes evident that the loser was never more than a parasite. Anyone who tries the experiment of such separation—and it is a highly interesting and profitable experiment—will soon become convinced that all these possibilities do actually occur.

From earliest antiquity music and poetry have been referred to as sister arts. We might add that the sisters were brought up together and were inseparable in youth, but as they have matured they have developed their own private concerns, until now they do not visit each other long or frequently. And this is perhaps just as well, for they tend to get on each other's nerves, and music, who was afraid to venture out

alone until she got well up in years, has lately developed a very domi-
neering attitude.

All this metaphorical statement is literally true. Among most primitive peoples poetry has always been chanted, and instruments have
been used only to accompany the chant. Though we know a good deal
about the mechanics, mathematics, and philosophy of Greek music, we
know very little about its artistic qualities; but we do know that the
poet and the lyre were almost inseparable. When they did separate, as
Plato observes, music almost ceased to exist, "for when there are no
words, it is very difficult to recognize the meaning of the harmony and
rhythm, or to see that any worthy object is imitated by them." [1] Therefore instrumental music is "exceedingly rude and coarse." Later, Greece
and Rome developed poetry intended only to be read, but not, it would
seem, much music independent of poetry (or dancing).

With the rise of the ballad, the folk-epic, and ecclesiastical music
in the Middle Ages, the tendency was for the union to become even
closer. The troubador, trouvère, scop, or Minnesinger was by definition
both poet and composer, and presumably a good deal of his composition of poem and music was simultaneously carried on. It is really only
during the Renaissance that the modern separation began, and the
insistence of Ronsard that poetry and music should go together is an
indication that the necessity of this union was no longer a self-evident
proposition. The increasing independence of music is shown in his
statement that unsung poetry is as bad as instrumental music: the poet
is to write with the musician in mind, "for poetry without instruments,
or without the grace of one or many voices, is no more satisfactory
than are instruments when they are not brought to life by the melody
of an agreeable voice." [2] But Ronsard was fighting a losing battle. In
spite of the attempt of the Italian founders of opera to rediscover the
integration of music and drama which had existed in Greek tragedy, in
spite of the example of such poet-composers as Campion, the two arts
drifted further apart. There have been distinguished exceptions, but
during the last three centuries the general rule has been that the poet
knows little about music and cares less, and that the composer, especially the composer of opera, regards the poet as merely a sort of
beater who must clear his path and stir up the game he intends to bag.

An Italian opera company was once visiting London and making a
great success with Verdi's *Otello*. One day the leading tenor came to
the manager in complete bewilderment. Everywhere he went, he said,
people kept saying "Shakespeare—*Otello*—*Otello*—Shakespeare." With

a mixture of despair and indignation, the tenor finally demanded, "Vat *ees* Shakespeare?" The manager stood lost in thought for a moment. "Shakespeare?" he shrugged. "Oh, he ees ze librettist." Wagner wrote his own plays in order to achieve a more perfect fusion of text and music, but one may be allowed to wonder whether he was not equally actuated by his obsession with being the whole show.

Remarkably little attention has been given to the relationship between text and music. The poets have studied their own craft to the extent of classifying meters, stanzas, types, and effects, and have at various periods of their history drawn up complete codifications of the rules of their art. Similarly, the musicians have worked out their elaborate systems of harmony, counterpoint, form, analysis, and orchestration. But anyone who looks for criticism on the musical setting of literary texts will be disappointed. Only occasionally is some poet, like Sidney Lanier or Robert Bridges, both willing and competent to deal with the problem. Both these poets wrote odes (Lanier's was called a cantata) to be set to music and performed at public celebrations. Both knew enough about the composer's problems to realize that a special sort of poetry would be required for such a purpose. And, finally, both were moved, partly by interest in the subject and partly by public misunderstanding of the poems so written, to write essays giving some explanation of their principles and methods.

It is interesting to notice that both poets, being perfectionists, were not too sanguine as to the possibilities. Lanier writes elsewhere that "The mixture of meaning and tone is merely mechanical, not chemical." [3] In the essay [4] on his text for a *Centennial Cantata* he is concerned with the fact that the development of the orchestra has changed some of the problems of vocal music, and this fact leads to his first general principle, that "In any poem offered by a poet to a modern musical composer, the central idea, as well as every important subordinate idea, should be drawn only from that class of intellectual conceptions which is capable of being adequately expressed by orchestral instruments." (This first principle is not far from a complete abdication of the poet in favor of the composer. Carried to its logical conclusion, it makes the poet simply the writer of a set of notes for a piece of program music.) The second principle, derived from the first, is that only general ideas can be used, since they alone are capable of orchestral expression. Lanier's final and least debatable point is that, if the proportions of chorus to orchestra will give the chorus any prominence, then "the words of the poem ought to be selected carefully with reference to such quality of tone as they will elicit when sung."

This last principle might seem too obvious to be worth mentioning were it not for the fact that it is very frequently ignored, not only by the poet writing for a composer, but, even less excusably, by the translator of a work which has already been composed. I have heard a mass sung in English, in which the last syllable of "Kyrie eleison" was the basis of elaborate and beautiful cadences. But the translator, presumably with the music before him, rendered the phrase "Lord, have mercy on us." Hence at each repetition, instead of dying out beautifully, the cadence closed with a hiss, *forte*. This is merely one of any number of possible examples of writers and translators who have written for music with apparent unconcern about qualities of sound.

Bridges is particularly concerned with a theory which he opposes, and hence he devotes a good deal of his essay to showing that a "declamatory" style is certainly not the best way to make a musical setting of a poem. But he is not too certain that there is any effective way, and the major part of his discussion is devoted to stating "what appear to me to be impediments in the way of this announced happy marriage of music and poetry . . ." [5] Since some of these impediments lie in basic differences between the two arts, we may well consider them in some detail.

The first crux comes in the question of repetition. We shall have to consider it more fully in the discussion of musical forms, but the essential difficulty is that music demands far more repetition than literature can tolerate. Hence the composer must decide whether he will indulge in the familiar and wearisome repetition of his poet's phrases, or whether he will leave his music with an effect of incompleteness. Bridges remarks that a declamatory setting, being based on the rhythms and inflections of speech, will simply intensify this difficulty, for the more the repeated passage suggests speech, the more obvious will the absurdity of its repetitions become. He offers no way out of this dilemma of repetition, and no completely satisfactory solution has ever been found, but a number of possibilities have been explored.

The most obvious of these is the stanzaic song. If the composer has chosen a poem written in a number of formally identical stanzas, he can compose the music for one of them, and repeat it for each successive stanza, thus achieving musical repetition along with textual variety. Folk-ballads, hymns, and a great many other types of songs use this device. There are, however, two considerations which keep it from being really satisfactory except in songs which do not aspire to a high artistic level. The repetition thus obtained is not really of the type which music demands, for it is merely mechanical and allows for no progress or heightening of effect. Also, the stanzaic song cannot present an organic union of words and music except in those rare cases, like *Drink to Me Only with Thine Eyes,* where the stanzas are very similar (if not identical) in content and mood. Otherwise, the composer must decide whether to set one stanza well and let the others take their chances with the same music, or whether to make a generally platitudinous setting which, not being particularly appropriate for any stanza, at least cannot be particularly inappropriate. Because of these difficulties, the *durchkomponiertes Lied* (the song composed all the way through instead of for one stanza only) has been the principal type of composition since Schubert's time.

More subtle solutions of the problem have been sought in the employment of repeated accompaniment figures, single lines of melody, or other parts of the general musical fabric, without any set scheme of formal return to earlier thematic material. If the poem itself has any unity of tone there will be ample possibility of such treatment, as we shall see in a later discussion of Schubert's *Erlkönig.* This method may still leave the composer wishing occasionally to repeat for purely musical purposes passages which poetically cannot bear the repetition, but at least it seems to be the most satisfactory compromise.

The conclusion of a piece of vocal music, particularly one of a declamatory nature, presents another difficulty. Many purely musical forms conclude with repetition, usually of the opening passages, but if such a pattern is used the previous problem remains. The use of climax is also a normal way of concluding a musical composition, but music is accustomed to work up to more climaxes in the same space of time than poetry can or should use. Besides, musical climaxes are usually more definite—so much so that they would appear exaggerated when imposed on the poem, and the poet usually cannot supply the climax almost at the end, where it is most appropriate in music.

Since we have already gone into some detail about the difference between musical and poetic rhythm, we need hardly pause over Bridges' contention that this difference presents a serious obstacle to the composition of good vocal music. The tendency is for music either to ignore the rhythms of its text, or to pay only very superficial respect to them: "Even the universally recognized fitness of the interpretation of a common measur in verse by the corresponding common measur in music depends much more on the power and satisfying completeness

of the musical form in itself than on any right relation which obtains
between words and music under these conditions." In his essays [6] on
chanting and speech-rhythms, Bridges attempted to obviate the difficulties by devising a more flexible notation for musical time, based
primarily on the idea of having a longer and a shorter time-value for
each type of note—longer and shorter quarter-notes, for example—the
difference being indicated by a difference in the actual size of the notes.
Along with this, various other complications of speech rhythm are indicated, so that, according to Bridges and some choir-directors who have
tried out his system, it is possible to represent accurately in musical
notation the normal rhythms of the texts of the psalms. So far as I
know, however, Bridges never suggested the extension of this system
beyond the chant. Its complications would certainly become unmanage-
able in concerted music of any degree of intricacy. Also, it may be
pointed out that his method did and could do nothing to reconcile
musical and literary rhythm. It merely enabled the latter to get revenge by forcing its rhythms on music, instead of itself being forced
into musical rhythms.

Bridges' next point has to do with the suggestive powers of the
two arts.

A certain disposition of ideas in words produces a whole result quite out of
proportion to the parts: and if it is askt what music can do best, it is something
in the same way of indefinit suggestion. Poetry is here the stronger, in that its
suggestion is more definitely directed. Music is the stronger in the greater force
of the emotion raised. It would seem therefore that music could hav no more fit
and congenial task than to heighten the emotion of some great poetic beauty,
the direction of which is supply'd by the words.

A declamatory method, however, cannot do this, for it competes with
poetry on its own ground and thus

renounces its own highest power of stirring emotion, because thatt resides in
pure musical beauty, and is dependent on its mysterious quality; for one may
say that its power is in proportion to its remoteness from common direct understanding, and that just in so far as its sounds are understood to mean something
definit, they lose their highest emotional power. It would follow from this that
the best musical treatment of passages of great poetic beauty is not to declaim
them, but, as it were, to woo them and court them and caress them, and deck
them with fresh musical beauties; approaching them tenderly now on one side,
now on another, and to keep a delicat reserve which shall leave their proper
unity unmolested.

The distinction between the *definite* and controlled suggestions of
poetry and the *indefinite* but often stronger emotional suggestion of

music is a basic one in the problems of program music. We need only note here that, as a consequence of this distinction, Bridges reduces the composer to what many musicians would consider a secondary rôle: he is not to take the poem as his raw material and try to make something of it. Rather, he is to take it as a perfect thing—much as a jeweler takes a diamond that has already been cut and polished—and to supply a setting which will emphasize its beauty.

Music can be particularly useful in helping to conceal the unmusical nature of "the bare ugly words which are the weakness and unkindness of language," but this must be done, not by imitating the effects of speech, but by being musical precisely where the poem is not. Also, we have already seen that the rhythms, pitches, and (in so far as they can be said to exist at all) the "tunes" of speech are far more restricted than are those of music; hence the composer who takes speech as his model is voluntarily surrendering the greater part of his art. The net result of Bridges' entire discussion is a complete condemnation of any musical setting which models itself on the inflections of the speaking voice. This point of view is the exact opposite of that of such critics as Combarieu, who, though making many reservations, find the ultimate nature of music in an extension of the emotional element of speech. Combarieu's general thesis is that all primitive language expresses a dualism consisting of (1) an intellectual concept and (2) an emotional attitude.[7] The separation of music and language has led to a specialization by which language tended to confine itself to the first of these elements, and music to the second. "Not only do the poet and the musician not speak the same language or obey the same laws; they do not even think with the same faculty."[8] A rigorous interpretation of this theory will, of course, admit the great difficulties in the way of effectively combining two such disparate arts, but it will also insist that only by such combination can anything be completely expressed. The aesthetics of music is full of such contradictions as these of Bridges and Combarieu. It is sufficient for our present purposes to recognize them without attempting the quixotic task of reconciling them.

One important consideration, however, goes far towards obviating many of the difficulties which beset the musical setting of poetic texts —a consideration which, to the best of my knowledge, no critic writing on this subject has mentioned. The sense of hearing lends itself very readily to the setting up of associations. From Ronsard through Gérard de Nerval and on down to Eugene O'Neill,* writers have testified to the ease with which music calls up events associated with it, even by sheer accident, at the time of previous hearings; and the associations of a first hearing are generally recognized as particularly powerful. The words sung to a piece of music have an inseparably close connection with the music itself in time and place, no matter what we may think of their relationship in terms of such aesthetic considerations as are raised by Lanier and Bridges. Though songs are occasionally transcribed for purely instrumental performance (or, less ambitiously, are simply hummed or whistled), the chances are that on both the first and most subsequent hearings of any piece of vocal music, we will hear it *sung*—that is, we will hear the text and its music together. A powerful association is thus set up by means of which, unless there is an intolerable and obvious inappropriateness, they soon seem to belong together. The difficulty of making the complete mental separation of text and music which was suggested at the beginning of this chapter is a clear proof of the power of such an association, and we shall see later that the *Leitmotiv* is a simple device calculated to take full advantage of it. The working of this principle is seen in the fact that one rarely, I believe, fully approves of a musical setting of an already familiar poem *at the first hearing*. The poem has its own associations already, and there is a strong tendency to resent the intrusion of the new ones. But after a few hearings of the song we find that we cannot read the poem without thinking of the music also. In the case of words and music we must revise the old adage and say that familiarity breeds consent.

It would be interesting for someone with sufficient time, apparatus, and "subjects" to check this association experimentally. He might have a considerable number of persons record their readings of certain biblical passages, including, for example, "Comfort ye, my people . . . ," "There were shepherds abiding in the field . . . ," and "I know that my Redeemer liveth. . . ." These recordings would then be analyzed for pitch and time relationships. Then, and not before, the experimenter would play for all his readers a series of musical pieces, including in-

---

* In *The Moon of the Caribbees*, Smitty has objected to some music because it brings him such "beastly memories." The Donkey Man has surmised that there is a woman in the case, and has said that the way to handle women is to knock them down if they don't obey you—and this is also the way to win their love. The conversation ends:
SMITTY (Pompously). Gentlemen don't hit women.
THE DONKEY MAN (Placidly). No; that's why they has mem'ries when they hears music.

strumental transcriptions of these passages from Handel's *Messiah*, and would simply have his readers identify the music if they could. (This process would check their real familiarity with the music far more accurately than would, say, asking them if they knew the oratorio.) The experimenter would then compare the recorded readings of those persons who knew the music with the recorded readings of those who did not. It is highly unscientific to guess the results of an experiment which has not been performed, but I feel certain that those readers who knew the music of their texts in *The Messiah* would, considered as a group, show far more uniformity in the time and pitch relationships of their readings than would the group who did not know the music, and that this uniformity would be in the nature of an approximation to the musical treatment.

With these general problems in mind, we can now proceed to the examination of some of the points of view which a composer may adopt in his setting of a literary text. It should, of course, be clear from the beginning that exact border lines cannot be drawn, and that no song is an absolutely pure example of any one method, but the analyses and discussions in the following chapters will show that there are some general types which can be clearly differentiated.

CHAPTER VI

The Literal Setting of Vocal Music

WHAT may be called the literal method of setting a poetic text to music consists of allowing the music to fasten on and exploit any word of the text for which musical analogies can possibly be found. The antiquity of this method is amply shown by the fact that almost since the beginning of independent musical criticism it has been scornfully attacked as a pointless and meaningless method of composing. Through the attacks themselves we can arrive at a clear idea of exactly what is involved in this type of vocal music. In the preface to *A Book of Ayres* (published in 1601 and containing Campion's first published songs), Philip Rosseter protests against both contrapuntal pedantry and literalness:

> But there are some, who to appear the more deepe, and singular in their judgement, will admit no Musicke but that which is long, intricate, bated with fugue, chained with sincopation, and where the nature of everie word is precisely exprest in the Note, like the old exploded action in Comedies, when if they did pronounce *Memeni,* they would point to the hinder part of their heads, if *Video,* put their finger in their eye. But such childish observing of words is altogether ridiculous, and we ought to maintaine as well in Notes, as in action a manly cariage, gracing no word, but that which is eminent and emphaticall.[1]

Rosseter, it will be noticed, does not necessarily condemn literal settings *in toto;* he merely objects to overdoing the thing, and particularly to applying careful attention to the literal rendition of every word instead of reserving it for the more significant ones only.

    Charles Avison (familiar to readers of Browning because of the latter's "Parleying" with him) goes much further. His *Essay on Musical Expression,*[2] published a century and a half later, makes a clear distinction between *expression* of the ideas of a poem and *imitation* of its words. Expression is regarded as the real aim of the composer, and imitation may be tolerated only in so far as it can contribute to this end. The entire essay is interesting as one of the first real attempts to grapple with the elusive problems of musical aesthetics, but we can quote here only a part of the section dealing with the literal setting of words:

And, as Dissonance and schocking Sounds cannot be called Musical Expression; so neither do I think, can mere Imitation of several other Things be entitled to this Name, which, however, among the Generality of Mankind hath often obtained it. Thus the gradual rising or falling of the Notes in a long Succession, is often used to denote Ascent or Descent, broken Intervals, to denote an interrupted Motion, a number of quick Divisions,* to describe Swiftness or Flying, Sounds resembling Laughter, to describe Laughter; with a number of other Contrivances of a parallel Kind, which it is needless here to mention. Now all these I should chuse to call Imitation, rather than Expression; because, it seems to me, that their Tendency is rather to fix the Hearers [*sic*] Attention on the Similitude between the Sounds and the Things which they describe, and thereby to excite a reflex Act of the Understanding, than to affect the Heart and raise the Passions of the Soul. . . . This Distinction seems more worthy of our Notice at present, because some very eminent Composers have attached themselves chiefly to the Method here mentioned; and seem to think they have exhausted all the Depths of Expression, by a dextrous Imitation of the Meanings of a few particular Words, that occur in the Hymns or Songs which they set to Music. Thus, were one of these Gentlemen to express the following Words of *Milton,*

> . . . Their Songs
> *Divide* the Night, and *lift* our Thoughts to Heav'n,

it is highly probable, that upon the Word *divide*, he would run a *Division* of half a Dozen Bars; and on the subsequent Part of the Sentence, he would not think he had done the Poet Justice, or *risen* to that *Height* of Sublimity which he ought to express, till he had climbed up to the very Top of his Instrument, or at least as far as the human Voice could follow him.

Precisely. The nature and dangers of musical imitation might be more sympathetically stated, but not more accurately.

Avison takes a good many flings at Handel, and certainly intends to include him among the "very eminent Composers" who "have attached themselves chiefly to the Method here mentioned." *The Messiah* had been well received in Dublin at its first performance ten years before Avison's essay appeared, but its English popularity dates from the Foundling Hospital performances beginning in 1750. Hence it seems reasonable to believe that *The Messiah* was one of the works against which Avison's strictures were directed—especially since it contains so

---

* *Divisions* is an old technical term for passages in which the notes of the basic time-scheme are greatly subdivided, such as a passage of thirty-second notes in 4/4 time. This is the point of Juliet's pun (*Romeo and Juliet*, III, v, 29-30):
> Some say the lark makes sweet division;
> This doth not so, for she divideth us.

much imitation of the kind which he condemned. For this reason we shall use *The Messiah* for illustrations of the literal setting of literary texts.

The tenor aria, "Every valley shall be exalted, and every mountain and hill made low; the crooked straight, and the rough places plain," will illustrate most of the general principles. It will be sufficient to give the melodic line alone, for the orchestra does little except to reinforce the voice or echo it during the pauses; also, by this method we shall avoid the vexed question of the additional accompaniments (two bassoons and two flutes are added to this aria) by Mozart *et al*.

We shall pass over phrase (A) for the moment, and return to it later. In (B) we have a triumphant emphasis on the word *be*, and then we come to the first version of the characteristic figuration of *exalted*. In this passage, of course, the meaning of the word is literal, and Handel takes it as literally as possible. There is an introductory brief descent, but the voice soon reaches the lowest note of the phrase (the tonic E), and then begins an elaborate progress upward with occasional brief fluctuations downward which serve only to emphasize the general ascent. This florid passage reaches its highest point on a G♯, from which it drops a major third and comes to rest on the E an octave above its lowest and almost initial point. (Throughout the aria Handel reaches the climax of exaltation on the last note of the accented syllable, and then drops slightly and comes to rest on the final *-ed*.) (C) continues the idea, but this time the process of lifting up is more rapid and decisive: the voice goes up by means of the steps of the tonic chord, holds the high E for emphasis, makes a brief flutter on up to F♯, and slides smoothly down to rest on B. In (D) the process is again long-drawn-out, and the general lines are much the same as those of (B), but the little figure which signifies exaltation by its ascending repetitions is different.

At this point the next part of the text is taken up for the first time, in (E). The phrase first mentioning a mountain makes a steep ascent of an octave to the accented syllable, and falls an octave sheer on the other side. The hill which follows is carefully differentiated: it is a whole tone lower than the mountain, it is almost symmetrical, and its contours are smoother. The "made low" with which phrase (E) concludes is an obvious and literal application of the idea. In (F), the crooked is represented by an alternation of two notes a tone apart, with the effect of sinuosity emphasized by the phrasing in pairs—all this is obvious contrast to the sustained half-note of "straight." After

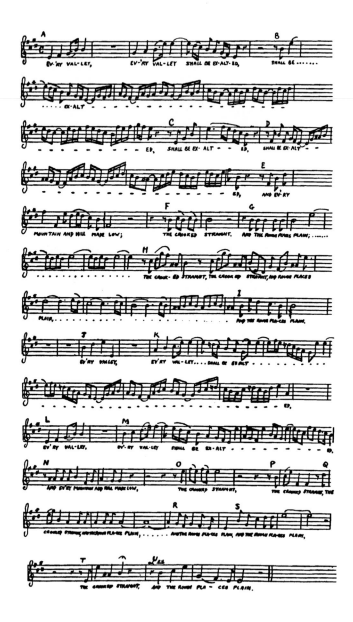

a half-rest, the same pitch and idea are continued into (G) (the rough places being passed over without notice for the moment), and the same B continues for a half-note into the word plain, which then leaps to the high tonic, a more exalted position. Here it is sustained for some time, keeping the E as its smooth level, but making slight and short undulations of a semitone: the rough places are to become slightly rolling prairie, not a dead level. Superficially, these undulations in (G) bear a resemblance to the representation of the crooked in (F), but their variation in pitch is only half as great, and they are smoothly phrased, thus making a sharp contrast with the rough phrasing of "the crooked." (H) represents the idea of crookedness in a more irregular fashion, and applies the same general configuration to the "rough places"; when that has been done, a different version of a generally smooth, but somewhat more undulating plain is given. We can even see some representation of roughness and plain-ness in (I) if we feel so inclined, but it is such a typically Handelian cadence that the words can hardly have influenced it.

After this cadence there is a general return to the material which opened the aria; hence it is now necessary to go back and consider (A). In the first statement of the text the musical imitations are the exact opposite of what might be expected. The twice-repeated "every valley" is an ascending figure in (A), and is higher the second time than the first. Similarly, the first occurrence of "shall be exalted" comes straight *down* the scale. The failure to imitate the idea of *valley* in (A) is probably due to purely musical (i.e., non-imitative) considerations: the ascending phrase makes a striking beginning and forecasts the general upward motion which plays such a conspicuous rôle throughout the rest of the aria. It is, of course, impossible to compose on exclusively literal principles. The failure to represent the idea of exaltation in this opening phrase, however, seems actually to rest on a principle of imitation involving the tenses of the passage. The valley is not yet exalted, but it *shall be;* hence the first statement does not represent the future fact. This interpretation is supported by the great emphasis placed on *shall be* at the opening of (B), and once the futurity of the process is underlined, the process itself can be represented.

With (J) a general return to the first part of the aria begins, and (J) is parallel to the first phrase of (A), but this time the valley is represented by a drop of an octave. (The same device was used for a *mountain* in (E), but there the emphasis was on the top, or highest note; mountains and valleys are really only different points of view, according to whether the attention is directed to the elevation between the depressions or to the depression between the elevations.) (K) is parallel to the second phrase of (A) and to (B), but the first half of the "exalted" phrase uses smooth descents offset by sharp upward jerks; the second half follows the general pattern of (B) and (D). (L) and (M) are parallel to (J) and (K)—and hence to the first part of (A) and the whole of (B)—(L) being, in fact, an exact repetition of (A), for formal rather than imitative reasons. (M) ingeniously combines the running descents and upward leaps found in (K) with the general idea of gradual ascent, for each of the descending figures ends on a higher note than its predecessor. It is almost as if the valleys are being jerked up but are sliding back down, though never going back to a position quite as low as that which they occupied before the immediately preceding lift. (N) includes only a very narrow range of pitch, but within that range the relationships are clear: *mountain, hill,* and *low* occupy three consecutive *descending* degrees of the scale. (O) repeats the figure of (F), and (P) and (Q) reproduce in a different form the essential ideas of crookedness, straightness, and plain-ness, this last quality being given particular emphasis by the fact that the word *plain* is sustained on the same note for seven beats. From this point onwards Handel is primarily concerned with repeating these phrases in such a way as to form an effective conclusion, but the sustained *plain* of (S) (six beats this time) and the unexpected A♯ of (T) still continue the imitative effect.

This analysis has been given in considerable detail in order to show that, though other considerations must necessarily enter in, the entire aria is really composed literally, and is devoted to a musical imitation of the ideas contained in the words *valley, exalt, mountain, hill, low, crooked, straight, rough,* and *plain.* A consideration of these words brings us to Avison's third rule as to how far music may be imitative: "As Music can only imitate Motions and Sounds, and the *Motions* only imperfectly; it will follow, that musical Imitation ought never to be employed in representing Objects, of which Motion or Sound are not the principal Constituents." [3] In this *aria* no words purely descriptive of sound occur, though *low* is used in its musical sense to illustrate the topographical meaning of the text. Also, from one point of view, only *exalt* refers to motion, but the idea of motion is involved in that of change throughout the text: the crooked and the straight are not static, but one is to be converted into the other. Furthermore, spatial relationships can be, and here are, transposed into temporal ones. Instead of *seeing* a crooked line all at once, we hear it by following its course.

The imitation of both sound and movement can be easily illustrated from other parts of *The Messiah*. As for sound, there is the obvious use of the trumpet in "The Trumpet Shall Sound," and there are also such passages as the following:

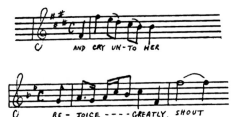

Counterpoint supplies even further possibilities of the imitation of sound. In "He Trusted in God that He Would Deliver Him" the text gives the words of the scorners in the crowd. The fugal structure of the chorus, by the confusion of words which it involves, gives an admirable imitation of the confusion of taunts from the mob. A similar use of counterpoint is made in "The Lord Gave the Word," where the phrase "great was the company of the preachers" gives, both by confusion of words and by its multiplicity of notes, a suggestion and to some extent an imitation of a great crowd. And we find imitation of sound and of motion combined in

Imitation of motion alone is equally common. A famous passage in Haydn's *Creation* shows how "with sudden leap the flexible tiger appears," and, later, how "in long dimension creeps with sinuous trace the worm." (Speaking of musical menageries, some animals are kind enough to have both their sounds and their motions imitable, and hence to give the composer his choice. In Handel's *Israel in Egypt* the frogs are represented by their hopping, but in Haydn's *Seasons* by their croaks shall ye know them.)

In *The Messiah* also there are numerous imitations of motion:

This shows the idea of ascent which we have already seen on the word *exalted,* and which can also be found in "Why Do the Nations" on "the kings of the earth rise *up*"; and in "For Behold, Darkness Shall Cover the Earth" on "but the Lord shall *arise.*" Other types of motion are shown by such phrases as the following:

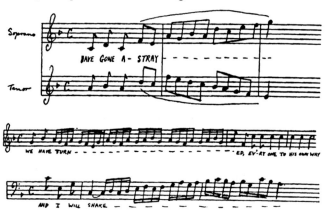

In the first of these examples the use of two voices enables Handel to embody the essential idea of the motion in the passage describing it, for going astray naturally implies separation from something. The second example not only has the obvious turning, but it suggests (and here we are on the borderline between imitation and expression, to use Avison's terms) the individual stubbornness amid the general confusion, in that when the voice has once finished the indecisive turning and decided on its way, it keeps to it with reiterated emphasis. Here again contrapuntal structure aids imitation, for always one voice is still "turning" while another discovers its own way and sticks to it.

Though there can be no question that Avison was right in placing some limitation on the ideas which can be musically imitated, we shall have to extend his categories. We have just seen that stubbornness can, to some extent, be imitated musically. Similarly, by using contrast, standing can be imitated, even though it is not, strictly speaking, a motion. Thus, in "I Know That My Redeemer Liveth," we find:

The word *stand*, sustained (against a moving accompaniment) for eight beats, is a clear case of imitation. We have already seen imitations of height, depth, and contour in the aria which was analyzed in detail. Furthermore, since a literal setting is very largely concerned with the words of its text, it is possible to illustrate them by other meanings of the same words—to make puns like the one suggested by Avison on *divide*. Actually, height and depth, if represented by high and low pitches, should probably be classified under this heading, for, in spite of the almost universal association of height with tones of rapid vibration-rates and depth with tones of slow ones, there seems to be no necessary logical connection between them.

Even when all allowances have been made for doubtful possibilities, the range of literal interpretation of a literary text is closely restricted. And its range of artistic effectiveness is even more restricted than its physical possibilities. Avison makes the excellent point that imitative effects in music are much the same as in poetry, and we have already noted both the difficulty of sustaining onomatopoetic effects and the risk of triviality involved in their extensive use. It must be conceded, however, that excellent music can result from literal settings. Even Avison did not say that the hypothetical setting of the lines he quoted from Milton would necessarily be bad; he merely implied that there would be no reason to expect it to be good. Handel's setting of "Every Valley Shall Be Exalted" is a good piece of vocal music and at the same time an extended example of literal setting, but there is no necessary causal relationship between these two facts. The truth probably is that Handel, being Handel, could write excellent music in spite of his conformity with a rather puerile approach to the problems of vocal music.

CHAPTER VII

The Dramatic Setting of Vocal Music

A LITERAL setting of a text seizes on all words which are capable of musical imitation and exploits their possibilities. A dramatic setting, on the other hand, pays little attention to the imitation of single words or ideas. It considers them in context and aims at suggesting or reinforcing the dramatic elements of the total situation. For this purpose it may occasionally use literal imitation, but that imitation will never be felt as an end in itself; it will be employed only in so far as it serves a larger purpose. Almost any word which is capable of musical imitation will illustrate the difference. The extreme literalist, for example, might illustrate the word *shout* by the same musical treatment, regardless of the particular situation in which it happened to occur. Not so the dramatic composer: his treatment of the word (or idea) will depend on a number of considerations far more specific than the general concept of a shout. He will be concerned as to who is shouting to whom, as to whether it is a shout for help or a shout of jubilation, as to whether it is a clear shout from a hilltop or a muffled one from the depths of a cave. Furthermore, he may ignore the word entirely if it occurs casually and in passing—if it is a mere mention of shouting which, in its context, does not demand that the act be performed. On the other hand, he may well present the imitation or suggestion of a shout even when there is no such word in his text, for the circumstances may easily imply a shout which the poet has not specifically mentioned.

A comparison with poetry may help to make the distinction clearer. Browning is famous for having publicized (though not invented) the "dramatic monologue." This is a poetic form in which, though there is only one speaker, the presence and even the remarks of other persons, as well as the immediate situation which called forth the speech, the speaker's character, and many other circumstances, such as the physical surroundings, are indicated. The dramatic monologue differs from the ordinary lyric in several respects. It is like a single speech taken from a play in that it includes the considerations just mentioned. Also, it does not show the poet speaking in his own person, as does the typical lyric; rather, it is dramatic in that the poet, like the dramatist, is speaking through a character and determining his effects not by his own ideas, feelings, or circumstances, but by a projection of himself into the ideas, feelings, circumstances, and character of his fictitious speaker.

Although a dramatic setting is not limited to monologue, it does have many characteristics in common with Browning's poetic form. It involves the same consideration of *all* relevant circumstances, and, perhaps even more important, it demands that the composer work, not from his own personal standpoint, but from a projection of himself into his characters or situations. Handel made such a projection, in an imitative way, in the noise and confusion of the mob in the chorus "He Trusted in God that He Would Deliver Him." Here we know who the speakers are, and under what circumstances their taunts are delivered. Furthermore, we know that their sadistic joy and malicious taunts find no echo in the personal attitude of the composer. If Handel had been composing in his own person at this point, the line just quoted would necessarily be a declaration of faith, and the following "let Him deliver Him if He delight in Him" would become something in the nature of a prayer. But Handel has remained true to the unsympathetic attitude of the mob and thus, in spite of serious restrictions involved by the fugal style of the chorus, has produced an essentially dramatic setting. "Every Valley shall be Exalted," on the other hand, involves merely the setting of the words with no consideration of speaker or circumstances, and thus is imitative without the dramatic element.

A further difference between the two approaches is made clear by two observations of Albert Schweitzer on Bach's handling of his texts. The first is that

Bach does not follow his text line by line, no matter how tempting the episodes it presents; he expresses the characteristic emotional content, the word that seems to him vital for the mood of the whole, in an eloquent melodic motive. He is sure that in so doing he has expressed the poem itself. . . . The first chorus of the cantata *Mache dich, mein Geist, bereit, wache, fleh und bete* (No. 115) is dominated . . . by a soaring, animated motive that symbolises the "wachen" (waking); the music will not be turned from its course by the concept of "beten" (to pray); all Bach does is to bring this home to us by a striking modulation.[1]

This method is in strong contrast to the literal one which snatches at single words. Later, in contending that Bach's settings of texts are pictorial, Schweitzer clarifies the questionable word by the statement that Bach's music "is very often a picture of a situation."[2] Now, the strict painter has a strong tendency to condemn a "picture of a situation" as something amounting to a misunderstanding, if not a perversion, of the painter's art; but any scene from any play may be aptly described in precisely these words. The added comment that Bach, though melodic, is also essentially declamatory helps to make the dramatic basis clear.

As we have already seen, the composer can make a reasonably good musical representation of a limited group of objects or ideas having sound, motion, or some other characteristic of music as a part of their nature. But the composer who aims at a dramatic setting cannot be contented with these. He may—in fact, he almost certainly will—use them as stage properties when they can serve his main purpose, but he must go far beyond them if he is to achieve that purpose. Thus "everything that suggests a motion that can be reproduced in a musical line is represented by Bach in music. He never allows words like 'ascend' and 'uplift' to escape him."[3] But the illustration of these words which can be imitated by obvious musical means is not an end in itself, and anyone who peruses Schweitzer's classifications of Bach's motives will find that literally descriptive ones are subordinate to motives of joy, grief, felicity, terror, peace, and other feelings which cannot be so literally imitated. These things are states of mind, the proper domain of the dramatist, and they are what Avison was demanding when he insisted on expression in music instead of mere imitation.

But how can music suggest these states of mind? Or, to ask the first question first, *can* it express them?

We must answer this question in the affirmative, though we may differ among ourselves as to the exact degree of precision which such suggestion can achieve. This statement is not a mere assumption, nor does it rest on critical authority, although even Hanslick—that inveterate enemy of program music—admitted the possibility. Ultimately, it rests on the simplest of experimental evidence: we know that it can simply because we know that it does. Within reasonable limits all hearers agree in their general characterizations of a specific piece of music as gloomy, merry, agitated, calm, or impetuous, however much they may disagree on such fine distinctions as the difference between melancholy, sad, and resigned music. It follows, then, that music clearly can suggest states of mind, and our next problem is to determine by what means it can suggest them.

Ultimately, the process is probably based on imitation and association. The imitation here is not the simple and obvious kind which makes the rhythm jump when the poet says "jump"—it is, so to speak, an imitation of fact rather than of word. Standing two hundred yards from a road (where facial expressions cannot be seen) one can still watch two persons walking and know that one is vigorous and the other exhausted. He can tell by the way they walk. The vigorous man has a regular, definite tread; he picks his feet up and sets them down with a clearly marked and strong rhythm. But the exhausted man totters as he moves; his feet have a tendency to drag; he is like young Ascanius at the fall of Troy, "following his father with unequal steps." There are, of course, other differences, such as the squared shoulders of the vigorous man and the drooping shoulders of the exhausted man, but the difference of walk alone is sufficient to distinguish the two men. This is basically a difference of rhythm—one of the primary attributes of music.

Now let us suppose that our observer is fishing on the bank of a creek under one of those old-fashioned wooden bridges which seem to be designed primarily as sounding-boards, and that first the vigorous and then the exhausted traveler walks over it. The rhythms which from a distance of two hundred yards were presented only to the eye will now be presented only to the ear, but the fisherman will know just as accurately which man is vigorous and which is weary. In this hypothetical case we have none of the confusion engendered by considerations of the composer's intention or the aesthetic maturity of the listener: we have simply a series of sounds which are, by the very nature of vigor and exhaustion, associated with them. And these sounds can be taken down in musical notation and reproduced by a drummer who has not heard them and does not know whence they are derived. Nevertheless, they are still clearly recognizable in their abstract significance. When the drummer plays one of them it will not reproduce a pictorial image of an exhausted man walking across a bridge, but it will carry with it a suggestion of weariness or exhaustion.

Similarly, there are forms of motion characteristic of other states of mind and body, and these also are available for musical suggestion.

Perhaps the most subtle of man's activities is speech, because as an implement of communication it has had to adapt itself to all his emotional states as well as his concepts. In fact, one school of aesthetics tries to make the rhythms and inflections of speech the ultimate basis of the entire art of music. This is certainly an exaggeration, but it is true that a great many emotional states are regularly accompanied by characteristic patterns of speech. "I think the woman down the street was cursing the cook this morning: I couldn't make out a word she said, but she sounded furious." This is a reasonable inference as to the state of mind of a speaker, drawn entirely from sound patterns which are quite independent of any particular words, and are therefore available for musical use. Similarly, a person whose words are unintelligible may *sound* pleased, surly, bored, frightened, doubtful, drunk, wheedling, etc. And in every case the composer can suggest the state of mind of this person by suggesting the non-verbal attributes of his speech.

Association plays its part also. We cannot be sure whether the footsteps of the exhausted man suggest exhaustion because some inevitable connection between the two lies hidden deep in the nature of things, or whether they suggest it simply because we have heard the sound before in connection with persons whom we knew to be exhausted. As stated here, the question is purely an academic one, but it becomes of some importance when applied to musical suggestion based on the patterns of speech. Music is erroneously supposed to be a universal language. Actually, we cannot understand or appreciate (they are really the same thing) the music of the Chinese without learning its language, nor can they, by the light of nature alone, understand ours. The same thing holds—whether accidentally or not it would be interesting to know—for the patterns of their speech. I have been told that an Occidental, overhearing a pleasant chat between two Chinese coolies, has the impression that one of them will probably spatter the other's brains on the wall in a moment. And even within the Western world, where music is more or less a common language, the patterns of speech vary from nation to nation, though never as startlingly as, say, between English and Chinese. Hence the musical suggestion based on speech is not so inevitable as one based on such a universal thing as walking. In recompense, however, the nuances of speech are much more subtle, and hence if they are grasped when the composer suggests them, their use can more accurately control the hearer's response.

Naturally, the conscious process in a hearer's mind has nothing of the elaborateness of our investigation of its causes. He merely hears certain musical effects and, without a rational process of any kind— without even thinking of a word to describe his impression—gets the feeling of a certain state of mind. It is probably only when pressed for an introspective explanation that he will assert that the music *means* anger. Otherwise, he feels it, precisely as he feels your anger if you bellow "Get out of here!" Only, in this latter case, there is a definable "meaning" as well as the impression of your anger. In the case of an "angry" passage in absolute music, the feeling of anger necessarily remains unattached to any specific person or situation.

All this explains the fact commented on by so many of the musical aestheticians that music presents emotions, or, better, "affections," only in the abstract, and without necessarily giving their causes or particularity. The unyielding advocate of program music sides with the half-crazed protagonist of Tolstoi's *Kreutzer Sonata* in regarding this fact as the curse of music. The defenders of absolute music, on the other hand, agree with Schopenhauer (who found music the only thing in the universe about which one could be enthusiastic) in declaring it to be music's prime glory. Having explained the fact, we need not be concerned here with the claims of either group of partisans.

The thing which language does best, however, is to give precisely this particularity which is beyond the reach of music. It cannot give us the sense of peace as strongly as can a fine composition of "peaceful" music, but it can tell us exactly who is peaceful, where, when, why, and in what surroundings. Thus the best course would seem to be for the poet and the composer to work as a team, the poet in general conveying those particularities which the composer cannot indicate, and the composer producing and suggesting those states of mind which the poet cannot so adequately or directly communicate. Wherever a piece of vocal music is found which is unquestionably better than either its music or its text alone, it will probably be found also to embody this division of labor.

It is highly desirable to end the theoretical discussion and test its generalizations by inspecting a good piece of vocal music on dramatic principles, but first it may be better to give concrete examples of the musical devices by which states of mind may be conveyed. Albert Schweitzer has made a very interesting analysis of the vocal music of Bach from this point of view, and has shown that certain rhythmic and melodic patterns almost invariably accompany certain ideas in the text. Erich Sorantin has made a more generalized study, using the works of a good many composers over a wide range of time and nationalities, and has attempted to draw up what might be called formulae for the musical expression of certain ideas.[4] There is always a danger of pushing this sort of schematization too far, and his work is not entirely free of such forcing, but the general thesis stands up well under examination.

Let us take a specific example. Lamentation, he finds, is expressed by a crescendo ascending passage leading to a diminuendo descending trochaic minor second, with slow tempo, minor harmony, and frequent pedals. I shall put this generalization to the most cruel possible test— that of coldbloodedly filling in the formula and seeing what results. To simplify matters, I shall use a short phrase (thus ruling out the assistance of the "frequent pedals") and I shall allow no harmony, and even no minor. Stripping the formula to its essentials thus, we must have an ascending passage to begin with. The scale of C major will do nicely, for it has no particular associations of any sort. No particular musical time is called for; hence the common 4/4 will do. Since slow time is required, I shall write it in quarter-notes and play it *andante*. It will take two bars of this to make the ascent through an octave; since no particular limits were placed on this ascent, that is a reasonable enough length and interval for it. Now we need a descending trochaic minor second. Since it must be trochaic, we must have a note to descend from on the first (accented) beat of the next bar; hence the simplest thing to do is to repeat the top C. To secure the trochaic effect both in time and in accent, we will make it a half-note and follow it by a quarter. Since a minor second is demanded, we must make this quarter-note the B immediately below. Adding expression marks to take care of the crescendo and diminuendo effects, we have the following passage:

In spite of its purely mechanical construction and its choice of the simple and obvious wherever a choice was allowed, we are now confronted by the fact that it *does* suggest lamentation. At least one of these theoretical formulae will work in practice.

Other characteristic figures can be used for joy, longing, love, persistency, etc. The idea of longing (Cf. Keats, "The music, yearning like a god in pain" [5]) is particularly interesting in that its musical expression depends largely on a harmonic effect and works by an obvious psychological equivalence. Longing is generally expressed by the use of mild and pleasant dissonances, such as the dominant seventh and dominant ninth chords. These chords are normally resolved according

to definite rules of harmony, and even the listener who knows nothing
of the rules is familiar with the practice to such an extent that one of
these chords seems to strive towards—to long for—its proper resolution. The story is told of a dissolute pianist who hated his early-retiring
neighbor across the hall. When the rake came staggering home about
three in the morning, he used to play the following sequence of chords
loudly enough to wake his enemy:

The conventional pianist would then lie awake, pitching and tossing in
a vain effort to get back to sleep, and would finally be forced to get up,
go to his own piano, and resolve the chord. That is longing with a
vengeance! The figure of persistency is the emphatic repetition of the
same note which we have seen Handel using for "Every one in his
own way."

Any theory which assigns definite external meanings to musical
figures runs the danger of being pushed too far, and few of the theorists
who have dealt with such classifications have entirely escaped this
danger. It seems unreasonable, for example, to assume that, because a
certain type of phrase can intensify the idea of longing when it is used
in conjunction with a text calling for that idea, the same musical phrase
in a purely instrumental composition is necessarily an expression of
longing. Similarly, it is no difficult task to pick up the score of a string
quartet and find that, according to a rigid interpretation of the formulae, in some passages each of the four instruments will be "expressing"
a different state of mind, and that these states of mind are incongruous
or contradictory, though there is no incongruity whatsoever in the
musical fabric which they combine to produce. Nevertheless, there is
unquestionably a considerable element of truth in the theories which
classify musical means of expression, and such classification serves a
very useful purpose in the study of music, if only it is not forced
beyond the limits clearly imposed on it by common sense and its own
nature.

We are now ready to see how all this theory of dramatic composition can be applied in the actual music of a song. Schubert's setting of

Goethe's *Erlkönig* will serve admirably as a specimen for study, both because it is generally considered one of the finest dramatic settings of a text and because it will already be familiar to most readers. It will not be necessary to reproduce the full melodic line of this song, but we shall require the full text. Also, the accompaniment, which could be ignored without any essential loss in our specimen from Handel, must here be considered as of at least equal importance with the singer Goethe's poem follows:

1. Wer reitet so spät durch Nacht und Wind?
   Es ist der Vater mit seinem Kind.
   Er hat den Knaben wohl in dem Arm,
   Er fasst ihn sicher, er hält ihn warm.

2. Mein Sohn, was birgst du so bang dein Gesicht?—
   Siehst, Vater, du den Erlkönig nicht?
   Den Erlenkönig mit Kron' und Schweif?—
   Mein Sohn, es ist ein Nebelstreif.—

3. "Du liebes Kind, komm, geh mit mir!
   Gar schöne Spiele spiel' ich mit dir.
   Manch' bunte Blumen sind an dem Strand,
   Meine Mutter hat manch gülden Gewand."

4. Mein Vater, mein Vater, und hörest du nicht,
   Was Erlenkönig mir leise verspricht?—
   Sei ruhig, bleibe ruhig, mein Kind:
   In dürren Blättern säuselt der Wind.—

5. "Willst, feiner Knabe, du mit mir gehn?
   Meine Töchter sollen dich warten schön;
   Meine Töchter führen den nächtlichen Reihn
   Und wiegen und tanzen und singen dich ein."

6. Mein Vater, mein Vater, und siehst du nicht dort
   Erlkönigs Töchter am düstern Ort?—
   Mein Sohn, mein Sohn, ich seh' es genau:
   Es scheinen die alten Weiden so grau.—

7. "Ich liebe dich, mich reizt deine schöne Gestalt;
   Und bist du nicht willig, so brauch' ich Gewalt."
   Mein Vater, mein Vater, jetzt fasst er mich an!
   Erlkönig hat mir ein Leids getan!—

8. Dem Vater grauset's, er reitet geschwind,
   Er hält in Armen das ächzende Kind,

Erreicht den Hof mit Mühe und Not—
In seinen Armen das Kind war tot.*

THE ERL-KING

1. Who gallops so late through wind and night?
   A father bearing his son in flight;
   He holds him tightly, breasting the storm,
   To bear him safely and keep him warm.

2. "My son, why bury your face thus in fear?"
   "Don't you see, father, the Erl-King draw near,
   The king of spirits, with crown and with shroud?"
   "My son, it is a wisp of cloud."

3. "My darling child, come, go with me!
   I'll play the finest games with thee.
   The brightest flowers grow on the shore;
   My mother has clothes of gold in store."

4. "My father, my father, but surely you heard
   The Erl-King's whisp'ring, promising word?"
   "Be quiet; there is nothing to fear:
   The wind is rustling through thickets sere."

5. "Wilt thou come with me, my boy, away
   Where my daughters play with thee night and day?
   For my daughters shall come in the night if thou weep
   And rock thee and dance thee and sing thee to sleep."

6. "My father, my father, but do you not see,
   His daughters lurking by yon dark tree?"
   "My son, my son, it is only the light
   Of old willows gleaming gray through the night."

7. "I love thee so, thy beauty leaves no other course,
   And if thou'rt not willing, I'll take thee by force."

* The following translation is submitted with some reservations. The translation of
any poem is necessarily a sort of cross-word puzzle because of the necessity of attempting to reproduce the form, the meaning, and the feeling of a work which was
conceived in a different form. When the poem has been set to music in its original
form the difficulty of matching syllables with the music and of making the right
words come out on the right notes for the expressive values of the poem is added to
the problems of meter, rhyme, sense, and atmosphere, and the problem becomes a
sort of three-dimensional cross-word puzzle. Any reader who can handle the original
text will, of course, always do well to ignore translations of songs unless the composer
actually set the translation rather than the original. Handel used the English Bible
for the texts of the *Messiah,* and German versions of that work run into difficulties
similar to those occasioned by an English version of the *Erlkönig.* Probably the
original Hebrew and Greek texts of the passages used by Handel could not be sung
to his music at all.

"My father, my father, he drags me from you;
Erl-King has seized me, and hurts me too."

8. The father shudders; he spurs through the wild.
His arms strain closer the weak, moaning child.
He gains his home with toil and dread—
Clasped in his arms there, the child was dead.

In spite of a good deal of discussion of "the artistic process," it is evident that there are as many different methods of working as there are artists. Schubert, unlike Beethoven, wrote with extreme facility, and the story is that he wrote the *Erlkönig* as fast as he could perform the mechanical operation of setting down the notes. Hence it must have been largely an intuitive process rather than the logical one which an analysis of the song might imply. Nevertheless, the perfect matching of text and music, plus the excellence of both, accounts for the place which this song holds in musical literature, and it is possible to some extent to explain this matching without necessarily implying that the act of composition *consciously* involved any elaborate logical approach to the problem. Schubert probably would have said that he simply *felt* that the poem ought to be composed as he did it, without ever *thinking why* it ought to be that way.

An examination of the text of Goethe's poem immediately raises several problems. It is stanzaic, but the changes of tone are such that obviously a setting which would repeat the same music for each stanza would be an absurdity. It would utterly destroy the dramatic nature of the poem instead of intensifying it. How, for example, could the first line be composed on this principle? What music could serve equally well for the narrator's opening question, the father's question, the child's successive screams, the Erl-King's light, cozening speeches, and the narrator's statement of the last stanza? A stanzaic setting would necessarily use either a first line which fitted one of these well and was absurd for the others, or one which was utterly colorless and hence inoffensive and pointless for them all. Such a setting is obviously out of the question.

The song will thus have to be composed all the way through. The stanzas of the poem, however, are symmetrically arranged, and cannot be simply run together; hence they will have to be clearly distinguished as formal elements in the structure of the song. Furthermore, most of the lines are "end-stopped"—that is, the end of a line usually coincides with the end of a sentence or phrase. This means that a speaker pauses at the end of the line, which thus becomes very clearly the logical and rhythmic unit of the poem; and a dramatic setting in music is inclined to be declamatory: hence the song will likewise respect the line as the unit of its structure and will observe the smaller pauses between lines as well as the larger ones between stanzas. The general structure of the song, then, is to follow closely that of the poem. The fact that this is a necessity rather than an accident is shown by Loewe's setting of the same poem: though differing in many respects from Schubert's, it likewise takes its structure from the poem in an almost identical manner.

Our consideration of the sharp differences in mood and content between different stanzas immediately leads to another problem. The composer is bound to reproduce and even heighten these differences. How, then, is he to unify them into one total effect—to make them into *one* song instead of into a series of loosely strung-together dramatic bits? Here we must remember Schweitzer's remark about Bach's habit of getting the tone of an entire situation and not allowing it to be interrupted by episodes which might lead a less effective composer astray. What background effect of the entire poem can be sustained appropriately through the different moods and rising tensions of the various speeches? The effect of speed and urgency, a rush which is both headlong and apprehensive. Since that is a concept of motion, it is translatable into musical terms, and as a matter of fact the first three bars of the piano introduction set the background for the entire composition:

The tempo-marking of *presto* is of the utmost importance. Combarieu remarks that in poetry the nature of an idea determines the speed of reading, but in music the speed of performance determines the nature of the idea.[6] Schubert uses this identical rhythmical figure as a background throughout *Die Allmacht* ("Omnipotence") but in that song it is played *lento solenne* and is used for an effect of power and majesty. In its *presto* form in the *Erlkönig*, however, it produces the almost opposite atmosphere of rushing and agitation. Occasionally one hears this steady rhythmic beat identified as an imitation of a galloping horse, but if Schubert had intended such imitation he could have easily done it much better with some such obvious rhythm as the one used for the purpose in that beloved old war-horse of the lamented cinema-organist, Von Suppé's *Light Cavalry Overture*. What he did clearly intend was a suggestion of the general idea of the poem rather than an imitation of any literal sound mentioned in its text. It is significant that these triplets rush on at their steady pace of twelve notes to the bar without a single break until they suddenly and most dramatically stop three bars before the end of the song: by varying the character of the accompaniment, particularly in the Erl-King's two wheedling stanzas, Schubert was able to keep his music appropriate to individual stanzas; but by maintaining this rhythmic figure unbroken he welded his diverse materials into one basic structure.

The phrase taken by the left hand aids in this effect, though it is not constantly used. There is in it a certain suggestion of the wind—possibly even an imitation of it—but it goes far beyond that and serves as a general theme for the ominous. It can and does disappear during moments of comparative calm, but it returns whenever the feeling of an impending fate is required. Taken together, the rhythmic figure and this theme of the ominous furnish almost all the material used in one of the most effective accompaniments ever written. An introduction of fifteen bars using, in addition to this material, only one or two octaves in the left hand succeeds in thoroughly establishing the mood of the poem before the voice enters. Thus the way is prepared for the opening question of the text: What is this headlong rush? The accompaniment goes on with the singer's question, the rhythmic figure occurring in chords and the figure of foreboding serving almost as punctuation, for it occurs in the middle of the first line (while the voice sustains the word *late*) and at the end of each subsequent line of the first stanza. It comes in twice during the pause between the first and second stanzas, in a five-bar passage which exactly repeats the first five bars of the introduction, and it is scattered through the second stanza even more liberally than through the first.

The voice takes the first line with the general rising inflection proper for a question, and the second line, containing the answer, has the general effect of a reversal of the first. The third and fourth lines are straight narrative and tend to follow (though with wider intervals of pitch and stronger rhythmic stress) the inflections which a reader would probably use. Special emphasis is placed on the crux of the entire situation by the use of three appogiaturas ("grace notes") on words meaning, literally, *boy, arm,* and *safe*. (Working out such effects without destroying larger poetical values is one of the impossibilities of the translation of songs.)

With the opening of the second stanza the dialogue begins. First we have the father's question, which also has a rising inflection, but is nevertheless clearly distinguished from the opening question of the narrator. That had a broad, swinging movement proper to excitement without personal concern, but this is a question of anxiety asked with a steady upward movement, largely chromatic, and pausing for reply with a tension reflected by the figure of the ominous, which appears twice in consecutive bars. The child is astonished, apparently, by such a question. He replies with a question of his own, and Schubert has emphasized Goethe's arrangement of the line, making the principal emphasis fall on *du*. The reason for fear is obvious to the child; hence his question in reply is, "Don't *you* see him too?" The musical direction for the two lines of the child's reply is *crescendo poco a poco*: the boy, in his anxiety and his attempt to convince his father by more exact description, talks louder and louder, but just before the end the melodic line puts what is almost a break into his voice. The father replies firmly and without excitement that it is only an illusion, and his attempt to quiet the child's fear is heightened by the interlude between this stanza and the next. This is made up of three bars of chords forming a beautiful and simple cadence, the whole played with increasing softness. This decrescendo effect serves a double purpose: it emphasizes the peace and comfort of the father's reply, with its temporary effect on the child, and it also makes a transition musically from the anxiety and comparative loudness of this stanza to the light, *pianissimo*, luring speech of the Erl-King which follows.

The Erl-King's speeches must be carefully differentiated from those of the father and child. The accompaniment points out the difference immediately. It keeps the rushing triplets which are necessary as a background for the whole song, but instead of having them on unbrokenly reiterated notes it divides them between the player's hands, the bass taking the first note of each triplet and the right hand playing the other two:

The melodic line of the first part of this third stanza is also quite different from anything that has gone before.

The first two phases are identical, and have the suggestion of a lullaby and even of a rocking cradle. The next phrase begins as a repetition, but rises higher and includes the little flourish of a triplet. There is another slight vocal flourish at the conclusion of this same stanza, but with these two exceptions the entire song is declamatory and confines itself usually to one, and at most to two notes to a syllable. Would it be going too far to say that these flourishes of the Erl-King's serve as a sort of warning to emphasize the speciousness and hypocrisy of the otherwise plausible effect of the luring lullaby? They seem to underline a sort of virtuosity: the Erl-King is so proud of his ability as a deluder that, like Tartuffe, he oversteps the limits of necessity and in pride of skill gives himself away for anyone who is not already ensnared.

The pause between the third and fourth stanzas is only a quarter-note in length, but that is sufficient, for the return of the accompaniment to its first form and volume is a sufficient indication of the shift. The stanza opens immediately with the child's cry—almost scream—of alarm. This cry

is a masterpiece of dramatic effectiveness. It is used twice again, each time with the same words, and its growing anguish is shown by a definite gradation both in pitch and in loudness: at each recurrence it begins one degree of the scale higher, and the volume changes from *mf* in this first occurrence to *f* the next time, and on to *ff* in the child's last scream. The word *father* is a sustained cry on its first occurrence, but the second one (each time that the cry as a whole occurs) has a break in the voice. All this is effective, but the greatest single element in the effect is the harmony, the clashing dissonance of C, D, and E♭, which suggests the idea of a scream far more effectively than any mere physical screaming on the singer's part could. This phrase is a good example of a perfect union between poetry and music by which both are gainers. Certainly no one but an old-style elocution teacher would actually scream the words when reading the poem, and certainly any such treatment of the text would be an artistic blemish. On the other hand, the musical effect is absolutely dependent on the text. For some incomprehensible reason, the *Erlkönig* has been transcribed in various ways for instrumental performance. (Liszt made a transcription for piano solo.) But no performance can make sense unless the words are either sung or very clearly—and line by line—present in the listener's mind. Even in the latter case this scream is sheer nonsense and gives only the impression that one of the players has made a bad mistake, for there is no *musical* justification for such an effect at this point. Schubert's setting of this passage is clearly an example of vocal composition which is better than either its text or its music taken separately.

The next phrase, "but surely you heard," repeats this outcry exactly except for two differences: the last bar has only one syllable, and that on a half-note, so that the break in the voice is not repeated; also, the phrase is sung *crescendo*. This repeats the effect of losing control under the stress of excitement and fear, and the same device is used in each of the child's speeches except the last. The question to the father follows the familiar pattern of ascending pitch (primarily a chromatic ascent), and there is a bit of literal imitation in the softening of volume in connection with the idea of whispering. The father's reply (the key here changes to C major) is similar to his other one, but with a crescendo on his explanation of the sound—an effect calculated, by the father himself, to make for confidence and reassurance. This is again followed by a cadence, though not as smooth or quiet a one as before.

The second speech of the Erl-King again keeps the rhythm of the accompaniment as a whole, but changes the general figure. This time the left hand begins with reiterated eighth-notes, one to each beat, with eighth-rests between them, but subsequently changes to a pattern of

The right hand maintains the steady triplets, but instead of repeating chords or notes it now has running figures of broken chords which give the effect of lightness and fantasy required by the speech. This effect is intensified by the general slow rise and fall (again the cradle-song suggestion) of the melodic line and its general rhythmic scheme of a quarter-note for the first and third beats of the bar and two eighth-notes for the second and fourth. In this stanza Schubert takes his only liberty with Goethe's text by repeating the last line. It is of an arresting nature in that its poetic rhythm is broken up by the series into that very rare thing, a line of amphibrachs:

Und wie—gen	und tan—zen	und sing—en	dich ein
And rock thee	and dance thee	and sing thee	to sleep.

The line already has a rocking motion, and Schubert intensifies it by his accent and time values. In fact, the change of rhythm in the bass, mentioned above, is calculated to bring out the full effect of this pattern, and is made for this line only. The line in itself is sufficiently arresting to bear repetition, but there is another reason also: it is not only the Erl-King's most seductive appeal, but, as we see later, it is also his *last* attempt to win the child by persuasion.

The sixth stanza is parallel to the fourth, both in words and in music, for the excellent reason that it is exactly parallel in situation. The only real difference is that the situation is now more serious, and hence the tension must be heightened. This is done by a general intensification of the musical means of expression already used: the child's cry is louder and is one tone higher; the tempo is retarded for half a bar just before the father's reply—a suggestion of difficulty in finding a comforting answer—and is sharply resumed as soon as the difficulty has been overcome; and the father's speech, with its stronger rhythm, wider intervals, and stubbornly repeated *A*, gives the impression that he is now trying to reassure himself as well as the child.

At the conclusion of this speech the opening accompaniment-figure is resumed at full volume, and is then repeated softly, making a longer interval between stanzas than has occurred for some time, as well as the suggestion of doom. The left-hand figure has not been heard since the second stanza: it set the general tone, but as long as the issue was in doubt it was dropped. Its return here is therefore particularly effective, and the softer repetition (still keeping the crescendo of the ascending half of the figure and the diminuendo of the descending half) suggests not a passing of danger, but a waiting with bated breath. In this atmosphere the seventh stanza begins very softly, but we know instantly that the Erl-King's tactics have changed, for there is now no change of accompaniment for his speech. His first line keeps—verbally—the familiar flattery, but this accompaniment prepares us for what is to come when, in the second line, he abandons his hypocrisy and, in a dissonant crescendo, grimly announces his intention of using force. That this is an announcement rather than a threat is shown by the child's cry—one beat later the Erl-King is already seizing him. This cry is the climactic intensification of the now familiar pattern, raised both in pitch and in volume. The following line, however, departs radically from the established scheme. It begins high, rises slightly as if in the interrogatory pattern, but then begins a descent and ends with an abrupt drop of a fifth.

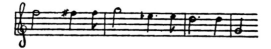

The suggestion of beginning in complaint and ending in collapse is clear enough and serves to reinforce the words, which characteristically represent the last words of the child—and Schubert so manages them that we at once realize that they are last words—as a complaint caused by physical pain. Some singers, influenced by the second line of the last stanza, make the final drop from *D* to *G* into a sob, thereby cheapening the effect and clearly demonstrating that literal imitation is inferior to dramatic suggestion.

The situation is now what it was at the beginning of the poem except that it is far more desperate. There we had a father riding headlong through the woods on a stormy night trying to get home with his sick child; now it is a dying child. This parallelism is clearly shown in the music, for on the last word spoken by the boy the left hand joins the right, fortissimo, in its opening and persistent figure, so that the insistent *G* is now hammered out over a spread of four octaves. For the most part, the final stanza retains this arrangement except when the left hand is needed for its own characteristic ominous figure. The father has no words of comfort now; he spurs on in grim silence, and the narrator concludes the story. After the first two lines of the stanza there is a pause in the voice which, by its mere existence, gives a suggestion of a lapse of time, and by its character—a reiterated C octave in the right hand against chromatically rising octaves in the left, all fortissimo—conveys the urgency and anguish of that interval. Then the narrator says that finally the father reaches home. The wild ride is over, and the accompaniment which has kept it before us since the beginning suddenly stops. For 145 bars there has been an absolutely unbroken beat of twelve notes to the bar, *presto*, and the accompanist also "erreicht den Hof mit Mühe und Not." This cessation is most effective. One can be startled by the cessation of a sound—or even awakened by it—as much as by its beginning. The father reins in his horse with the conclusion of the ride, and just as the physical urgency is concluded the mental shock of being able really to see the child's condition comes. All this is adequately conveyed by the *quiet* and the *shock* simultaneously produced by the cessation of the established accompaniment. The last line is daringly given in recitative. From the point of view of instrumental music this also is an absurdity, but it is dramatically perfect. The ride has ended, the child is quiet, nothing external makes a sound or movement, and the father is left to the silence of his own discovery. Hence we have the voice in a recitative: "Clasped in his arms there, the child"—and here there is a pause of the suspended heartbeat when the truth is realized, a pause poignantly filled in with a soft diminished seventh chord—"was dead." The inevitable has happened, the Erl-King has won, and there is no further word to say. Two chords put the seal of finality on the discovery.

It would be possible to carry this analysis of the dramatic element in Schubert's setting much further, to consider in detail each individual line and phrase of the poem, and to show how the composer contributed to it a heightening of effect beyond the power of the poet alone. Such an analysis, though multiplying examples, would contribute nothing different in principle from what we have already seen, and it would lead to a grave danger. The deluding thing about strict logic in such cases is that it is likely to mistake the possible for the inevitable.

Most detective stories depend on some such fallacy. The reader is given a set of circumstances, but is himself unable to solve the crime with the evidence at his disposal. When the amateur hero of the story does solve it, the reader is naturally impressed, and he accepts the solution as proof of the detective's superior analytical powers. Every detail fits, and the author hastens to corroborate the detective's solution by some new and definitive piece of evidence, such as the criminal's confession. The trick lies in leading the reader to mistake *a* possible solution of the problem for *the* unique solution, and to abandon as inferior any solution of his own which, though equally logical, is not allowed by the author.

A good deal of artistic criticism runs into exactly the same fallacy. In an essay entitled *The Philosophy of Composition,* Poe tells, or pretends to tell, how he wrote *The Raven.* "It is my design," he writes, "to render it manifest that no one point in its composition is referrible either to accident or intuition—that the work proceeded, step by step, to its completion with the precision and rigid consequence of a mathematical problem." And he does show precisely that. By strict logical steps he decides the best length, the form, the subject matter, the locale, the participants, and even such details as the necessity of a refrain, the determination to use a refrain of one word only, and the realization that that word would *have* to be "Nevermore!" He goes on to say that the details of the writing of each stanza can be explained on similar principles. All this is most convincing as long as the reader follows docilely where Poe chooses to lead him. But the flaw is that the logic is too perfect. If it held good, any poet setting out to write a poem would necessarily do one of two things: he would make one or more obvious blunders in the course of his work—or he would write *The Raven.*

The analytical critic must not draw his logic so tight that it strangles creative activity. There is good reason to think that Poe's essay was suggested by such statements as those of Coleridge to the effect that "poetry, even that of the loftiest and, seemingly, that of the wildest odes, had a logic of its own, as severe as that of science; and more difficult, because more subtle, more complex, and dependent on more, and more fugitive causes" [7]; and that "nothing can permanently please, which does not contain in itself the reason why it is so, and not otherwise." [8] The flaw is that for the first of these statements Poe tried to give the impression that he had neatly pinned down all the subtle, numerous, and fugitive causes. And for the second he went far beyond the legitimate meaning, which is (to use Coleridge's example) that all the parts of a work of art must combine to make a harmonious whole—that if the form is that of verse, the tone must be that of poetry, etc. Poe tried to demonstrate not only that his poem was consonant with itself, but that it was unique in being consonant with the nature of things in general.

What light do Coleridge and Poe throw on our discussion of Schubert's *Erlkönig*? They remind us that, excellent and dramatically effective as that song is, it is not the inevitable and only effective way of setting the poem. Interesting confirmation of this statement is found in the excellent setting of the same poem by Loewe. Since this version and Schubert's were entirely independent of each other,* they are good illustrations of different possibilities in the setting of the same text. We have already seen that Schubert took full advantage of the dramatic elements of Goethe's poem and thus was essentially concerned with its characters and situations. Loewe, of course, does not entirely ignore this element, and the rapidity of speech (for it is much more nearly speech than song) in his version gets the effect of urgency achieved by Schubert's accompaniment. In general, however, Loewe is more interested in the fairy-story and folk-literature aspects of the poem than in its human relationships, and his setting is designed to bring out such possibilities. Therefore, instead of the constantly varying melodic line of Schubert, he uses almost throughout the entire composition a somewhat sing-song pattern in which the same general contour is repeated for each successive line. In the "My father, my father" passages he seeks an effect of tense excitement rather than terror and anguish. In fact, there is hardly a phrase of his setting which resembles the corresponding phrase of Schubert's. Nevertheless, it is an effective setting and an excellent one. The general preference has chosen Schubert's version, and hence it is impossible—as well as somewhat invidious—to attempt a ranking of the two on their relative merits, for most critics have probably become at home with Schubert's song before hearing Loewe's, and therefore the established association works strongly in favor of Schubert. Nevertheless, we can grant that Schubert's version is superior (Schubert is usually superior to Loewe) without disturbing the important point that the two versions demonstrate the possibility of strikingly different good dramatic settings of the same text.

The *Erlkönig* of Goethe offers far more dramatic possibilities than do most poems, and for that reason it has been useful for a demonstra-

---

* Schubert composed his version in the winter of 1815 and it was sung at his old school on the evening of its composition—without too much success, especially since the dissonant cry of the child had to be explained away somehow by the teacher of harmony. Apparently the song was not performed again until Dec. 1, 1820 (in a salon of musicians) and Jan. 25, 1821 (first public performance). It was published shortly after the latter date.

Loewe's setting was composed in 1818. He had been in Halle when Schubert's song received its first performance (and only one before 1820) at the school in Vienna. (Grove's *Dictionary*, Articles "Loewe" and "Schubert.")

tion of the dramatic composition. We must now consider, however, the task of setting texts which do not present such opportunities. Frequently an excellent lyric offers no differentiation of characters or real change of situation. In such cases the composer cannot go beyond two principles in the relationship between his music and the text. The first of these is merely the mechanical necessity of a certain correspondence of syllables to notes which will enable the text and the music to be put together, though it is impossible to draw a line between the mechanical and the dramatic in such matters as the emphasis given to particular words and phrases. Beyond this pointing up of the rhetoric (in the good sense of the word) of the poem, the composer can and must achieve a general correspondence of mood and atmosphere. This whole question of mood, in both music and poetry, rather tends to defy analysis, but we need not fall into the dogmatism of some pseudo-scientists by denying the existence of everything which we cannot explain. Even if music alone cannot create a sharply defined mood which will be identical for all members of an audience—and this is a hotly debated point—it can certainly reinforce a mood controlled by the greater precision of language. And since such reinforcement is a matter of situation and human experience we are justified in classing it as dramatic.

When a composer's text is of such nature that it demands only a mechanical matching plus a general correspondence of mood, it leaves him far greater freedom for purely musical effects than does a text which demands constant attention. Hence it is not surprising to find that, other things being equal (though in specific examples they never are), the less detailed the relationship between text and music is, the better the music, considered separately, is likely to be. We have already noticed that some of the finest effects in Schubert's *song* are absurdities in any *instrumental* transcription. "Drink to me only with thine eyes," on the other hand, can well afford to be divorced from its text and played by a string quartet.

The intricacy of possible relationships between text and music is well illustrated by the strangely haunting *Ein Ton* (usually translated as "The Monotone") of Peter Cornelius. He wrote both text and music, and, regardless of the historical fact of which was put down first, each was predicated on the other. The ten simple lines of the poem are based entirely on a musical idea: the poet constantly hears, in his heart and mind, one single tone. He wonders whether it is the last breath of his beloved, or the bell that sounded for her funeral, and it seems to him to be her soul descending in love to sing his grief to rest. The basic concept of the text is a musical sensation which becomes a poetic symbol.

The music fits perfectly: the accompaniment begins with a twice-repeated single note, a *B* in the middle of the treble clef. Then the voice enters, and the melody of the entire song is simply this one note. If one is inclined to be skeptical as to whether the repetition of a single note can be properly termed a melody, he need only hear this song in order to be convinced that, in this case at least, it can. The fact is explained by the poetic reason that this repetition is a dramatic illustration of the text and by the musical consideration that this note enters into such interesting and constantly shifting relationships with the accompaniment that it is never monotonous and hardly seems to be the same note. At the conclusion of the vocal part the *B*, in various registers, becomes an ever-present note in the piano score, which closes with two sustained, soft repetitions of this note alone. In this song the balance between poem and music is beautifully kept. Does the music illustrate the idea of the text, or does the text explain the peculiar structure of the music? The question is unanswerable, for each serves as an explanation or illustration of the other, and either music or text, considered alone, is intriguing, but gives a sense of incompleteness. This song offers an example of the ideal and very rare combination of music and literature to form one indivisible work of art.

Throughout this discussion of vocal music it has been assumed that the text comes first and the music is added later. This assumption is the result of fact rather than theory: whether a composer uses a text already written by someone else or writes his own text, his general practice is to have the words in their final form (barring some repetition of phrases) before beginning work on the musical setting. There are, of course, exceptions, but their rarity and their peculiar nature serve only to emphasize the general statement. Poets—or perhaps versifiers is a more accurate term—frequently take some familiar tune and write verses to be sung to it, but these verses are very likely to be parodies of texts for which the music was composed, or undistinguished efforts in which the relationship is purely mechanical. Thus Cäsar Flaischeln wrote nearly sixty pages of poems designed to be sung to various tunes which he names along with the titles of the poems.[9] That the relationship is purely mechanical is shown by his *Silvesterlied*, which, he suggests, may be sung to any of five different tunes, or may use a different one for each stanza. By straight mathematics, then, five stanzas may be sung according to any one of 125 musical schemes, and by considering them all equally good Flaischeln merely demonstrates that they must be all equally bad. The writing of texts more specifically designed for music already in existence is fairly common. To cite only a few examples, all the *Geistliche Lieder* of Klopstock are written for familiar hymn-tunes; H. W. von Gerstenberg wrote two monologues to be sung to the same piano-fantasy (selecting different melodies from the right-hand part) of C. P. E. Bach; [10] Theodor Körner [11] wrote verses for music by Paisiello and Paer, and for various folk-songs; Auguste Dorchain has a *Chant militaire* [12] for music by Widor; de Musset wrote a text to music by Mozart; [13] and Leigh Hunt wrote a *Serenade*, "suggested by the music of Cherubini's trio 'non mi negate, no.' " [14] More recently, Rachel Field wrote a text for Schubert's *Ave Maria* in Walt Disney's *Fantasia*. A few such texts, like the "Going Home" sometimes attached to the *Largo* of Dvořák's *New World Symphony* and the religious text which, for church purposes, has replaced the original text of Handel's *Largo* (from *Xerxes*) have become popularly established, but musicians, doubtless under the influence of both historical purism and superior taste, still regard them with condescension.

The patriotic song seems to be the only type in which texts written for already familiar music have had any consistent success. The theme used for a set of variations in Haydn's *Emperor Quartet* became, with the addition of suitable texts, the "Gott erhalte Franz den Kaiser" of Austria and the "Deutschland, Deutschland über Alles" of Germany. Also, its illegitimate and deformed offspring include about half the Alma Mater songs of American colleges and universities. *The Star-Spangled Banner* is simply a patriotic text attached to the English drinking-song, *To Anacreon in Heaven*. With the addition of words the choral middle section of Sibelius' *Finlandia* became so politically powerful that Finns living in Russia were forbidden to sing it; and when Elgar, writing a coronation ode for Edward VII, attached A. C. Benson's words to the trio of his own instrumental *Pomp and Circumstance, No. 1*, the resulting song met with such popular favor that now, forty years after its first appearance, *Land of Hope and Glory* is in fact, though unofficially, the national anthem of England.

It is easy to see why the composition of texts for music already written should be the exception rather than the rule, and why the most successful examples of such a process should be patriotic songs. We have already seen that in most vocal music the text gives the external situation or idea, and the music reinforces the implications of the words. Hence it is necessary to begin with the general idea which the text expresses and then to add the musical reinforcement and suggestion. Bridges' statement that the best musical treatment of passages of great poetic beauty is "to woo them and court them and caress them" applies here with full force. A man cannot well woo and caress and court in the abstract with the hope that some helpful person will find the lady to whom his advances are most appropriate and kindly insert her under his caresses. He must find the woman first, and then, in accordance with her nature, determine the course of his own wooing. Patriotic songs offer an easy exception because they do not generally have that close connection between words and music found in what is generally called the "art-song." They demand, above all, a good, swinging, marching tune, and the rather standardized words of national pride can easily be attached once the tune has been found. (It is worth noticing that *The Star-Spangled Banner* lacks these qualities, and therefore has never been a national anthem in any except an official sense. Throughout its history the United States has been vainly searching for a real national anthem, and with the advent of *God Bless America* the situation became desperate.) In the case of Haydn, Sibelius, and Elgar a non-aesthetic association was doubtless at work also: the national pride in a great composer, the feeling that he is a voice of all his people, naturally makes it particularly easy to view any suitable piece of his music as *per se* an expression of the glory of his nation, and thus suggests the addition of patriotic words.

CHAPTER VIII

The Dilemma of Opera

"STRICTLY speaking," said Schopenhauer, "one might define opera as an unmusical invention for the pleasure of unmusical people." [1] Though few of us would be willing to speak quite so strictly, we cannot deny that there is a certain amount of truth in the statement. We can even see a definite application of Schopenhauer's definition of opera in terms of its admirers. Opera has established itself as a great adjunct of society —meaning those persons whose trivial activities are reported with awe in the "society pages" of our newspapers—and even in our cartoons and comic strips the society woman gushing over an opera has become a stock figure.

Why doesn't she occasionally go to a symphony concert instead? There are two clear reasons. The first is that the professional society woman is, paradoxically enough, entirely dominated by the herd instinct, and a great deal of her activity is devoted to the serious business of making a clearly visible difference between her own small herd and that large one which she views as the vulgar masses. She does not go to any music except opera because none of her friends do. And this is a long-established custom by which the performance of an opera is an event in the lives of the smart set, but that of a symphony is not. Various historical causes have contributed to the setting up of this tradition, but its ultimate source is our second reason: a symphony is sheer unrelieved boredom for anyone without a certain minimum of musical interest and appreciation, but an opera offers many nonmusical distractions. Hence the person who feels that one *should* be interested in music in order to show that one is "cultured" (in the shoddy sense which the word has recently acquired) finds that opera is the least obnoxious form on which to display one's interest. And it is the congregation of such people at the opera which ultimately accounts for that institution's great social prestige.

Looking at opera from the composers' viewpoint gives another sort of evidence that it is something essentially different from other music. In a way, of course, it is simply vocal music, and hence comes under the discussion of that form which has occupied the past two chapters. Yet we find outstanding composers of vocal music who either, like Schubert, had no particular success with their half-hearted attempts at opera or, like Brahms, felt that a composer *should* write at least one opera, but never quite brought themselves to the point of doing it. In fact, though many composers have done excellent work in such unrelated types as the song and the symphony, there are only a few who have been outstanding both in opera and in instrumental music of any type whatsoever. What peculiar characteristics of opera so sharply differentiate it in the minds of both composers and audiences from other music, and especially from types like the song and the oratorio or cantata, with which it seems superficially to have so much in common?

The primary difficulty is one of complication. In any sort of vocal music a struggle between the text and the music is likely to ensue and, as we have already seen, a perfect combination of the two arts is a rarity. Opera has this difficulty plus a great many others. Acting and the dance must be included also, along with the art of the set-designer, scene-painter, and costumer. Each of these has its own principles and its own proper effects, and what one needs at any given time is likely to be ruinous to some other.

We may consider briefly the complications produced by adding only one art, acting, to the already difficult combination of music and literature. In the first place, there are purely mechanical difficulties. Any verisimilitude on the stage depends on the willing acceptance of a number of conventions, but the addition of music increases these a thousand-fold. (I speak here of the addition of music because the play is already a combination of literature and acting: an opera can be equally well viewed as a cantata which is acted out or as a play which is sung.) The plot demands some statement from the dying Siegfried, and the literary stage could handle the situation reasonably well, though even there the problem is grave enough. "I have observed," comments Dryden, "that in all our tragedies the audience cannot forebear laughing when the actors are to die; it is the most comic part of the whole play." [2] If it is difficult to die and speak at the same time without appearing ludicrous, what can poor Siegfried do when he has to *sing* a long passage with a spear sticking between his shoulder-blades —and presumably into his lungs? And this example is taken intentionally from Wagner, who managed with less of this type of absurdity than almost any other operatic composer. Other scenes are far worse—the famous quartet in *Rigoletto*, for example, with two persons inside a shack thinking they are alone, two outside spying on them, and all four singing away full blast in slickly contrived harmony. Such scenes make absolutely impossible "that willing suspension of disbelief for the moment, which constitutes poetic faith." [3]

These things may seem to be slips which reasonable care on the part of the composer and librettist (whether they be the same person, as in *Götterdämmerung*, or two different ones, as in *Rigoletto*) might have avoided. But the inherent falsity goes far beyond these isolated conspicuous examples; it pervades every note, every word, every gesture. The mechanical difficulties of timing require two conductors (one for the orchestra and another for the singers), and their problems of coordination are likely to lead to a certain woodenness. The singers must try to sing and act at the same time—a difficult enough feat if they could do both separately—but they are normally chosen purely as singers and hence have to muddle through the acting as best they can. They must act and sing *and* watch the conductor *and* try to maintain positions in which good singing is possible. For these reasons the action of standard operas has become absolutely stereotyped: every gesture, every step, every bit of stage business is performed at the same instant in the same way by every singer who performs the rôle. This mass production system has the great advantage of interchangeability of parts, for an opera company which finds itself in difficulties can wire for a tenor and know that he can fit into the production, just as the car owner can order a new crankshaft and know that it will fit his motor. But this mechanical performance naturally belongs in the machine and not in the work of art.

The nature of opera also inclines it towards the theatrical rather than the dramatic. This fact is reflected in the forced and absurd situations, the exaggerated *statement* of emotional crises which are neither communicated by the opera nor *felt* by the audience, and the frequent incoherence of an opera as a whole. Aristotle's dictum that "the poet or 'maker' should be the maker of plots rather than of verses" [4] is systematically ignored, and another statement of his prophetically tells why. "Of all plots and actions," he writes, "the epeisodic are the worst. I call a plot epeisodic in which the episodes or acts succeed one another without probable or necessary sequence. Bad poets compose such pieces by their own fault, good poets, to please the players; for, as they write show pieces for competition, they stretch the plot beyond its capacity, and are often forced to break the natural continuity." [5] Since practically every step in the development of opera, from its first appearance during the Italian Renaissance through the reforms of Gluck and Wagner, has styled itself an attempt to return to the greatness and effects of Greek tragedy, it is not inappropriate to apply Aristotle's criticism to the results. All too often the librettists have been those bad poets who are perfectly capable of writing episodic plots by their own uncompelled triviality, but even the good ones have had to write to please the players, who are more intent—as are at least large portions of their audiences—on sensational scenes, showy production, and opportunities for the display of individual virtuosity than on the creation or performance of works of art.

The matter of individual display is not a mere sneer; it is apparently a necessary condition of operatic performance. The instrumental virtuoso has occasionally made an unenviable reputation for himself by his vanity and showmanship, but he is usually a soloist whose only fault is to consider his own dexterity more important than the composer's music. Orchestral players are practically anonymous, and this fact goes far towards securing balanced effect, even under the baton of the occasional virtuoso-director. If the leader of the bull-fiddlers dragged his instrument out to the center of the stage and there played what Berlioz characterized as "the dance of the elephants" in the Scherzo of Beethoven's *Fifth Symphony* under the beams of three spotlights, an entirely new set of problems in orchestral music would arise. Opera, the only branch of music which consistently operates under the disastrous Hollywood "star" system, has these problems and more besides. Being both instrument and performer, the singer takes somewhat to himself and tremendously to herself double the credit which any instrumentalist can demand. No opera-goer with an aesthetic sense can fail to be constantly irritated by music which is written and performed with the sole purpose of personal aggrandizement for one of the singers. Probably the most scathing statement of this attitude is found in Coleridge's *Lines Composed in a Concert Room,* in which the descriptions of music, performer, and audience make it clear that the concert was operatic:

> Nor cold, nor stern, my soul! Yet I detest
> These scented rooms, where, to a gaudy throng,
> Heaves the proud harlot her distended breast
> In intricacies of laborious song. [6]

Even so great a devotee of opera as Mr. Ernest Newman could not refrain from uttering a proposition (which he tactfully suggested as merely the suspicion of a hypothetical person) that "a long experience of singers . . . may lead you to believe you can formulate a sort of natural law that the higher the voice the lower the intelligence." [7] And the best advice he can give his hypothetical critic on this matter is: "Don't think these blasphemous things, Joseph, or if you do, don't say them." The entire background of Berlioz' delightful *Les soirées de l'orchestre* is one of contempt for the great body of operatic literature. Berlioz tells how he spent the winter in a provincial town, and went every night to the opera-house, where he passed the evening in the orchestra pit with the obstreperous members of the orchestra. They (with the exception of the serious bass drummer) spent their time swapping yarns in order not to have to listen to the stuff they were forced to play. Frequently they would stop entirely, and the conductor would lean over to join in the conversation while he vaguely beat time for the singers. Neither the cast nor the audience ever seemed to notice the absence of the orchestra. Occasionally, when a really good work was performed, the orchestra would play instead of talking, but such occasions were distressingly rare. One evening Berlioz himself was doing the talking when horrible sounds from the stage—"un grand air de prima donna," in fact—interrupted them. Thereupon he remarked:

That singer up there reminds me of one of my neighbors in the Rue d'Aumale in Paris. Having decided to become a diva right away, she practised as long as she had strength to utter another note—and she was very strong. One morning a milkman, passing under her window on his way to town, heard her piercing voice and sighed, "Marriage is not all a bed of roses." Towards the middle of the afternoon the sympathetic milkman passed the same place on his way home, and once again heard the screams of the indefatigable singer. "Oh God!" he cried, crossing himself; "Poor woman! It's three o'clock, and she's been in labor since morning!" [8]

Such slurs on opera in general and the prima donna especially might be multiplied indefinitely, and no one would take any particular one of them very seriously. Considered all together, however, they do prove that opera has tended to provoke a certain scorn and irritation in discriminating critics. This feeling is doubtless due to the cross-purposes and compromises involved in any attempt to combine so many arts into one integrated whole. Since these problems, in so far as they differ from those of vocal music in general, result from the admixture of arts other than music and literature, we need not be concerned with them beyond pointing out their existence.

There are some elements of Wagnerian opera, however, which have especial interest for the student of relationships between music and literature. Most persons feel that, generally speaking, this form is more impressive and satisfying than French, Italian, or earlier German opera. Though its preeminence is due to a number of causes, only two of them are of immediate concern. The first has to do with the libretto. Many composers have protested against the insipidity of the stuff given them by the professional writers of opera texts; others have preferred colorless words which could offer no competition with their music. These latter have been, in general, flabby or showy composers unworthy of serious attention, and such reformers as Gluck have always insisted on good texts of at least equal importance with the music. In a letter to the *Mercure de France* Gluck left no doubt as to his stand on this matter:

No matter how great the composer's talent may be, he will never compose anything but mediocre music unless the poet excites in him that enthusiasm without which any work of art is feeble and languishing. The imitation of nature is the recognized goal which all the arts should set up for themselves; it is the goal which I seek to attain. As far as possible, my music, always simple and natural, aims only at the greatest expression and reinforcement of the declamation and poetry.[9]

But he was only a voice crying in the wilderness, and before the time of Wagner few libretti could be considered even passable from a literary standpoint.

Wagner wrote his own. He had the great advantage of being a poet of considerable ability, and this ability is clearly shown by the fact that any history of German literature discusses him, on the basis of his libretti, as a poet. Also, such works as *The Ring* and *Tristan* make good reading, even though they were not intended for this purpose. But this fact is probably accidental and irrelevant. The important thing is that these works were written *for* music by a person who knew what sort of thing the composer needed. From a purely literary point of view Wagner's verse is based on early Germanic poetry. This is the source of the alliteration, the freedom in the use of unstressed syllables, the loosely-thrown-together "paratactic" constructions, and even the meter.

The earliest Old English, Old Norse, and Old High German poetry had a line of four stresses divided into halves by a pause somewhere between the second and third of these. The two halves, bound together by various types of alliteration of stressed syllables, employed varying numbers and arrangements of unstressed ones. Wagner prints each half-

line as a line, but otherwise his pattern is essentially the same: even the
three-stress lines which he scatters here and there have some precedent
(though not exactly as he used them) in Old English poetry. This form
is particularly suited for musical treatment in that it offers great rhythmic variety according to the number and position of its unstressed syllables, the alliteration gives a coherence of verbal sound which in no
way interferes with the musical effects of the composer, and the loose
syntax breaks the text up into easily assimilated phrases. This last point
can be clearly seen by considering how impossible it would be to give
any adequate musical setting to the long and intricate periods of *Paradise Lost*. There is also a certain historical appropriateness in the use of
this form of verse for such a work as *The Ring*, but that is a minor
matter: probably very few of those who hear Wagner's operas and feel
his effective combination of music and text are aware of the system
of versification employed in either early Germanic poetry or Wagner's
libretti.

Wagner also had a great advantage in that he wrote his own texts.
If someone of equal or greater poetic ability had written them in the
same form, the result could still not have been as good. The individual
style which makes a particular composer's or poet's work recognizable
is, to a certain extent, discoverable by formal technical analysis, but
above and beyond this lies the individuality of the creator, and if a
man is gifted in two arts, his work in both will have similarities ultimately referable to the nature of the man himself. Thus Wagner's
words are, by the test of style alone, the best possible ones for his
music. But beyond this lies the conception of the entire work, and the
advantage here is perhaps even greater: Wagner's general attitude towards the story of Tristan or Siegfried can be shown in both play and
music, and he can decide which things can best be expressed by one
and which by the other. For all these reasons it would be a fine thing
for any composer to write his own texts, if only he could. Even though
this is impossible, the influence of Wagner is shown in the subsequent
demand that libretti be entrusted to such recognized poets as Hugo
von Hofmannsthal and Edna Millay.

Another particular advantage of the Wagnerian opera is its use of
the Leitmotiv. This device was, of course, no invention of Wagner's: it
had been used, in one form or another, by many composers before his
time. Since the Leitmotiv is a musical theme associated with some
external, or non-musical person, idea, situation, etc., and repeated when
that thing is to be designated or suggested later, its exact definition in-

volves a question of degree. How specific must the association be, how distinctive must the theme be, and how often must it be repeated before it can be called a Leitmotiv? Though some fine distinctions may be made, there can be no doubt that the Leitmotiv of Wagner and the *idée fixe* of Berlioz are really only two different names for the same principle. In general, the longer work gives more scope for the use of the Leitmotiv, but if we approached Schubert with the prepossessions of the tabulators of Wagnerian themes we might well refer to the ascending left-hand figure of the *Erlkönig* as the Motive of Foreboding, and to the child's cry as the Motive of Terror. And why cannot the melodic and rhythmic themes which Schweitzer finds Bach using again and again to express certain concepts be called—incongruous as the term may sound—the Leitmotivs of Bach? Without further laboring the point, we may note simply that Wagner's use of this device was, like most "new" techniques in art, merely a systematic exploitation of a familiar principle.

Wagner himself associated the Leitmotiv with literary antecedents and pointed out the fixed Homeric epithet as a parallel. We may go further than this, and say that the Leitmotiv is essentially a literary (or verbal) device adapted to the needs of music. This remark can be easily substantiated. A word is simply a spoken sound or a group of such sounds which have come to possess, in the minds of a group of persons who are in general agreement on such matters (that is, who speak the same language) a comparatively fixed meaning. Most children invent words of their own, and to the inventor such words, in so far as they have privately understood significance, are real words. When parents sternly tell a child that one of his combinations of sound is not a word, they simply mean that he cannot communicate anything by its use because other persons do not attach any external significance to it.

But this is to consider language among people who have already acquired it. A consideration of the process of acquisition will illuminate the workings of the Leitmotiv. The child is given a toy rabbit, and the person who gives it to him makes that set of sounds which is represented in writing as "bunny." At first the sound is simply interesting for its own sake, and the child may repeat it, but without attaching any meaning to it. During the next few hours or days, however, this sound is repeated whenever that particular toy is the center of attention, until an association between the two is formed. Finally, a few days later, the child drops the rabbit behind the radiator, vainly tries to recover it, and finally comes to his mother and pleadingly says, "Bunny." The process is now complete: the sound has been used in the presence of and in obvious connection with the object so frequently that an association has been set up by means of which the sound alone can "stand for" the absent object. In short, "bunny" has ceased to be merely a collection of sounds and has become a word. The toy rabbit is an object, and is easily associated in this way. But similarly the child learns "hot" by painful association with that same radiator and thus (making no distinction between the parts of speech as yet) acquires a more abstract word referring, not to an object, but to a sensation. And he soon learns "bad"—a simple enough word in appearance, but one bearing the complicated significance of a type of conduct differentiated by its relationship to the conduct, demands, and interests of others. By now the way is open for an association between sound and the most abstract concepts of the human mind; and from "bunny" to "bad" is probably a greater mental advance than from "bad" to such terms as "passivity" and "aestheticism."

The Leitmotiv is the exception to the earlier statement that musical sound differs from linguistic in not having a fixed meaning, for the Leitmotiv is nothing more or less than a musical *word*. It is deliberately created by the composer, and is taught to the spectator-auditor (both relationships are necessary) precisely as a child is taught his first words. The Siegfried horn-theme is, on first hearing, merely an interesting and pleasant grouping of sounds—is, in short, "pure" music. But it is used in connection with a certain man who blows a horn, and thus an association is built up by which it comes to *mean* this man, and to stand for him when neither he nor his horn is physically present. It is now a word in music in precisely the same way that *Siegfried* is a word in language. This process of establishing an association can obviously be extended, like its linguistic parallel, from persons and objects to situations and abstract concepts. Thus a glance at Wagnerian analyses shows musical words for such things as the power of love, a dragon, care, anger, hatred, scorn, hopelessness, conjugal love, light, inseparability, and even such a specific combination of abstractions as longing for death.

The process of establishing these meanings is somewhat obscured by the fact that one usually comes to Wagner after having reached a certain maturity in the use of language, and hence is likely to use linguistic keys (analyses, *names* of motives, etc.) for a clarification of the musical words. Nevertheless, it cannot be doubted that if a child were brought up from infancy in a Wagnerian theater, the meanings of the principal themes in Wagnerian opera would seem to him as obvious and as inevitable as the meanings of such words as "dog," "hungry," and "bad." An adult learning a foreign language does not get his associations directly, as does the child; he uses dictionaries and thus employs the language which he already knows as a key to the one he is trying to learn. And this is precisely what the opera-goer does when he begins to learn the Wagnerian language: he gets a guide which will explain the Wagnerian words (themes) in terms of the words which he already knows in his own native tongue. Actually, then, a list of the Leitmotivs in Wagnerian opera is nothing more than a Wagnerian-English or Wagnerian-German dictionary.

As words, the themes of Wagner can also shift their emphasis or meaning according to the context in which they are used, and can gather significance as the situation of which they are the symbols develops. Thus a theme which is at first the name of a physical thing (a magic drink, or love-potion) comes to mean a person (Isolde) who is primarily affected by that potion, and to refer to the relationship and attitudes which spring from the drinking of that potion. If space and the scope of this book permitted, it would be interesting to make a detailed investigation of this shift of meaning and emphasis. Certainly the shifts found in words according to context could be found, but I believe that the process would go far beyond that. The language of *The Ring* has not only its existence, but its historical development in that work, and I feel certain that all the ordinary processes of semantic change which words exhibit in the course of centuries—specialization of meaning, generalization of meaning, etc.—could be shown to take place in the course of the history of Wagner's musical themes. A study of the use of the Leitmotiv from a philological point of view would doubtless throw a great deal of light both on Wagner's own creative processes and on the vexed question of significance in music.

This linguistic use of musical themes opens up a fascinating, but improbable possibility. We have seen how composers of vocal music can suggest, with the aid of a text, certain states of mind and physical objects. Wagner uses something of a similar method except that the performance of his works on the stage makes language not so necessary as a guide: instead of depending on already recognizable general effects in music and controlling their exact significance by means of the text, he can present the themes along with the persons, objects, or ideas and situations, and thus build up his own more exact musical words.

These themes have a significance only for the works in which they occur, but suppose that Wagner's work should become so basic a part of human experience that people would attach his meanings to his themes wherever they might occur. Suppose further that his method should become so widely practised that composers would take over his already established themes along with his meanings for them, and at the same time develop new themes of their own. In this way it would be possible to develop a language of music, in which musical phrases would have the exactness of words. Thus it would become possible to whistle "I'll meet you in the coffee-shop at three this afternoon" and have it as perfectly comprehensible as the words now are. Furthermore, an art could arise which would be both poetry and music at the same time rather than a putting together of two separate arts; and the poet of this art would be concerned, not with communicating his experience and at the same time working out his patterns of rhyme, meter, and verbal sound in general, but with the combining of his musical phrases so that they should simultaneously convey a clear meaning of the sort which we now associate with words and produce a texture of purely musical beauty.

I have actually seen the very crude beginnings of such a language used by a musician who happened to be an expert chess-player. At the chess club he gave underhanded assistance to his less expert friends (when they were playing against non-musical opponents) by hanging around and humming, ostensibly to himself. But he hummed themes associated with titles or persons, and these themes, though they could not tell a player what to do, actually did tell him where to concentrate his attention. Thus themes of Mark simply meant "king"; those of Isolde meant "queen"; and the opening bars of the *Poet and Peasant Overture* (in German the pawn is *der Bauer*, "the peasant") meant "pawn." Complete musical directions for chess would need only one theme for each piece and one for each number from one to eight.

But these are idle speculations. The essential thing is that Wagner's development of the Leitmotiv enabled him to add, as it were, another dimension to dramatic art. Since the beginnings of drama its writers have struggled with the problem of conveying things which no one would normally say. To some extent actions and facial expressions can achieve this end, but frequently something must be communicated for which they are entirely inadequate. By its very nature literature expresses itself in words, but drama is confined to the words spoken by the participants in the plot. What is the dramatists to do with the unrevealable secrets of his characters, their. thoughts which are not in accord with what they can say in a given situation? The answers—unsatisfactorily enough—have been such conventions as the soliloquy and the "aside," the *confidante* of Corneille and Racine whose real purpose in the play is simply to be told things that can be told to no one else, and such mechanical devices as O'Neill's masks which the characters put on and take off according to the nature of their speeches in *The Great God Brown* and his hardly more satisfactory distinction between words and spoken thoughts in *Strange Interlude.*

"Music expresses whatever one can neither say nor refrain from saying," * wrote Victor Hugo. He meant this as merely a vague panegyric on music in general, but it applies with absolute literalness in Wagnerian opera. The characters can speak only that which they can reasonably say under any given circumstances, but their attitudes, their recollections and associations, and even the things which they deliberately refuse to say can be dealt with by the music. One striking example will amply illustrate the possibilities of this method. Mark, returning from a hunt shortly after dawn, has found Tristan and Isolde together. His unbounded confidence in Tristan makes the discovery of their guilt a heavy blow to him, and he is both sorrowful and bewildered. In a long speech he reproaches Tristan, but is himself more in sorrow than in anger. He closes by asking who can explain the undiscoverable, mysterious reason why such things should come to pass. Tristan replies, "raising his eyes pityingly to Mark,"

> O König, das
> Kann ich dir nicht sagen;
> und was du fragst,
> das kannst du nie erfahren—

"O king, I cannot tell you that; and you can never know the thing you ask." What else could Tristan say? Any account of the potion would seem only a weak and ineffective attempt to avoid his responsibility and lie his way out of a difficult situation. Thomas Mann comments [10] that psychologically it is not necessarily the potion itself, but Tristan and Isolde's belief that they have drunk death, which frees their latent passion. But the belief still holds, and Mark is simply incapable of understanding a passion like theirs. Tristan's reply to Mark is a dramatically adequate refusal to discuss a situation which explanation can only make worse.

* "Ce qu'on ne peut dire et ce qu'on ne peut taire, la musique l'exprime." Hugo, *William Shakespeare*, II, iv.

On the non-musical stage the refusal could be given, but not the necessary recollection of the very thing which cannot here be said. If Tristan were a character in *Strange Interlude,* he might turn towards the audience and say, "It was that damned potion we swallowed, but I can't expect *him* to swallow *that.*" Music can do far more. Before Tristan replies at all, in the pause after Mark's question, the English horn softly gives out the Tristan-motive, and as the last note of this sounds the oboe comes in with the theme of the potion (which is also the theme of Isolde), the bassoons giving a mysterious harmonic background.[11] Thus the history of the hero, the potion, the heroine, and their relationship pervades the whole scene. Tristan speaks only the words that can be spoken, but the music carries the unspoken thoughts and the fatality of the situation, Mark being, of course, innocent as to any particular significance in it. (For that matter, except for sounds which are commented on, like hunting horns, the characters are not supposed to hear the music which accompanies their words and actions.) During the pause halfway through the speech of Tristan quoted above, these two themes are again heard. Tristan says no more to Mark. Once again his theme sounds, in a modified form, and after this the potion theme is repeated lingeringly. Then comes the recently established theme of the inseparability of the lovers, and Tristan turns to ask Isolde whether she will follow him into the dark land of night.

All this takes place in considerably less than one minute after the conclusion of Mark's question. In drama alone the scene would be ludicrous: a man, caught seducing the wife of his master and friend, refuses to answer the husband's very reasonable question; instead, he turns to the wife and continues his courtship in the husband's presence. Obviously, this will not do. In a narrative poem something of the feelings and thoughts involved could be given, but such procedure would impede the action. Only by the Leitmotiv—by the flashes of association and recognition which have already been built up around these themes —can a scene such as this be made really effective.

We shall have occasion later to see that this device, though really literary in its nature, has been borrowed back into literature from Wagner's music. And it is quite possible that the historical importance of Wagner—aside from the artistic value of his works—will ultimately rest not on his sensational orchestration or his grandiose attempts to create an all-embracing form of art, but on his development of a technique by which composers and poets can say some things which before Wagner were incommunicable.

CHAPTER IX

Repetition and Variation

THUS far we have been considering the raw materials out of which both music and literature are constructed, and the combination of the two arts in vocal music. The rest of our investigation will concern the influence of each of these arts on the other, and the occasional use in one art of features which are standard in the other, even where there is no reason to assume direct influence.

The most convenient method of approach will be to note certain forms and principles wherever and whenever they occur rather than to attempt a historical survey of the interrelationships between the two arts. But before beginning such a classification we may note a few significant historical facts. Since, broadly speaking, instrumental music does not come into its own as an independent art until about 1600, little influence of one art on the other is to be expected before that time. Nor does the rise of instrumental music immediately bring about such interrelationships: when it began to assume a position of prominence it was too busy exploring its own resources to be concerned with those of a different art; and it could hardly exert any appreciable influence on so well established an art as literature before it had fully developed its own capacities. Though occasional writers like Milton [1] are influenced by instrumental music, they are sporadic phenomena until the first stirrings of the romantic movement. Irving Babbitt [2] and other writers have had a good deal to say about "the romantic confusion of the arts," and have pointed out that the romanticists were very much concerned with the possibilities of transferring techniques, effects, and even subject-matter from one art to another. That interest has come down to the present, and in the case of music and literature it has been growing steadily since the beginning of the romantic movement.

There is one theory which offers an excellent explanation of this fact. It has been pointed out [3] that the arts tend to move in regularly repeating cycles, achieving maturity in the same order with each new epoch of civilization. At any particular time one art is in a dominant position, and the others have a tendency, perhaps unconsciously, to look up to it and imitate it. Thus Dante's *Commedia*, written during the dominance of architecture, is architectural both in its own structure and in its detailed presentation of the architecture of its setting. Likewise, when the artistic hegemony had passed to painting in the Renaissance, writers like Ariosto and Spenser produced strongly pictorial poems. According to this cycle-theory, music is the dominant art of the nineteenth and early twentieth centuries, and writers have tended to take it as a model and inspiration. Thus the famous dictum of Walter Pater [4] (actually anticipated by Schopenhauer [5]) that *"all art constantly strives towards the condition of music"* seems to be true enough of Pater's own period, but false in its use of the word "constantly." Pater's explanation of the phenomenon is theoretical rather than historical: "For while in all other kinds of art it is possible to distinguish the matter from the form, and the understanding can always make this distinction, yet it is the constant effort of art to obliterate it." Certainly it is true that in music, more than in any other art, form and substance are inseparable, but there is good reason to believe that the assumption of such an identity as the ultimate goal of art is peculiar to the aesthetics of the romantics and their successors.

Since the literary aping of music is the particular product of our own age, it will be better to consider it first. And since it is impossible to distinguish form from content in music, we shall naturally find that this imitation has frequently taken the course of borrowing or adapting musical forms for literary purposes. In order to see how and to what extent writers have been able to do this, we must examine the structural features on which musical forms are based and see what correspondence or equivalence exists between them and the structural devices of literature.

There is probably no profounder single remark on the essential nature of art than that of Coleridge about the Imagination: [6]

This power, first put in action by the will and understanding, and retained under their irremissive, though gentle and unnoticed, control, *laxis effertur habenis*, reveals itself in the balance or reconcilement of opposite or discordant qualities: of sameness with difference; of the general with the concrete; the idea with the image; the individual with the representative; the sense of novelty and freshness with old and familiar objects; a more than usual state of emotion with more than usual order; judgement ever awake and steady self-possession with enthusiasm and feeling profound or vehement; and while it blends and harmonizes the natural and artificial, still subordinates art to nature; the manner to the matter; and our admiration of the poet to our sympathy with the poetry.

Some of Coleridge's specific examples are applicable only to poetry (of which he is actually writing), but the general principle—that the imagination, as distinguished from the mere power of fancy, is a *creative* power able to reconcile opposite or discordant qualities into one organic whole—holds for all the arts. So do many of his more particular statements. We may be able to make intermediate explanations in terms of orchestration, thematic development, etc., but ultimately the difference between the finest climaxes of Beethoven's symphonies and the too-frequent passages in which Tschaikowsky throws a hysterical fit with the cooperation of a large orchestra lies in the fact that while both composers had "a more than usual state of emotion" and "feeling profound or vehement" (probably only the latter in Tschaikowsky's case), Beethoven also had "more than usual order" and "judgement ever awake and steady self-possession" along with his feeling. What is hysteria except a display of emotion unchecked by judgment or restraint? Principles like these obviously apply to all the arts equally.

The most widely applicable of Coleridge's examples of reconciliation of opposite qualities, however, is that of "sameness with difference." No work of art from epigram to epic, from cameo to sphinx, from bagatelle to symphony, can exist unless it combines these two opposite qualities. For it must have sameness in order to be *a* work rather than an accidental jumble; and it must have difference in order to avoid complete monotony, or, to make an extreme example, to consist of anything more than mechanical repetition of the first word, note, or stroke of the brush. And since music does not have content independently of form, the necessity is particularly obvious in musical structure.

As long as musical sound consists solely of repetition, the monotone, it remains formless. On the other hand, when music goes to the other extreme and refuses to revert to any point, either rhythmic, melodic, or harmonic, which recollection can identify, it is equally formless. Repetition and contrast, therefore, are the two twin principles of musical form. They are found asserting themselves in the most primitive examples of the folk-tunes of all nations, and are not to be escaped from by the most daring innovators in modern music.* [7]

* From Grove's *Dictionary of Music and Musicians.* By permission of The Macmillan Company, publishers.

Neither sameness nor difference, taken alone, can be profitably discussed, for both dead monotony and utter chaos are absolutes which, by their very nature, defy analysis. Therefore it will be best to consider two pairs of attributes, each of which involves, with different emphasis, both of these qualities. Repetition and variation, considered as one principle, includes both exact repetition and repetition with a difference, thus placing the principle emphasis on the sameness of material, but at the same time allowing for change in its presentation. Balance and contrast, likewise considered together, forms a principle placing the emphasis on difference, but allowing for a structural or proportional sameness in the concept of balance. Before considering the attempts of authors to adopt the forms established by composers, we must see how these structural principles of music apply in literature and how far their application differs in the two arts. It is obvious that these devices, thus stated, cannot always be sharply distinguished, for one will always contain aspects of the other. Thus a theme followed by a variation on that same theme will, from one point of view, be a repetition involving variation; on the other hand, it will form two sections balanced against each other. It will also involve contrast as well as repetition: in so far as the variation is identical with the original theme, repetition will occur; but in so far as it is different there will be an element of contrast. Nevertheless, the distinction between the two principles of repetition and variation, on the one hand, and balance and contrast, on the other, can be clearly enough made for our present purposes.

Repetition and variation can be seen in the smallest real structural units of both literature and music. In rhythm, for example, the basic pattern of the bar or the line is repeated indefinitely, but is sufficiently varied on successive repetitions to remain interesting. Even in smaller subdivisions than the poetic line the same thing holds true, for the line is defined in terms of a certain type of foot repeated a certain number of times. Similarly, 4/4 time can be broken up into two half-bars repeating the same pattern with a difference in the strength of the accent, and such time schemes as 6/8, 9/8, and 12/8 are readily broken down on a similar principle. Some types of irregular time, such as the 5/4 of the second movement of Tschaikowsky's *Sixth Symphony*, apply the variation within unity in a slightly different way. Here a secondary accent is necessary, and no equal division of five beats can be made: hence the bar may consist of a two-beat group followed by one of three beats, or this order may be reversed. In other words, the five-beat bar is repeated indefinitely, but there is frequent variation in the position of the secondary accent, which may come on either the third or the fourth beat.

Poetry has a particular type of repetition on which the structure of many different forms depends. Rhyme, alliteration, and assonance all demand both repetition and variation in order to exist at all. Rhyme is an identity of sound in the stressed vowels of two words and in all sounds following these vowels, and assonance is an agreement of these vowels only. Alliteration, in the narrower sense of the word, is an agreement of initial sounds of words or of their stressed syllables. The important point here is that each of these definitions demands repetition of some sounds and difference of others. *Book* does not rhyme with *book* because the words are identical and the element of difference (or variation) is non-existent; but it does rhyme with *hook* or *crook*.* Similarly, we ordinarily demand some difference between sounds in words as well as a prescribed repetition of some sounds before we speak of alliteration or assonance. Since a poetic form like the Italian sonnet can be almost entirely defined in terms of meter and rhyme scheme, it is evident that its structure is very largely based on repetition and variation.

These are purely formal repetitions and variations of sound, but the existence of a meaning apart from sound allows other possibilities in poetry. A favorite one, especially in certain early poetry of various nations, involves the use of different words to repeat, with difference of emphasis or shading, the same basic idea. Frequently this device appears simply in a fondness for accumulating synonyms. Thus when Helenos advises Hector to go into Troy to ask Hecuba to make sacrifices to Athene, in the hope that the goddess may protect them from

---

* During some periods of literary history identical rhyme has been allowed and even always cultivated, but almost always with the idea that the words which are identical in sound must be sharply separated in meaning. Thus Chaucer, in *The Book of the Duchess,* can write

> Certes, I nil never ete breed,
> I make a-vowe to my god *here* ("here")
> But I mowe of my lorde *here!* ("hear")
> (lines 92–94)

Or he can describe Fortune as

> The traytresse fals and ful of gyle,
> That al behoteth and no-thing *halt,* ("holds to" a promise)
> She goth upright and yet she *halt.* ("halts, limps")
> (lines 620–622)

Dante's refusal to rhyme the name of Christ with anything except itself is a piece of theological symbolism quite independent of the technique of versification.

the attack which Diomed is leading, he says: "Thus she may perhaps hold back from sacred Ilium the son of Tydeus, the savage spearman, the mighty inspirer of flight" *—three synonyms for Diomed. These two lines are considered sufficiently effective to be repeated in almost identical form nearly two hundred lines later. The same device is a great favorite with Old English poets in general, and especially with the anonymous author of *Beowulf*. When the hero of that poem arrives at Hrothgar's court and asks to speak with the king, a retainer replies (and the synonyms, which must be placed together in modern English, are scattered along through the sentence): "Since you request it, I will ask the friend of the Danes, the prince of the Scildings, the divider of spoil, the famous king, about your voyage, and will quickly bring you the answer which that good man sees fit to give me." † This one sentence contains five different terms for Hrothgar, and, with a sort of virtuosity evident also in the Homeric passage, does not include his actual name at all. The prevalence of such synonyms in Old English poetry, together with the poets' ingenuity in creating new ones by compounding words or inventing metaphors, shows clearly that such varied repetition of an idea is deliberately sought as an ornament of poetic style.

The same device is familiar in biblical poetry, in which synonymous phrases or sentences are used, but their parallelism makes for an effect of balance which will be discussed later. There is, however, a remarkable passage in *Judges* which must be considered here. Deborah's song describing Jael's killing of Sisera gives the climax of the entire action in an unprecedented series of repetitions: "At her feet he bowed, he fell, he lay down: at her feet he bowed, he fell: where he bowed, there he fell down dead." ⁸ From a logical point of view this verse is hardly more than an incoherent stammering, but the repetition, with its shifts of rhythm and grouping and its climactic final word, is extremely effective.

A somewhat different use of the repeated word is found in a fine

---

* ἅι κεν Τυδέος υἱὸν ἀπόσχῃ Ἰλίου ἱρῆς,
ἄγριον αἰχμητήν, κρατερὸν μήστωρα φόβοιο....

(Iliad, VI, 96–97 and 277–278.)

†   Ic þæs *wine Deniga*,

frean Scildinga	frinan wille,
beaga bryttan,	swa þu bena eart,
þeoden mærne	ymb þinne sið,
ond þe þa andsware	ædre gecyðan,
ðe me *se goda*	agifan þenceð.

(Beowulf, 350–355.)

sentence from Sir Thomas Malory describing the final disposition of
King Arthur's sword: "Then Sir Bedivere departed, and went to the
sword, and lightly took it up, and went to the water side; and there
he bound the girdle about the hilts, and then he threw the sword as far
into the water, as he might; and there came an arm and an hand
above the water and met it, and caught it, and so shook it thrice and
brandished, and then vanished away the hand with the sword in the
water." [9] The long and otherwise straggling sentence is held together
by the repeated emphasis on *sword, water,* and *hand* in such a way that
each subdivision of the sentence is dominated by one of these words,
and the three are combined to round off the period as a whole.

So far we have been considering the repetition of single words or
phrases, or of single ideas which can be expressed by such simple means.
When we come to larger repetitions in literature we find that they are
very likely to be of a structural character. This is true of those poetic
forms—ballade, rondeau, villanelle, pantoum, triolet, etc.—which demand the repetition of certain passages at specified places, and of the
use of the refrain, whether exactly repeated or varied, in ballads. In
addition to these purely formal repetitions, others are made entirely
by the writer's choice. Homer and the folk-epic in general are full of
them. In Book VI of the *Iliad* alone three passages of three lines or
more each are repeated with some changes, and they may well be used
as a typical example.

The first one (which we will call A) contains the synonyms for
Diomed which we have already noted, but they are only a small part
of it—the entire passage is twelve lines in length. At its first occurrence
Helenos tells Hector to go and ask Hecuba to pray to Athene. When
Hector does ask her, he repeats almost the identical speech of Helenos.
And, finally, when Hecuba goes to Athene's temple to make her offering,
the poet himself describes the scene in language so similar to the
earlier passages that it is unquestionably to be considered as a repetition. The other two passages in question are shorter, and in each case
the varied repetition follows almost immediately after the original
statement. The second one (B), in the excellent and almost literal
translation of Lang, Leaf, and Myers, will illustrate the method:

But when he came to Priam's beautiful palace, adorned with polished colonnades
—and in it were fifty chambers of polished stone, builded hard by one another,
wherein Priam's sons slept beside their wedded wives; and for his daughters
over against them on the other side within the courtyard were twelve roofed
chambers of polished stone builded hard by one another, wherein slept Priam's

sons-in-law beside their chaste wives—then came there to meet him his bountiful mother. . . .

The passage which we will call C occurs when Hector asks the serving-women in his own house whether Andromache is in this place or in that, and they reply, repeating his words with negatives, that she is not in this place or in that, but on the great tower. These three passages illustrate different uses of repetition. The first spreads over a considerable part of the Book, and helps to tie together one sequence of actions in spite of intervening episodes. The second is really a verbal imitation of the architectural symmetry which it describes, and the third shows what is probably a pleasure in the negative repetition entirely for its own sake. The order of these passages (ABBAACC) shows clearly the larger importance given to the longer passage and its unifying effect.[10]

Another frequent type of poetic repetition is found in fairly elaborate metaphors or similes. We shall see later that poetic tolerance of repetition is comparatively slight, and the figure of speech offers an excellent way to increase that tolerance, for figures can be parallel (or identical) in their basic meaning, and yet, by employing different imagery, can give an effect of freshness and variety at each reappearance of the idea. Burns, in *Tam O' Shanter*, is obviously amusing himself with the device when he gives a series of similes to inculcate the moral idea of the transiency of pleasure,[11] and Wordsworth is—for once—not taking himself too seriously when he tells how he likes to "sit and play with similes" to describe the daisy.[12] Shelley devotes a stanza each to four similes based on the skylark,[13] and Omar Khayyám (or, rather, Fitzgerald's arrangement of his originally independent quatrains) shows human helplessness in the hands of an inscrutable deity by comparing men successively to the puppets of a silhouette show, the pieces in chess, and the ball in a polo game—all moved from without by forces which they cannot fathom.[14] Perhaps the best example of this type of poetic repetition is to be found in Shakespeare's seventy-third sonnet:

> That time of year thou mayest in me behold
> When yellow leaves, or none, or few, do hang
> Upon those boughs which shake against the cold,
> Bare ruin'd choirs, where late the sweet birds sang.
>
> In me thou seest the twilight of such day
> As after sunset fadeth in the west,

Which by and by black night doth take away,
Death's second self, that seals up all in rest.

In me thou seest the glowing of such fire,
That on the ashes of his youth doth lie,
As a death-bed whereon it must expire,
Consum'd with that which it was nourish'd by.

This thou perceiv'st, which makes thy love more strong
To love that well which thou must leave ere long.

Here the three quatrains are all metaphorical expansions of one simple statement: "I am growing old"; but they give no impression of redundancy or prolixity, for each has its particular imagery. Autumn, twilight, and a dying fire all carry with them associations of decline and approaching death, but they also present different shadings of the idea, and what we have here is really a set of variations on a theme.

The larger literary forms may occasionally be bound together by repeated passages, but in general they involve repetition and variation of plot rather than of words or images. Thus *Beowulf* is divided into two episodes separated by an interval of half a century, and the episodes are similar in their general nature. In the second half of the poem, however, the rôles are shifted: in the fight with the dragon Beowulf plays the part which Hrothgar had played in the Grendel episode, and Wiglaf plays the part taken by Beowulf in that earlier adventure.[18] Similarly, the sub-plot in Elizabethan drama is a variation on the main plot, bound up with it and influencing it, but essentially running its own parallel course. In *King Lear*, for example, the story of Lear and his daughters is repeated with minor variations in the story of Gloucester and his sons.

To attempt any complete classification of the types and functions of repetition in literature would be a mere work of pedantry, for the types merge into one another, and the economy of means practised by all great art frequently causes the same thing to have a number of different functions. Enough has been said about literary repetition to serve as a basis for comparison with that employed in music, and other examples and principles will necessarily be considered in connection with the attempts of writers to employ various forms borrowed from music.

In music also the principle of repetition and variation is all-pervasive. It occurs, as has been noted, in the very basis of musical time. Once a phrase has been stated, a great deal of its extension and development will take the form of repetition beginning on different degrees of the scale, in different registers, with different instruments, with alterations of time and intervals, with different harmonization—in fact, with any conceivable sort of variation, or often without any variation at all. The standard larger forms of music, such as the fugue, rondo, sonata, etc., cannot be adequately defined except in terms of patterns of repetition. Even the forms which do not have predetermined patterns of this kind have their own individual patterns: Chopin's *Scherzo in B Flat Minor*, for example, has no standard pattern, but it does consist of several sections, each of which is repeated at least once during the course of the composition. Like poetry, music uses these repetitions for a number of different purposes and for effects ranging all the way from the merely mechanical to carefully prepared and tremendous climaxes.[16]

The general principles of repetition are much the same in music and in literature, but there is a conspicuous difference in degree. In general, music demands far more repetition than poetry can tolerate. Examples of musical repetition are so frequent that it is not worth while to cite them. The fact that musical notation has and frequently employs a sign to indicate the repetition of an extensive section (as well as manuscript signs for the repetition of single bars) speaks eloquently. However, it is worth while to point out the extent to which music actually does make use of the same material over and over. I have just run through the score of Chopin's *Funeral March* and made a tabulation of the repetitions of individual bars. The results show that, though the composition runs to a length of 108 measures, it contains only 38 *different* measures.* One of these is used 8 times, 14 of them are used 4 times each, 1 is used 3 times, 19 are used twice each, and 3 occur only once each. These three cannot be repeated. They are the last measure of the first section (which must lead into the trio), the last of the trio (which must lead back to the first section), and the last of the entire composition. But these figures do not indicate the full extent of the repetition, for they ignore the repetition of a measure on a different degree of the scale, with one of the notes doubled an octave lower, or with any of the numerous minor changes which do not affect its general nature.

Another composition will serve for an example of the repetition of

---

* This count was made on the strictest possible basis, and did not consider two bars as the same unless they were absolutely identical. Thus bar 4 and bar 10 were not counted as repetition because the introductory "grace note" in bar 10 is lacking in bar 4.

general idea and contour. Grieg's *Ase's Death* (from the first *Peer Gynt Suite*) is entirely made up of repetitions of one rhythmic phrase four measures in length—ten occurrences of it, and one approximation. This phrase has two general melodic contours. For its first six occurrences it has a generally ascending line, and with each repetition it rises in pitch and increases in volume. In the latter part of the composition the same rhythmic phrase embodies a descending melodic line, which is lower and softer with each successive repetition, and fades out falteringly and very softly the last time it is heard. After these eleven repetitions of the four-measure rhythm, one final measure (consisting of one repetition of the preceding chord) is added. And that is all there is to the composition—four measures of rhythm to which two different melodic and harmonic ideas are attached. These two examples were chosen more or less at random, and are typical. Certainly there is no reason to believe that the *Funeral March* is at all unusual in its use of repetition; and though *Ase's Death* does perhaps show a greater limitation of material than many other pieces of the same length, it could hardly be called a remarkable instance of economy.

We have already seen that the repetitions involved in the measure and the foot correspond closely, and that the poetic repetition of sound on which such devices as rhyme and assonance are based is purely formal and seldom extends beyond a few lines. Even such forms as the ballade and chant royal, which extend a rhyme-scheme or set of rhyming words over the entire length of a poem, can hardly be considered as exceptions to this statement, for they are, in comparison with the epic and drama, extremely short literary forms. For this reason the following discussions of repetition will ignore these repetitive elements and be confined to the repetition of lines, refrains, or ideas in poetry, and to the roughly equivalent repetition of thematic material in music.

We immediately notice one significant difference. In literature the formal repetition of specific parts of the work at predetermined points is confined to such forms as the ballade, rondeau, triolet, etc. It is no part of the plan of such works as the drama, the epic, and the novel. In music, on the other hand, forms like the prelude, nocturne, bagatelle, and impromptu can be defined without any mention of repetition, for though it usually plays a considerable rôle in such compositions, its use is entirely a matter of choice with the composer. But it is impossible to give any account of sonata form, or of the form of passacaglia, rondo, or fugue without telling what is repeated at what point. In literature, then, the shorter and slighter forms are based on repetition, but the larger ones are "free" in this respect; in music the shorter and slighter forms are "free," but the longer and more imposing ones require a certain amount of formal repetition. This fact furnishes further evidence for the earlier statement that music tolerates and even requires far more repetition than does literature.

The principal reason for this difference seems to lie in the nature of the two arts and to go back to the general indivisibility of music into such categories as form and content. Repetition without variation is strictly limited in poetry by the fact that one remembers an idea even though the words in which it was embodied may have escaped the memory; hence the idea alone is usually sufficient for the further purposes of the work, and there is no need to repeat the exact wording until that has become established in the mind. It also follows from this principle that variation in literature does not, as a general rule, alter the feeling of redundancy which extensive literary repetition is likely to produce. The exact words are not established in the reader's mind as are the exact notes of a musical theme, and therefore when the idea is repeated in a different form he is not aware of—and hence not interested in—the difference. In fact, unless he has a really extraordinary memory he cannot tell whether a recurrent literary idea is an exact repetition of a variation unless he turns back to the earlier occurrence of the idea and makes a comparison.*

In music there is no such difficulty. A speech or idea repeated in different words gives an impression of prolixity, but a musical theme "divided," augmented, diminished, transposed, reharmonized, reorchestrated, or varied in any of the almost infinite possible ways seems to be more of a new thing than a repetition. Even unchanged repetition is far more tolerable than in poetry because of the necessity for fixing the exact form (not merely the general idea) of a theme in the listener's mind, in order that he may follow its subsequent development. All these considerations help to explain the fact (which will become in-

---

* Strictly speaking, it is obviously impossible to say something over in different words, for the change of even a single word will necessarily make a slight change in the total things said by a passage. But though there may theoretically be no possibility of separating form from content in literature, we all recognize that in practice we can and do make such a separation far more definitely in verbally than in musically presented material.

creasingly evident) that the poet * will usually repeat, either exactly
or with variation, only small parts of his work, while the composer will
construct the major portion of his work out of repetitions and variations.

There is also a historical consideration which may help to explain
this difference. We have already commented on Homer's use of repetition, using only average examples to illustrate it. It may be worth while
to look at an extreme one. In the opening of Book II of the *Iliad*, Zeus
summons a messenger who is to go to Agamemnon as a false dream.
In five lines Zeus tells him what to say, and the messenger immediately
appears before the general and carries out the god's instructions, expanding the five lines to eleven, primarily by means of additions at the
beginning and end. Shortly thereafter Agamemnon awakes, calls his
chiefs together, and reports the message verbatim except for the
omission of the last line and a half. Within the first forty-seven lines
of Book II this substantial passage occurs three times and thus occupies
more than half of the total space. Vergil would never have written such
a passage; in fact, he makes far less use of repetition in general than
does Homer. In *Beowulf* and, later, in the English and Scottish ballads,
we again find extensive repetitions of this general nature, but in
Chaucer they are not frequent, and they are not to be found at all in
many later writers. Except in cases where some special point is obviously to be gained, recent and contemporary writers do not repeat
themselves in this way. Evidence could be multiplied at great length,
but the general point is clear: extensive repetition is a characteristic of
the early stages of literary art, and it tends to disappear as the art
becomes more mature and more self-conscious. (I speak historically,
and do not mean to imply that being more mature necessarily means
being aesthetically better.)

Music is in one sense probably coeval with literature, but its development as an independent art is so late that we need have no hesita-
tion in calling it, in its present form, the youngest of the arts. It is
highly possible that the difference with respect to repetition comes
not only from differences in the nature of the arts, but also from the

---

* English greatly needs some word like the German *Dichter* for the writer of imagi-
native literature, whether in prose or verse. We have no word which applies both to
Cervantes and to Milton except such all-inclusive terms as *writer* and *author*, and
they include the writer of the newspaper sports-page and the author of a recipe-book.
Similarly, we need a word like *Dichtung* for the literature itself. Where no distinction
between prose and verse is required, I shall feel free to use *poet* and *poetry* in this
broad sense.

accidental fact that recent music is in a much earlier stage of development than is recent literature. At any rate, there is some evidence to support such a view. Performers and audiences alike seem to find the formal repetition demanded by fairly recent composers excessive, and to feel that the composer is more honored by the breach than by the observance of his instructions to repeat certain extensive passages. The repeat-marks often found at the end of the exposition section of a movement in sonata-form, for example, are often ignored in present-day performance. Also, later composers seem not only to specify less of this formal repetition, but to repeat themselves in general somewhat less than did their predecessors. If this tendency continues, and if literature remains stable in this respect, five centuries from now the difference in the use of repetition in music and literature may be far less striking than it now is. Nevertheless, there seems to be sufficient difference in the nature of the two arts to insure that music will always make more extensive use of repetition than will literature.

CHAPTER X

Balance and Contrast

LIKE repetition and variation, balance and contrast can be found in all the arts, on all levels, and on all scales. Perhaps the principle is most obvious in architecture, where the requirements of physical stability reinforce the aesthetic demand for a certain balance and symmetry of parts; but it is no less active in other arts. In the rhythmic structure of the temporal arts the balance and contrast between stressed and unstressed sounds is the basis of the foot and bar. In both arts the principle extends from this small beginning through balance of phrases, sections, and such larger divisions as books, acts, and movements. We shall consider the pervasiveness of balanced structure in literature because it happens to be mechanically simpler to quote verbal illustrations than musical ones; but we should remember that, with some slight reservations to be noted later, precisely the same principles and the same kinds of examples are to be found in music.

Perhaps the most familiar example is that of Hebrew literature as rendered in the King James Bible. Over and over again one finds verses divided into halves which say much the same thing in different words (thus employing repetition and variation), and carefully balanced off against each other:

> The heavens declare the glory of God; and the firmament sheweth his handiwork.
> Day unto day uttereth speech, and night unto night sheweth knowledge.[1]

The whole of the third chapter of *Job* is based on the same device and shows such intricate possibilities of balance and contrast that it is worth quoting in full:

1. After this Job opened his mouth, and cursed his day.
2. And Job spake, and said,
3. Let the day perish wherein I was born, and the night in which it was said, There is a man child conceived.

4. Let that day be darkness; let not God regard it from above, neither let the light shine upon it.

5. Let darkness and the shadow of death stain it; let a cloud dwell upon it; let the blackness of the day terrify it.

6. As for that night, let darkness seize upon it; let it not be joined unto the days of the year, let it not come into the number of the months.

7. Lo, let that night be solitary, let no joyful voice come therein.

8. Let them curse it that curse the day, who are ready to raise up their mourning.

9. Let the stars of the twilight thereof be dark; let it look for light, but have none; neither let it see the dawning of the day:

10. Because it shut not up the doors of my mother's womb, nor hid sorrow from mine eyes.

11. Why died I not from the womb? Why did I not give up the ghost when I came out of the belly?

12. Why did the knees prevent me? or why the breasts that I should suck?

13. For now should I have lain still and been quiet, I should have slept: then had I been at rest,

14. With kings and counsellors of the earth, which built desolate places for themselves;

15. Or with princes that had gold, who filled their houses with silver:

16. Or as an hidden untimely birth I had not been; as infants which never saw light.

17. There the wicked cease from troubling; and there the weary be at rest.

18. There the prisoners rest together; they hear not the voice of the oppressor.

19. The small and great are there; and the servant is free from his master.

20. Wherefore is light given to him that is in misery, and life unto the bitter in soul;

21. Which long for death, but it cometh not; and dig for it more than for hid treasures;

22. Which rejoice exceedingly, and are glad, when they can find the grave?

23. Why is light given to a man whose way is hid, and whom God hath hedged in?

24. For my sighing cometh before I eat, and my roarings are poured out like the waters.

25. For the thing which I greatly feared is come upon me, and that which I was afraid of is come unto me.

26. I was not in safety, neither had I rest, neither was I quiet; yet trouble came.

Such verses as 25 have the division into halves, but that is a very minor part of the total balance. The first two verses, being introductory narrative, are not under the stress and excitement of Job's magnificent curse: they confine themselves to a balancing of short compound predicates. Job's first utterance, however, forms a highly complex structure. The third verse lays the groundwork by balancing two curses, one di-

rected at the day and the other at the night. Verses 4 and 5 take up
the first half of verse 3 (the curse on the day) and consist of *three*
parallel members each. Logically the members of these two verses are
the same, and hence there is a series of six balanced imprecations on
the day; but by syntax and punctuation the two verses are kept separate so that they form a balanced group of three against three. Verse 6
now takes up the *night* (the second half of verse 3) and makes a series
of three parallel curses for it—parallel both to each other and to those
already leveled at the day. Verse 7 continues in the same vein, but
abandons complete symmetry by using only two parallel members instead of three. Verses 8 and 9 now balance and combine these separate
imprecations: the day is to be made like the night, and the night to
be infinitely dark and accursed; hence the day and night can now be
considered together. The two logically parallel elements of verse 8 are
grammatically not quite parallel, and they are balanced against the
three exactly parallel elements of verse 9 (the second of which, "let it
look for light, but have none," contains its own balanced structure).
Thus the general principle is kept, but there is sufficient irregularity in
the symmetry to maintain interest—Coleridge's "sameness with difference" again. This section of Job's speech is closed by verse 10, which
explains the reason for all the accumulation of curses in earlier lines.
But since these were all parallel elaborations of verse 3, it follows that
verse 10 is really parallel to verse 3: drop out the intervening verses of
elaboration, and the result will be two verses, each balanced within
itself and each balanced against the other. Within this general scheme
there are, of course, minor points of balance (such as "darkness and
shadow" in verse 5) but even if we ignore them we find an elaborate
structure based entirely on balance and contrast. Using numbers for
the verses and letters for their subdivisions, and bracketing together
parallels, we get a symmetrical diagram of this passage.

But verse 10 is more than a conclusion for the previous section. It
also serves as a starting point for the next division: the curse on the
night "because it shut not the doors of my mother's womb" leads directly, and by the same principle of balance, to the query "Why died
I not from the womb?" and that question touches off the subject
matter for the rest of the chapter. An analysis of this remainder, on
the principles of the one already made for the earlier passage, will
show that it too is simply an elaborate application of the one principle
of balance and contrast.

This chapter is, of course, an extreme example, and its particular effectiveness is made possible by the dramatic situation in which it occurs. Job has been deprived of his children and his property; he has been smitten with sore boils from sole to crown. Even under these afflictions he has rejected the kindly suggestion of his wife that he curse God, and die. Instead, he has seated himself in the ashes, and his three friends and comforters (as he believes them to be at this point of

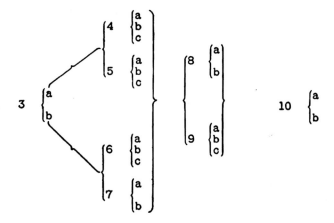

the story) have come to him. "So they sat down with him upon the ground seven days and seven nights, and none spake a word unto him: for they saw that his grief was very great." For a week, then, Job has been revolving these things in his mind, but has kept silence. When he finally does speak, the pent-up curses and questions break loose in a torrent, and the vehemence and naturalness of his multiplied imprecations, though organized by an intricate structure, are sufficient to conceal the mechanics of that structure from any reader who does not deliberately search for it.

Many of the patterns based on balance and contrast have become formalized and established as regular poetic types. Perhaps the best example of such a form is the Petrarchan, or Italian, sonnet. The Elizabethan sonnet has three quatrains and a final couplet, and this arrangement frequently leads to an organization like that in the example quoted from Shakespeare: the quatrains vary one main idea, and the couplet makes a final comment. There is a certain disproportion between the three quatrains on the one hand and the couplet on the other, for by the time the couplet is reached, it is likely to be either very obvious or else (if the idea is not obvious) too cryptic. (I once heard an Oxford Professor of Poetry toying with the idea of getting out an edition of Shakespeare's sonnets in which all final couplets would be omitted.) The generally recognized superiority of the Italian sonnet seems to be the result of a better arrangement of balance and contrast. This form has a general division into octave and sestet—a division which gives a better balance to the two contrasted sections without making an absolute and dead symmetry. Furthermore, there is a tendency for the two quatrains of the octave, though bound by rhyme into a single unit, to be balanced one against the other, and for the two tercets of the sestet to form a similar balance. One of Rossetti's sonnets will illustrate the pattern.[2]

> When do I see thee most, beloved one?
> When in the light the spirits of mine eyes
> Before thy face, their altar, solemnize
> The worship of that Love through thee made known?
>
> Or when in the dusk hours (we two alone)
> Close-kissed and eloquent of still replies
> Thy twilight-hidden glimmering visage lies,
> And my soul only sees thy soul its own?
>
> O love, my love! if I no more should see
> Thyself, nor on the earth the shadow of thee,
> Nor image of thine eyes in any spring—
>
> How then should sound upon Life's darkening slope
> The ground-whirl of the perished leaves of Hope,
> The wind of Death's imperishable wing?

This subdivision of octave and sestet, though not obligatory is remarkably common. A brief turning through Edna Millay's *Fatal Interview* indicates that seven out of the fifty-two sonnets follow this pattern exactly, and most others approach it, but without such complete regularity. In all the arts, once a form or principle has been thoroughly established and generally understood, it does not require such obvious treatment as it did in its earlier stages. Thus the paintings of Cimabue have an exact balance, figure for figure; but after the Italian Primitives the principle of balance was well enough understood to be less mechanically employed. If we look at the sonnets of Petrarch (though he certainly cannot be called a "primitive" in the sense in which that term is applied to Cimabue) we find that departures from this rigid scheme are rare indeed. Petrarch's first ten sonnets all follow it exactly, and it is only very occasionally that one finds a sonnet like No. 245, in which the sense of the first quatrain runs over two words into the second. Later writers of sonnets have achieved some of their finest effects by such slight departures from absolute and (what is perhaps more important) expected symmetry. Milton's sonnets are the most consistent and the finest examples of this deliberate playing about the exact symmetry without strictly observing it. Thus the theoretical pattern calls for the main break in thought to come exactly at the end of the eighth line, at the division between octave and sestet. But in Milton's sonnets on the massacre of the Piemontese and on his blindness the division comes a few words early (*within* the eighth line), and in those to Cromwell and to Cyriak Skinner it runs over into the sestet and comes a bit late (*within* the ninth line). Milton employs the same principle even more extensively in the smaller subdivisions into quatrains and tercets.

The Italian sonnet happens to be the standard form in which the principle of balance and contrast is most clearly established. A great many poems, however, are based on the same principle, often so unobtrusively that their structure is likely to escape attention. A. E. Housman's *Epitaph on an Army of Mercenaries* is a good example: *

> These, in the days when heaven was falling,
> The hour when earth's foundations fled,
> Followed their mercenary calling
> And took their wages, and are dead.
>
> Their shoulders held the sky suspended;
> They stood, and earth's foundations stay;
> What God abandoned, these defended,
> And saved the sum of things for pay.*

A great deal of the effectiveness, and even the apparent simplicity, of this poem lies in the fact that the second stanza is, line for line, a contrast to the first—"when heaven was falling . . . their shoulders held the sky suspended," etc.

A use of larger contrasting sections forms the basis for Andrew Marvell's *To His Coy Mistress*. The poem is particularly interesting in that the first two sections are not only contrasted in sense, but have a corresponding difference in tone. There is a juxtaposition of the flippant and the serious which few poets would dare, and yet a great part

* From *Last Poems* by A. E. Housman. Copyright, 1922, by Henry Holt and Company.

of the success of the poem as a whole lies in the successful balancing of
these opposites. Certainly the beginning of the second paragraph gains
a great deal of its impressiveness from the shift of tone.

> Had we but world enough, and time
> This coyness, lady, were no crime.
> We would sit down and think which way
> To walk, and pass our long love's day.
> Thou by the Indian Ganges' side
> Shouldst rubies find: I by the tide
> Of Humber would complain. I would
> Love you ten years before the flood,
> And you should, if you please, refuse
> Till the conversion of the Jews;
> My vegetable love should grow
> Vaster than empires and more slow;
> An hundred years should go to praise
> Thine eyes, and on thy forehead gaze;
> Two hundred to adore each breast,
> But thirty thousand to the rest;
> An age at least to every part,
> And the last age should show your heart.
> For, lady, you deserve this state,
> Nor would I love at lower rate.
>
>   But at my back I always hear
> Time's wingèd chariot hurrying near,
> And yonder all before us lie
> Deserts of vast eternity.
> Thy beauty shall no more be found,
> Nor, in thy marble vault, shall sound
> My echoing song; then worms shall try
> That long-preserved virginity,
> And your quaint honour turn to dust,
> And into ashes all my lust:
> The grave's a fine and private place,
> But none, I think, do there embrace.
>
>   Now therefore, while the youthful hue
> Sits on thy skin like morning dew,
> And while thy willing soul transpires
> At every pore with instant fires,
> Now let us sport us while we may,
> And now, like amorous birds of prey,
> Rather at once our time devour,
> Than languish in his slow-chapt power.
> Let us roll all our strength and all
> ₁Our sweetness up into one ball,
> And tear our pleasures with rough strife,
> Thorough the iron gates of life;

Thus, though we cannot make our sun
Stand still, yet we will make him run.

The final section, it will be observed, makes complete the reconciliation between the two contrasting themes and tones. Thus the work as a whole is a strict example of the thesis, antithesis, and synthesis of philosophic disquisition.

Even the largest literary forms may be based on a division into contrasting sections. A great deal of the effectiveness of Sir Thomas Malory's eight-hundred-page *Morte D'Arthur* rests on the gradual development of such a contrast. In the first twelve of its twenty-one books we have accounts of Arthur's origin and rise to power, of his founding of the Round Table, and of the adventures of his knights. This part is primarily the story of a group of brave, rather happy-go-lucky adventurers who fought any man at the drop of a hat, met and slew by their own human strength giants, pagans, and monsters, and lay with the lady of the castle wherever they visited. But a change is coming. "The thirteenth book," says Caxton's preface, "treateth how Galahad came first to King Arthur's court, and the quest how the Sangreal was begun." With the quest of the Grail the atmosphere changes. Knights begin to represent virtues, and the giants they slay come to stand for errors and sins. Adventure begins to fade into allegory; the condition of a knight's soul has more to do with his success than the strength of his good right arm, and the knight now tends to repay the hospitality of his hostess with prayer and fasting. Also, treachery breaks into this moralized world, and the last hundred pages or so are a magnificent decline, a gorgeous sunset of Arthur and his court, until finally Arthur is mysteriously borne away and the few survivors of his knights and ladies become monks and nuns. One lays the story down at the end of the final twenty-first book with a feeling that here, at least, Swinburne is amply justified: "Thou hast conquered, O pale Galilean; the world has grown gray from thy breath."

The use of contrast cannot be so clear-cut and obvious in a work of this scope as in a short poem; and the account given above must not be taken to mean that there was no treachery or allegory before the Grail came into the story, or that there was no secular adventure afterwards. The effect here is not that of a sharp division, but rather of a gradual shift of emphasis, and it is only in retrospect that the reader is aware of the turning point. Nevertheless, the generalization holds that the total effect of the book depends on the two contrasting sections and that the Grail is the pivot on which the shift is made.

The same principle governs the construction of the *Nibelungenlied*. Throughout the first half of the poem Siegfried and Kriemhild are the hero and heroine of the story, and the murder of Siegfried, together with the ensuing treatment of Kriemhild, makes Hagen and Gunther very definitely the villains. In the second half Kriemhild, always longing for a revenge which seems beyond her reach, marries Etzel (Attila) with this one object, invites Siegfried's murderers to his court to visit her, and has them destroyed there. But she pursues her revenge with such inhuman singleness of purpose and such a use of her husband and his people as mere pawns, and the killers of Siegfried defend themselves so gallantly and long against overwhelming odds, that the rôles are reversed and the sympathy of the reader changes entirely. Once again the turning-point is clear even though the contrast between the two sections is gradually developed.

There are, of course, many kinds of contrast in literature besides the use of balanced and contrasting passages or sections of a work. Frequently one character is a "foil" for another—an opposite who by his very difference intensifies the traits of both. The wise and the foolish virgins will serve as examples, or Ariel and Caliban, or, to descend to the recent, Scarlett and Melanie. Similarly situations, settings, events —any elements that enter into literature—can be intensified by the use of balance and contrast.

In music the same principles hold. We shall soon have occasion to see how even a short and simple tune depends on them. The same thing is true on a larger scale of all musical types and forms. And, as in literature, any elements of the art can be employed to produce balance and contrast. Thus a composer may pair off loud and soft, fast and slow, high and low, staccato and legato, strings and woodwinds, major and minor, sound and silence—the possibiliti re almost infinite. In music also a distinction can be made between that balance of contrasting sections which is entirely a matter of preference for the writer and that which is an essential characteristic of an established form. Broadly speaking, every set musical form involves at least the use of two contrasted elements for its theoretical pattern, and demands a great use of free contrast for any successful working out into an actual piece of music.

Before we take up the relationship between musical and literary forms it will be worth while to look at a simple melody. In the chapter from *Job* we saw how far balance and contrast (and, of course, repetition and variation) may enter into even a short literary passage. It is necessary to see the same principles as they apply in the small musical unit. Our discussion of musical forms will use the "theme" or "section" as the smallest unit. But a theme itself may be a far more complicated structure than a casual listener might suspect, and it will necessarily be constructed on the same principles as the larger forms in which it is considered as a single unit. For this purpose the theme of the first movement of the Mozart piano *Sonata in A* will do perfectly. It is a very simple, singable tune with an unpretentious accompaniment; so certainly it will not have complications of any unusual sort. Also, it is, considered as a whole, the unit out of which the entire movement is constructed: it is a theme used as the basis for a set of variations. Since Mozart's repeat-marks are now usually ignored in performance, they will not be included here, and analysis will be facilitated by setting up the music in units of four measures each.

The first point to notice about this theme is that the 6/8 time falls into clearly separated half-bars of three eighths each, and these half-bars are kept separate throughout, with never a note held over and never a rest on the first beat of either half. This means that, even before as large a unit as the measure has been achieved, there is a regular balancing of one half against the other. The first bar as a whole is also balanced against the second, which is rhythmically identical with it, but is a contrast in pitch and harmony: the melody is one tone lower, and the first bar is based on the chord of the tonic while the second is on the chord of the dominant—the most simple and obvious of harmonic changes. The third bar keeps the general rhythmic scheme of alternate quarter and eighth notes, but it contrasts with the first two in its lack of the sixteenths; and the fourth bar makes a compromise between these two slightly different rhythmic patterns by letting the upper voice have two sixteenths on the second beat while the others keep the rhythm of the third bar. It also summarizes and compromises in its harmony by going from tonic to dominant to tonic to dominant—a more rapid change than we have had before, but still keeping to the two chords which, with one exception, have been the entire harmonic basis up to this point. The third and fourth bars set each other off in that one has the ascent of the melody and the other its descent. Also, these two bars together balance the first and second.

We have now seen the principal elements in the structure of the four-bar unit on which the entire melody is based, but two other points remain to be noted. Since the music is to a certain extent contrapuntal as well as harmonic, we cannot merely consider the top voice as the

melody and ignore the others except in so far as they combine to form
chords. We note immediately that the middle voice is one single note
reiterated on the basic rhythmic pattern almost to the end of the

phrase (at which point the bottom voice takes it an octave lower). The
lower voice is, up to this same point, an exact parallel to the upper
voice (or "melody") except that it is an octave and a third lower. Thus
we have the parallel movement of these two voices throughout, and the

intervening and contrasting repetition of the middle voice. In the fourth bar this pattern is broken up in order to terminate the phrase.

The next four bars parallel and balance the first four. The first half of this second phrase is an exact repetition of the first half of the first phrase. Its third and fourth bars, however, while balancing the corresponding part of the first phrase, are different: the ascent and descent are equal, and a greater effect of finality is achieved by closing on tonic harmony and using an eighth-rest before the third section. This changed repetition of the original four bars involves a great complication of the structural relationships, for not only does the second phrase contain within itself all the relationships of the first, but each part has its own relationship of identity, balance, or contrast with the corresponding part of the first phrase.

The third four-bar unit is designed primarily as contrast to the first and second. It makes a slight change in the rhythmic pattern by using a basic scheme of six eighth-notes to the bar, but in its first two bars this figure is confined to the accompaniment, and the melody keeps the pattern of the first two bars of the preceding phrases—that is, the melody of bars 9–10 has practically the same rhythmic pattern as that of bars 1–2 and 5–6. Bar 10 is, both in its ascent and descent and in its harmony, a reversal of bar 9. With bar 11 the changed rhythm shifts to the melody, leaving the accompaniment to fill out the broken chords. On the third beat of bar 12 occurs the only chord not in the initial key —the dominant seventh chord of the dominant. It is touched on very lightly to mark the farthest point of departure before the return of the now very familiar initial theme. Bars 13–16 give us once again the initial four bars, with a graduated set of repetitions, for 13–14 are an exact repetition of 1–2, but 13–15 are also an exact repetition of 5–7. Bar 16 leads into a two-bar tail-piece which gives a final flourish and completes this entire section.

It is now apparent that comparatively elaborate systems of repetition and contrast were used to build up four-bar phrases, and that these in turn were combined to produce a larger unit whose structure might be described by the formula AABA. (Mozart's repeat-marks really make it AA AA BA BA.) We need only remember that varied repetitions of this completed unit form the entire first movement of the sonata in order to see how the same structural principles which govern the bar or phrase also apply to the section, movement, or entire composition.

Two other attributes of music, tonality (or key) and mode (or scale-form, most familiar in the distinction between major and minor), remain to be briefly considered. They play an important part in the structure of musical forms. In general a melody like that of Mozart will give its B section further contrast by putting it in a different key from the A section. When we come to consider such forms as the sonata we shall find it impossible to define them at all without speaking of key-relationships. Important as these are in musical structure, they have no literary equivalents. The popular differentiation of major as gay and minor as sad is made in direct defiance of a great many familiar compositions, and such distinctions as that between "somber" keys using flats and "brilliant" keys using sharps are equally meaningless.

Poets consciously trying to follow musical patterns involving these elements have sometimes ignored them, and have sometimes substituted changes of meter, imagery, general tone, etc., but none of these devices can be considered as a real equivalent. If it were practicable for a poet to shift from one language to another he might come closer to the effect than in any other way, but he still would not achieve it. The difference in sound between a major and a minor is really much like the difference in taste between an onion and a tomato. It is a plain enough difference, but one capable of description only in its own terms: no one would be likely to contend that an onion tastes cheerful and a tomato tastes plaintive. The last wrd that can be said on the matter is that they taste different in precily the same way that the taste of a tomato differs from that of an onion.

CHAPTER XI

Theme and Variations

WE ARE now in a position to investigate those poetic forms which are related to the standard forms of music. We shall find some which are independent developments in the two arts, and others which show the attempts of writers—particularly during the last century—to borrow established musical structures and adapt them to literary uses.

Since the nomenclature of types in both arts is confused, we must first decide what constitutes a form. In literature the types are classified according to structure, scope, medium, content, and mood or tone, taken singly or in almost any possible combination. Thus the structure of an Italian sonnet is alone sufficient to identify it. In its earlier history it was necessarily a love-poem, but Milton freed it from all restrictions of subject-matter. And in this case the form is so clearly defined that the scope or length is automatically a part of the definition. Drama, on the other hand, is defined entirely in terms of medium: anything acted out by speaking characters is drama, whether it be in prose or verse, whether it be tragic or farcical, or whether it be a two-minute skit or a trilogy of ·five-acters. A satire may take any form, since the classification is entirely a matter of tone and content. On the other hand, the novel, the novelette, and short story agree in being prose works with at least a backbone of narrative, but any of them can treat any subject in any sort of way, and the three types are differentiated by their length and scope. It is inevitable that these classifications should overlap in every conceivable way. A tragedy may be a drama with a certain type of content, or it may be a novel (witness Dreiser's *American Tragedy*) with the same type of plot and approach. Thus we are often forced to fall back on double names and speak of the elegiac couplet, the tragi-comedy, and the dramatic monologue. To attempt a complete classification would only lead to the pointless pedantry of Polonius: "The best actors in the world, either for tragedy, comedy, history, pastoral, pastoral comical, historical pastoral, tragical-historical, tragical-comical-historical-pastoral, scene individable, or poem unlimited. . . ." [1]

In musical terminology a similar confusion reigns. The gigue, waltz, and sicilienne are defined by their rhythm; the fugue, sonata, and rondo by their structure; the symphony, concerto, and string quartette (all in sonata-form) by their medium; the nocturne, scherzo, and serenade by their general tone; and the prelude, ballade, and bagatelle by the whim of the composer at the moment of christening his work. Furthermore, some names are used in both arts: the rondo (Anglicized and accented on the first syllable) is a musical form, but the rondeau (with French pronunciation) is a poem; and the ballade is either a very strictly organized poetic form or an extremely free and indefinable sort of music.

For our investigation of structural similarities and reciprocal influences between literature and music, the word *form* will be used exclusively to denote an established structural pattern such as is found in the fugue or in the Italian sonnet.

The first of these forms is the characteristically musical theme and variations. As its name implies, it is based entirely on repetition with variation, and consists of a theme given out first in its simplest version (as a general rule) and then repeated with as many different treatments as the ingenuity, patience, or interest of the composer may suggest. Each variation, of course, departs from the original theme in some specific and consistent way, so that it forms an intelligible unit in itself. Thus the first may take the melody unchanged in the bass, against a running triplet-figure in the upper voice or voices; the second may take it at half-speed in a minor key; the third may syncopate it and ornament it with brilliant runs and flourishes, etc. There is a general tendency for the later variations to depart further from the original theme than the earlier ones, for with each new variation the general idea of the theme becomes more thoroughly established in the listener's mind, and he thus becomes able to follow more radical departures from it. The first movement of the Mozart *Sonata in A* (the theme of which was reproduced above), the *Harmonious Black-smith* variations of Handel, the second movements of Beethoven's *Kreutzer Sonata* and Schubert's *Death and the Maiden Quartet*, Mendelssohn's *Variations sérieuses*, and Elgar's *Enigma Variations* may be cited as familiar examples. There are also numerous movements, like the finale of Beethoven's *Eroica* and the third movement of his *Ninth*

Symphony which, while not pure examples of the theme and variations, are very largely based on that form.

We have already seen that repetition with variation is a basic literary device also, but it has never been an independent literary form except under the direct influence of music. The examples cited earlier were incidental devices in various works, not separate literary compositions consisting of variations on a theme. The earliest example that I know which seems to be under musical influence (though this cannot be proved) is Eve's morning song to Adam in *Paradise Lost;* [2]

> Sweet is the breath of morn, her rising sweet,
> With charm of earliest Birds; pleasant the Sun
> When first on this delightful Land he spreads
> His orient Beams, on herb, tree, fruit, and flour,
> Glistring with dew; fragrant the fertil earth
> After soft showers; and sweet the coming on
> Of grateful Eevning milde, then silent Night
> With this her solemn Bird and this fair Moon,
> And these the Gemms of Heav'n, her starrie train:
> But neither breath of Morn when she ascends
> With charm of earliest Birds, nor rising Sun
> On this delightful land, nor herb, fruit, floure,
> Glistring with dew, nor fragrance after showers,
> Nor grateful Eevning mild, nor silent Night
> With this her solemn Bird, nor walk by Moon,
> Or glittering Starr-light without thee is sweet.

The deliberation with which Milton gives out a positive theme and follows it with a detailed negative variation, together with his general knowledge of music and interest in it, makes it at least reasonable to believe that he had the musical analogy in mind when he wrote this passage. But it is still simply a short passage in a larger work, and we have to come down to the early years of the nineteenth century before we find literary examples of the theme and variations as an independent form written in imitation of music.

Among the many eccentric works (as well as some very solid ones) of Ludwig Tieck is a play called *Die verkehrte Welt* [3]—"The Topsy-Turvy World." For this play he conceived the idea of writing a verbal prelude ("Symphonie," he called it) and of using verbal passages in lieu of music between the acts. The last of these entreacts is a "Menuetto con variazioni" consisting of a statement of a theme, followed by three variations on it. The idea here is clearly to compete with the musical form and to use the same methods for the production of a literary work.

An excellent illustration of this type of literary theme and variations comes from John Gould Fletcher: [4]

STEAMERS

Maestoso

Like black plunging dolphins with red bellies,
The steamers in herds
Swim through the choppy breakers
On this day of wind and clouds.
Wallowing and plunging,
They seek their path,
The smoke of their snorting
Hangs in the sky.

Like black plunging dolphins with red bellies,
The steamers pass,
Flapping their propellers
Salt with the spray.
Their iron sides glisten,
Their stays thrash:
Their funnels quiver
With the heat from beneath.

Like black plunging dolphins with red bellies,
The steamers together
Dive and roll through the tumult
Of green hissing water.
These are the avid of spoil,
Gleaners of the seas,
They loom on their adventure
Up purple and chrome horizons.

Various other writers have attempted the same thing. Théophile Gautier's *Variations sur le Carnaval de Venise* [5] has the particular interest of being based, as the title indicates, on the silly little tune know as "The Carnival of Venice" and of imitating the tune rhythmically in the first line of the second variation. From among the fairly numerous other examples of this form of poetic rivalry with music we may cite Grace Hazard Conkling's and Robert Hillyer's poems entitled *Variations on a Theme,* [6] Richard Plattensteiner's *Wasser-Lied* [7] and *Wolken-Symphonie* [8] (each with the subtitle "variations on a familiar theme") and Mme. Merens-Melmer's *Thème et variations.* [9] Saccheveral Sitwell has even followed the common practise of composers by taking another writer's theme and composing a set of variations on it. In *The Cyder Feast and Other Poems* [10] he thus employs themes from Herrick, Pope, and Milton; and in another book he writes three variations,[11] each about a page in length, on two lines from Peele:

> God, in the whizzing of a pleasant wind,
> Shall march upon the tops of mulberry trees.

This set of variations brings up the problem of length. In music there may be a difference of tempo, and a theme may be somewhat extended or compressed, but in general any variation is approximately the same length as the original theme. The use of *divisions*, as in the andante of Beethoven's *Fifth Symphony*, enables a composer to subdivide his notes and thus put in, as it were, more detail within the same compass. In poetry the logical analogy of this process is the addition of detail, but since there can be far less difference in the durations of words than in those of notes, the result is always a lengthening of the treatment and a consequent disproportion between the theme and its variations. This is a fundamental difficulty, and one on which many poets have wrecked themselves. A variation of a two-line theme should itself be approximately two lines long if it is to keep anything resembling the musical effect; but Saccheveral Sitwell's extension of the two lines to approximately a page in each of the variations results in something totally different. The proportion is like that achieved when a composer takes a theme from someone else and uses it as the subject of a fugue.

Another difficulty lies in distinguishing the variations from each other. We have already remarked that in music each one has its own particular type of departure from the original, and hence its own particular character. This effect is essential to the success of the form, for without it the variations cannot be kept separate and the result is a pointless alteration which is neither variation nor systematic development. The poets have given little attention to this problem. It is possible to view the subject from a different standpoint, or to adopt a different tone, but they seldom do so. Perhaps the best solution might be the process of clothing the same basic idea in different figurative treatments, as did Shakespeare in the "That time of year" sonnet, but the writers of deliberate themes and variations in poetry have seldom adopted this method either. The use of different meters, rhyme-schemes, and stanzaic forms for different variations is another obvious possibility which has not been sufficiently explored. In general, writers of the literary theme and variations seem to have felt that the originality of the attempt (they apparently arrived at it independently for the most part) was sufficient to carry their poems along without any very serious effort to get beyond the bare idea of doing something roughly like the musical form.

Some of the most interesting examples of poetic variation were written, not as themes with variations, but as separate poems, without any idea of the musical analogy. Thus Friedrich Hölderlin's collected poems contain a number which exist in two versions each, the second usually labeled as a variation. These pairs simply represent an original poem and a later reworking of it (called a variation). It is interesting to note that here also the variation is usually considerably longer than the original poem, and frequently it contains most of the lines of the first version, unaltered, but interspersed with further material and elaborations of ideas that had been first stated in simpler form. There are, however, some cases in which the second version condenses the first. In a way, any poem of which two versions have survived might be considered an example of variation in this sense, but few such pairs of versions would give, as do Hölderlin's, a suggestion of the effect of a theme and variation when read together. This peculiarity is probably due to the relationship between what is kept and what is changed: if too much is kept unchanged in the second version the effect will be merely that given by an occasional glance at the footnotes of a variorum edition; and if too little is kept the effect will be that of two entirely independent poems which happen to have something of the same general idea—like the two competitive sonnets of Keats and Leigh Hunt on the subject of the grasshopper and cricket. It happens that these reworkings of Hölderlin's have the proper balance of sameness and difference to suggest the musical effect, though this was not the intention of the author.

The final difficulty with the theme and variations as a literary form lies in preserving a reader's interest. Generally speaking, a musical variation of a theme gains in interest from the very fact that we have already heard it before in a different form; whereas a literary variation, because of the possibility of separating what is said from the words which say it, tends to be less interesting for the same reason. This problem has been beautifully solved in what is probably the vastest and at the same time the most successful use of the theme-and-variation form in literature, Browning's *The Ring and the Book*. The

first of the twelve books of this poem states the theme, describing the
poet's finding of the documents dealing with an old Roman trial for
murder, and going on to give the facts in the case as presented in the
documents—

> pure crude fact
> Secreted from man's life when hearts beat hard,
> And brains, high-blooded, ticked two centuries since.

The beautiful daughter of poor parents had married an old count, lived
with him for a while, and then run away with a young priest and returned to her parents, at whose home the count, following her trail,
had found her, killed the parents, and mortally wounded her, though
she lived long enough to give her testimony. The next ten books give
ten variations on these crude facts, each book presenting the interpretation put on them by some person or group of persons, all the way
from the principals in the action to the idle gossips. Thus we have the
story told by Half-Rome, The Other Half-Rome, Tertium Quid, Count
Guido Franceschini (the husband and murderer), Giuseppi Caponsac-
chi (the young priest), Pompilia (the wife), Dominus Hyacinthus de
Archangelis (the Count's lawyer), Juris Doctor Johannes-Baptista Bot-
tinus (lawyer for the prosecution), The Pope, and Guido (in a last
appeal). The final book, a coda, is itself a similarly constructed set of
variations dealing with the outcome of the trial and the execution
of Guido and his confederates. Remembering the frequent occurrence of
an andante with variations in musical literature, we see that Browning
is clearly conscious of the borrowed structure of his poem when, a few
lines before the end, he writes of the relativity of truth, saying of man

> That all this trouble comes of telling truth,
> Which truth, by when it reaches him, looks false,
> Seems to be just the thing it would supplant,
> Not recognizable by whom it left—
> While falsehood would have done the work of truth.
> But Art,—wherein man nowise speaks to men,
> Only to mankind,—Art may tell a truth
> Obliquely, do the thing shall breed the thought,
> Nor wrong the thought, missing the mediate word.
> So may you paint your picture, twice show truth,
> Beyond mere imagery on the wall,—
> So, note by note, bring music from your mind,
> Deeper than ever the Andante dived,—
> So write a book shall mean, beyond the facts,
> Suffice the eye and save the soul beside.

Philosophically considered, no one's account is true—not even the crude facts, which lie by their very crudity. The first statement of the theme is itself only one form of the idea, and might as well be called the first variation; and at the end we have an idea of the theme which is truer than any particular statement of it can be.

The secret of Browning's success in sustaining interest throughout a long set of variations, when most writers who have attempted it have become tedious by the second page, lies in this very fact. Most writers take some slight lyrical thought and try to vary it, but end by merely repeating it. Browning's subject, however, is of sufficient complexity to admit of real variation, and his variations are dramatically interesting. His theme is not the events that led up to the murder, but the human tensions and relationships, and these must necessarily differ according to the character and relationships of the interpreter. The average poetic variation says the same thing again in different words, but each of Browning's says something different within the same framework of events. His success lies in the fact that he has devised a way of making each variation a new revelation of the implications of his theme—as it is in music—rather than another rehashing of an already tedious story.

In spite of such occasional successes as Browning's, however, we must admit that variation is in general a more successful poetic device when used incidentally as a part of some other structural pattern than when employed as the basic principle of a work.

CHAPTER XII

ABA Form and the Rondo

A GREAT many musical works have the general plan of a first section, a contrasting middle section, and a return to the first section for the conclusion—a structure usually known as the ABA form. This form, unelaborated, is the basis of hundreds of small musical compositions; and various types of extension and elaboration of the same principle give sonata form, fugue form, and the structure of most overtures and a great many symphonic poems. Hence it may well be considered as the fundamental musical form. The simple ABA form, however, is sufficiently distinct from these elaborate applications to deserve separate consideration. Its prevalence in movements from dance-suites is amply shown by the frequency with which such directions as *Da capo al segno* and *Da capo al fine* are found in their scores. These directions can, of course, be used only if the final section is an exact repetition of the first. In such cases—and they are remarkably common—the cost of engraving and printing music can be cut to two thirds by the simple expedient of indicating that the first section is to be played again at the conclusion. Chopin's *Funeral March* is a familiar example of such structure. The A section is the march, with its chords and heavy rhythm in a minor key. The trio,* as is usual in this form, is designed to furnish a strong contrast: it is a song-like melody in a different key (the relative major of the previous minor), with an accompaniment of widely-spaced broken chords. After the trio, the march (A) is repeated exactly as it appeared before, except that the last chord is changed to provide a conclusion instead of leading into the trio. The same thing may be found in practically any of the gavottes, passepieds, etc., in the suites of Bach.

No exact line can be drawn between this type of composition and the even more frequent form in which the repetition of the A section

* *Trio* is the standard name for the contrasting middle section (B) of the march, minuet, and various other types of compositions which are usually written in simple ABA form.

is not exact. In the example from Chopin we had to allow the final chord to be different. In Gluck's *Gavotte from Iphigenia* (well known in the form of Brahms' transcription for piano solo) a few notes are added to make a slightly different rhythmic effect in the conclusion, and the last phrase is taken an octave higher. In Beethoven's *Minuet in G* the notes are exactly the same in the second occurrence of the A section, but the omission of the repeat marks within this section makes it only half as long as on its first appearance. From examples like this it is an easy step to others in which the changes are greater—to Chopin's *Fifteenth Prelude*, for example, with its A section considerably modified as well as shortened at the conclusion. Thus we need not be greatly concerned with the question of whether the repetition is exact, and we may define the simple ABA form comprehensively as a fairly short composition which uses one type of thematic material for the beginning and end, and a different type for the middle, aiming at a definite contrast between these sections. Repetition may, of course, be used within these divisions, and they may be built up on patterns similar to those of the composition as a whole.* But it is only in the expansions of this simple form that any particular construction of the individual sections is *de rigueur*. The proportion between them is, however, relatively fixed, and though a certain amount of latitude is allowed, the general principle is that the three sections shall be of approximately equal length. Where there is a disproportion in length it usually takes the form of a shortening of the A section at the end.

How far is this basic form applicable in poetry? In considering this question it will be useful to make a distinction between independent poetical uses of the form and those written under the influence of music.

Many poets have used an ABA form without any influence of music —or at least without any demonstrable influence. Four poems of Catullus,[1] for example, have the first line and the last line identical. Catullus seems to have considered such repetition more a matter of satirical emphasis than of lyricism, for in each case the repeated portion is a foul insult or, at its very mildest, a caustic remark. A more lyrical use of the same type of repetition is found in the eighth *Psalm*, in an anonymous Italian poem of the thirteenth century,[2] in one of Goethe's songs of Mignon,[3] in Uhland's *Schäfers Sonntagslied*,[4] and in

* For example, the form of the Mozart theme (as we considered it, without the repeat-marks) is AABA. The same is true of the trio of the Chopin *Funeral March*. And this same AABA pattern, with eight bars to each section, is the almost invariable formula for the choruses of our current song-hits.

Théodore de Banville's *Nous n'irons plus au bois*.[5] Three poems of Keats—*Lines on the Mermaid Tavern, Bards of Passion and of Mirth*, and *La Belle Dame sans Merci*—repeat the beginning for a conclusion, as do Poe's *Dream Land* and Alfred Noyes' *The Highwayman*. Frequently a four-line stanza is the repeated unit: this is the case in Blake's *The Tiger*, Sir Philip Sidney's *First Song* (from *Astrophel and Stella*),[6] Baudelaire's *Hymne*,[7] "A la très-chère, à la très-belle," and one of Chamisso's songs,[8] as well as one or two of the examples mentioned earlier. This list, though by no means exhaustive, is sufficient to show that the ABA form has been employed from time to time by poets of widely different periods, nations, and languages, and that it is to be regarded as a natural poetic form quite independent of any suggestion from the practice of music.

There is, however, one important difference between this poetic form and the musical one—a difference evident in all the examples mentioned above and almost * any others that might be cited. In poetry the A section is considerably shorter than the B section—usually not more than one third as long, and frequently far less than that. Thus the musical balance by which the A section is the principal and emphatic part of the composition, with a middle section thrown in for contrast, is entirely reversed. The repeated part of the poem tends to become little more than a motto or refrain used for a beginning and conclusion, and the middle section contains the body of the poem. This difference is a clear result of the limitation on repetition in poetry, and writers uninfluenced by musical analogies have stayed within the limits of effective poetic repetition. Thus they have produced a form which is mechanically similar to the musical one, but is totally different in emphasis and effect. Conrad Aiken does have one poem [9] in which the entire last page is identical with the first, but the proportion is still kept, for the complete poem is seventy-five pages long. And the return of one page after an interval of seventy-three pages does not seem nearly so repetitious as Baudelaire's return of one stanza after an interval of three stanzas.

We can draw further conclusions about the ABA form in poetry by noticing what happens when a poet undertakes to deal with a musical composition having this structure. Sometimes the poet simply prefers to omit a third of the composition from his poem in order to make it fit some established poetic form. Thus Mary Alice Vialls writes

---

* One exception is Theodor Storm's *Die Nachtigall* (Insel-Bücherei, No. 242, pp. 13–14). The poem consists of three five-line stanzas, the A section being the entire first stanza and being exactly repeated to form the third.

a sonnet [10] on the *Tannhäuser Overture*, but begins with the middle section of the music, using that for the subject of her octave and the return of the A section for her sestet. Another of her sonnets, this one [11] on Chopin's *Nocturne, Op. 37, No. 1*, violates its subject by the opposite distortion, a refusal to include the repetition of the A section. This poem considers the first subject of the nocturne (an accompanied melody in G minor) as a questioning of pilgrims struggling along the barren track to eternal death. The sestet interprets Chopin's second subject (a chorale-effect with close harmony, in E flat major) as advice to return to the fold and to the faith. The poem ends here for the double reason that it is a sonnet and that, if the author were to follow the music in its return to the first subject, she would have to reverse her edifying moral.

More usually, the poet does try to follow the musical structure, but is driven to certain departures from it. The Polish poet Ujejski is a good example. He wrote a set of eleven poems [12] based on compositions of Chopin, and clearly had the intention of following the music as closely as was poetically possible. In fact, he identified the compositions by giving the opus numbers, and even imitated poetically such things as the characteristic rhythm of the mazurka. In spite of this clear intention of basing his poems on the music, Ujejski evidently felt that poetry would not stand for the extensive repetition demanded by the typical ABA form. The poem on Chopin's *Funeral March* [13] is a good evidence of this difficulty. As we have already noted, the A section is exactly repeated in Chopin's music, but the poet cannot allow this. He distinguishes the main sections of the composition clearly by using different meters and stanza forms, and he uses enough repetition (the last few lines of both the trio and the conclusion of the poem repeat earlier passages) to give something of the musical suggestion. After the trio, however, he resumes the poetic form of the march for the return of the A section, but he does not repeat. Instead, he begins more or less where he left off for the trio, and heightens and develops the themes used for the first occurrence of the A section. The fact that this procedure is clearly more effective than a literal repetition like that in the music is clear evidence of the difficulty which poets experience in any attempt exactly to follow the musical form.

This method of either developing or varying the A section when it reappears is common in poets who have written about musical compositions in this form. Robert Underwood Johnson does the same thing in his poem [14] on Chopin's *Fifteenth Prelude*. And a particularly fine example is to be found in d'Annunzio's *Sopra un Adagio di J. Brahms*.[15] The unidentified adagio is clearly an ABA form, and d'Annunzio's poem both follows and motivates the structure. His first stanza brings out an Ozymandias-like theme of desert and desolation, with ruins and a vacant throne as the center of interest. The contrasting middle section is a vision of former glories of the fallen empire, and when this vision fades there is a return to the original scene of desolation, which is described in much the same terms as before, but with slight changes of wording and imagery which are clearly a verbal equivalent of musical variation.

Ujejski's poem suggests another possibility in the poetic use of ABA form, since it distinguishes the two sections by the use of different meters. The same thing is true of Meredith's *Tardy Spring*.[16] A number of poems have been written, both under musical influence and independently, which use one meter or stanza at the beginning and end and a different one for a middle section, but have no verbal repetition. Whether or not we should consider these as examples of ABA form is largely a matter of interpretation and emphasis; and the central problem is really that of separating form and content in poetry. If there is a straight development of idea throughout a poem of this form, there is a parallel with music in the mechanical pattern, but not in the content. In music we classify as ABA form only those compositions which repeat or vary the original thematic material in the final section. For example, if a composition were to consist of a march, a waltz, and another march entirely independent of the first one, it would not come under the ordinary definition of ABA form. But such structure would parallel that of most poems which have merely the contrast in form. If there is any justification for the contrast there will necessarily be some similarity in mood or spirit between the two sections using the same poetic structure, but unless there is repetition or variation of subject-matter we do not have ABA form. The resemblance in tone between two parts of a poem, like that between two independent marches, is insufficient.

We may conclude, then, that this form is used in independently written poetry only with the proviso that the repeated section be reduced to a position of relative unimportance, and that it is used in musically inspired poems with a considerable feeling of constraint and difficulty. In other words, the pattern is never quite at home in poetry, though it is absolutely fundamental in music. Evidence from the other side clinches this point: poets working with music tend to suppress or disguise an ABA structure when they are confronted with it; but composers dealing with poetry tend to supply one where the original material lacks it. Thus Liszt, in his three piano solos (originally written as vocal settings) on sonnets of Petrarch, violates the sonnet form by using a free ABA structure, precisely as Mary Alice Vialls violated ABA structure by using the sonnet form. Out of a great many possibilities, one further example will suffice. Matthias Claudius wrote a poem [17] called *Der Tod und das Mädchen* (*Death and the Maiden*) in which the first stanza is the maiden's cry of fear and her plea to Death to spare her, and the second (and last) stanza is Death's comforting reply that he is no monster, but a gentle deliverer. Poetically, this makes a perfect balance, but when Schubert came to make a song out of it he evidently felt that, from a musical point of view, something was lacking. The stanzas would naturally be quite different in their musical treatment, and Schubert simply wrote a short instrumental introduction using the theme of Death's stanza—thus making the poetic contrast of two things into the standard musical form of ABA.

The musical form known as the rondo is really nothing more than a series of simple ABA forms telescoped together by the use of the same material for the A section in each. Since its length is indeterminate, the simple rondo form may be schematically represented as ABACAD . . . A: it has one principal section which begins and closes the work (or movement), and is repeated throughout in alternation with different subjects of an episodic nature. (There is also an elaborated rondo form in music, but this simple one is more directly related to literature and hence is more important for our purposes.) This musical form is adequately defined when we add the observation that, as might be expected, the A section may, at any appearance, be either exactly repeated or varied.

As a matter of fact, this form is older in poetry than it is in music: any poem with stanzas and a chorus is in simple rondo form if only the chorus precedes the first stanza. Burns' *Green Grow the Rashes, O* is a perfect example, its chorus and five different stanzas giving it the form of ABACADAEAFA, and this type of structure is common enough in the folk song and in poetry written in imitation of it.* In these stanzaic songs with a chorus the stanza and chorus are likely to

---

* The music of such a song is, of course, not a rondo unless each stanza has its own different music. Normally there is one musical setting for the chorus and another which is repeated for each stanza, thus giving the form ABABAB . . . A—a simple alternation.

be approximately the same in length, and thus the musical proportion by which the sections of a simple rondo are about equal is kept.

It is interesting to note that poems of this type devote slightly more than half their length to repetition of one section, and that such an amount of repetition is far more than poetry will usually allow. The explanation lies in the fact that these poems are composed more to be sung than to be read. Burns frequently wrote his poems for specific Scottish tunes, and the writers of the Elizabethan lyric often had their music already in mind when they wrote their words, or, failing this, definitely intended that their poems were to be set to music and sung.

The habit of inserting songs in plays is interesting evidence on this point, though the significance is largely obscured by present-day performances. The actors of Elizabethan drama were normally competent singers—as was any Elizabethan gentleman—and those of the children's groups, for which such dramatists as Lyly wrote, were professional singers. Thus the songs which our modern actors try to get out of the way as unobtrusively as possible were originally high spots of the entertainment, much like the songs of our present musical films. The influence of writing for music can be seen throughout the Elizabethan lyric,[18] and the frequency of repetition in various forms is one result of such influence. A good example of the form as used by Burns, but two centuries earlier, is the anonymous *Fain Would I Have a Pretty Thing.*[19] Another Elizabethan example, William Browne's *A Welcome,*[20] is worth quoting in full:

> *Welcome, welcome! do I sing,*
> *Far more welcome than the spring;*
> *He that parteth from you never*
> *Shall enjoy a spring forever.*

> He that to the voice is near
> Breaking from your iv'ry pale,
> Need not walk abroad to hear
> The delightful nightingale.
> *Welcome, welcome, then . . .*

> He that looks still on your eyes,
> Though the winter have begun
> To benumb our arteries,
> Shall not want the summer's sun.
> *Welcome, welcome, then . . .*

> He that still may see your cheeks,
> Where all rareness still reposes,

Is a fool if e'er he seeks
Other lilies, other roses.
Welcome, welcome, then . . .

He to whom your soft lip yields,
And perceives your breath in kissing,
All the odours of the fields
Never, never shall be missing.
Welcome, welcome, then . . .

He that question would anew
What fair Eden was of old,
Let him rightly study you,
And a brief of that behold.
Welcome, welcome, then . . .

The particular interest of this poem lies in the fact that two forms are run together. It is a rondo in its use of one fixed stanza alternating with differing ones, but these different stanzas are themselves a set of variations on one theme. I know of no exact musical equivalent of this plan, but the early part of the slow movement of Beethoven's *Ninth Symphony* is an approximation to it.

Sometimes this combination of rondo and theme and variations is carried even further in poetry by using a plan similar to this, but varying both elements, with the result that a poem consists of two alternating themes each of which is varied at each reappearance. Conrad Aiken's morning song of Senlin [21] illustrates this method. The themes are differentiated both in form and in content, appearing thus in their first statements:

It is morning, Senlin says, and in the morning
When the light drips through the shutters like the dew,
I arise, I face the sunrise,
And do the things my fathers learned to do.
Stars in the purple dusk above the rooftops
Pale in a saffron mist and seem to die,
And I myself on a swiftly tilting planet
Stand before a glass and tie my tie.

Vine leaves tap my window,
Dew-drops sing to the garden stones,
The robin chirps in the chinaberry tree
Repeating three clear tones.

These two themes are alternated, with the A theme predominating both in length and in frequency of reappearance, so that the form of the poem is AB AAB AAAB. Both themes are varied, but, as would naturally be expected, the A theme is varied extensively, whereas the B theme has only slight verbal changes. An even clearer example by the same author is found in a poem [22] describing the reflections of a man at a concert. The interminable chatter of his companion is made to alternate with the stream of ideas suggested by the music whenever he gets a chance to listen to it. It is probably no accident that a form of this sort is used in connection with a description of music.

More sophisticated poetry, and particularly poetry not specifically connected with music, often uses the rondo form, but with the same general reservations found in the poetic ABA form. In other words, the usual thing is to reduce the A section until it no longer forms an equal balance with the episodes. Thomas Lodge, in *Phoebe's Sonnet* [23] (which is not a sonnet in the formal sense of the term), has reduced the repeated element to exactly half the length of the episodes—six lines for the thrice-repeated A section and twelve lines each for the B and C sections. Usually, the disproportion is even greater, but in its context in *Rosalind* this song is supposed to be sung—in fact, to be "scornfully warbled out." Two examples from ancient literature make the repeated element only a refrain occurring at irregular intervals throughout the poem. Bion's *Lament for Adonis* [24] opens with two lines which form the basis of the A section, but they are repeated with different combinations of phrase and with variations, and the recurrences of this material usually do not exceed one line. The anonymous *Pervigilium Veneris* [25] (which, by the way, can be sung very effectively to the choral theme of Beethoven's *Ninth Symphony*) has an A section of the single line, "Cras amet qui numquam amauit quique amauit cras amet!" which recurs at intervals of from five to fifteen lines * throughout the poem. Examples of a two-line A section alternating with considerably longer contrasting divisions are found in Greene's *Sephestia's Lullaby*,[26] Hebbel's *Requiem*,[27] and Nietzsche's haunting poem of autumnal melancholy, *Der Herbst*.[28]

In all the poems thus far mentioned, the form has been the author's invention; at least, it has not been a standardized thing like the sonnet. There are, however, several poetic forms based on the idea of the rondo and involving formal repetition of predetermined passages at certain points. The exact patterns and their names vary, but the general type includes some unnamed forms and various forms of the

---

* Some scholars believe that the refrain was supposed to be repeated after each four lines of the text.

rondeau with different amounts of repetition. In all these poems there are three occurrences of the opening theme, and thus the form is ABACA. The length of the A section varies from two lines to one word, with various intermediate possibilities. Sometimes, as in many examples [29] by Charles d'Orléans (d. 1465), a two-line refrain is repeated in the middle of the poem, but only its first line is used at the end. A reversal of this process by repeating only the first line in the middle of the poem, but both the first and second lines at the end, gives the triolet —long known simply as the rondeau, and one of its simplest forms. A fine early example of this form is a *Rondeau* by Guillaume de Machault († 1377):

> Blanche com lys, plus que rose vermeille,
> Resplendissant com rubis d'Oriant,
> En remirant vo biauté non pareille,
> Blanche com lys, plus que rose vermeille,
> Suy si ravis que mes cuers toudis veille
> Afin que serve à loy de fin amant,
> Blanche com lys, plus que rose vermeille,
> Resplendissant com rubis d'Oriant.

The fixity of this pattern of rhyme and repetition may be seen by leaping more than five centuries to Thomas Hardy's *Birds at Winter Nightfall*: [30]

> Around the house the flakes fly faster
> And all the berries now are gone
> From holly and cotoneaster
> Around the house. The flakes fly!—faster
> Shutting indoors that crumb-outcaster
> We used to see upon the lawn
> Around the house. The flakes fly faster,
> And all the berries now are gone! *

This triolet—as well as a number of those of Austin Dobson, Robert Bridges, and most modern poets—shows a certain uneasiness about purely formal repetition; and because of this dissatisfaction with it, the modern examples of the rondeau form tend to demand that, if possible, the syntax, meaning, or emphasis be changed when the exact words are repeated.

Among the numerous possibilities of the general rondeau form is one cultivated by Chaucer which uses three lines for a refrain, repeating two of them in the middle and all three at the end—really an

* From Thomas Hardy, *Collected Poems*. By permission of The Macmillan Company, publishers.

expansion of the idea of the triolet. A song [81] sung by the birds in honor of St. Valentine's day at the end of *The Parlement of Foules* is a good illustration, and it is worth noting that immediately before this poem Chaucer gives an indication of the tune to which it was sung.

> Now welcom somer, with thy sonne softe
> That hast this wintres weders over-shake,
> And driven awey the longe nightes blake!
>
> Seynt Valentyn, that art ful hy on-lofte;—
> Thus singen smale foules for thy sake—
>   Now welcom somer, with thy sonne softe,
>   That hast this wintres weders over-shake.
>
> Wel han they cause for to gladen ofte,
> Sith ech of hem recovered hath his make;
> Ful blisful may they singen whan they wake;
>   Now welcom somer, with thy sonne softe,
>   That hast this wintres weders over-shake,
>   And driven awey the longe nightes blake.

The *Rondeaux* [82] of Christine de Pisan show a reduction of the repeated section to a single line, and one [83] by Villon repeats only the single word. In general, however, the rondeau has become standardized between these two possibilities, and most examples now repeat the first half of the first line. Austin Dobson's *In After Days* is typical of hundreds of examples from Clement Marot [84] to the present:

> In after days when grasses high
> O'er-top the stone where I shall lie,
>   Though ill or well the world adjust
>   My slender claim to honour'd dust,
> I shall not question nor reply.
>
> I shall not see the morning sky;
> I shall not hear the night-wind sigh;
>   I shall be mute, as all men must
>   In after days!
>
> But yet, now living, fain would I
> That some one then should testify,
>   Saying—'He held his pen in trust
>   To Art, not serving shame or lust.'
> Will none?—Then let my memory die
>   In after days!

Perhaps the most widely known poem in this form today is *In Flanders'
Fields*—which, according to a recent newspaper article, McCrae wrote
as an experiment with a new verse-form which he had invented!

The possibilities of the rondeau have been elaborated at some
length in order to show that it is a basic poetic form as well as a musical one. Here again, however, it must be observed that the poet tends
to allow less repetition than the composer, and consequently both to
reduce the length of his repeated portions and to vary their meaning
even when the conventions of his form forbid varying the words themselves.

Two other poetic forms, while not exactly corresponding to the
rondo in music, are applications of its general principles. The first of
these differs from some of our earlier examples only in that it does
not begin with the repeated section—it is the musical form except that
it drops off the initial A section and begins with B. In the case of the
stanzaic song with a chorus it obviously makes little difference whether
the chorus occurs before the first stanza or not. The really significant
use of this form is found in poems like Rossetti's *Sister Helen*, in which
the refrain keeps its general character, but allows constant variation so
that each recurrence has some particular application to the preceding
stanza. Such a refrain, whether fixed or varied, can be highly effective,
but too often it becomes a merely mechanical, pointless, and banal
repetition. The use of the refrain among the Pre-Raphaelites supplies
good examples of both excellence and bathos. Pointless or tedious uses
of the device are well illustrated by Rossetti's *Troy Town* and William
Morris' *Two Red Roses Across the Moon*—the latter and its type being
dealt with once and for all by Calverly's *Ballad* [35] with its italicized
refrain:

> The auld wife sat at her ivied door,
>> (*Butter and eggs and a pound of cheese*)
> A thing she had frequently done before;
>> And her spectacles lay on her aproned knees,

etc., etc., etc.

Considerably more interest attaches to the poetic form in which the
A section is subdivided, with now one part and now another repeated
throughout the poem. A fine irregular use of this method is found in
Lorenzo de' Medici's *Trionfo di Bacco ed Arianna*,[36] which begins with
the four lines:

> Quant' è bella giovinezza
> Che si fugge tuttavia!

Chi vuol esser lieto, sia:
Di doman non c'è certezza.*

The third and fourth lines of this refrain are used at the end of each
of the eight-line stanzas (and are always introduced and prepared for
by the preceding rhyme-word *tuttavia*); but the first two lines do not
recur until the conclusion of the entire poem. Thus the form is a combination of the rondo and simple ABA form, and the first two pairs of
lines, in reverse arrangement, also serve as the last two.

This type of repetition is standardized in the poetic form known as
the villanelle. Its structure is absolutely fixed: there are only two
rhymes, and the first and third lines are used alternately as refrains for
the following three-line groups, and are then combined in succession to
close the four-line group at the end of the poem. Oscar Wilde's
Theocritus is a fine example:

O singer of Persephone!
In the dim meadows desolate
Dost thou remember Sicily?

Still through the ivy flits the bee
Where Amaryllis lies in state;
O singer of Persephone!

Simaetha calls on Hecate
And hears the wild dogs at the gate;
Dost thou remember Sicily?

Still by the light and laughing sea
Poor Polypheme bemoans his fate;
O singer of Persephone!

And still in boyish rivalry
Young Daphnis challenges his mate;
Dost thou remember Sicily?

Slim Lacon keeps a goat for thee,
For thee the jocund shepherds wait;
O singer of Persephone!
Dost thou remember Sicily?

The success of this poem lies largely in the fact that its tone and content are admirably suited for its rather artificial form. A passionate or

* How beautiful is youth
Which is always fleeting!
Let him who wishes be happy now:
There is no certainty of tomorrow.

vehement villanelle would be an impossibility, but the tone of nostalgia and the series of scattered recollections which form the poem lend themselves readily to the division into short sections with recurring conclusions.

Although the peculiar character of the villanelle is more conspicuous than that of the rondeau in general, a certain similarity between the simple rondo and the various poetic forms based on the same principle lies in the fact that neither considers itself too seriously. The musical form tends to be longer, but both are usually graceful compositions relying largely on lightness of touch and dexterity in the solution of technical problems for their effects.

For the sake of completeness, the elaborated rondo form in music should be mentioned. This calls for the use of a central, unrepeated theme, some variation of the B theme on its second appearance, and a very free treatment of the A section in the coda, where it makes its final appearance. The form is thus A B_1 A C A B_2 A. It has been standard since the time of Beethoven—the finale of his *Sonata Pathétique* is a good example—but so far as I know no poet has attempted it.

CHAPTER XIII

The Fugue

THE fugue is usually considered the most intellectual of musical forms. Such a characterization is accurate enough, but the common corollary that it is therefore a tedious or uninteresting form is very far from the truth. Naturally, a poor fugue is as tedious as a poor sonata or a poor march, but because of its very perfection of form a good fugue can be one of the most satisfactory forms of art, emotionally as well as intellectually. Only the listener whose approach to music is purely sentimental—and there are far too many of his type abroad in the land —will object to the rigid formal requirements which govern at least considerable portions of any fugue. As a matter of fact, the fugal pattern is one of the most effective devices known for building up a climax and its attendant excitement.

In this connection it is interesting to note that one critic (I forget who), wishing to oppose the theory that music is *merely* a sort of stylised formalism, deliberately chose the most formal pattern of all as his example. His line of argument was interesting. Suppose, he said, that any competent and uninspired student who has learned his counterpoint takes one of Bach's best fugues as a model. Suppose that he writes—as he probably can—a theme of his own which is, in itself, as good as Bach's. Then suppose that he takes Bach's fugue as his formal pattern and follows it exactly, using the same order for entrance of voices, the same key-relationships, the same types of counterpoint at the same places. When he gets through, he will have a correct academic exercise, and no more, but Bach's fugue, with exactly the same formal pattern, will be a great and stirring piece of music. Even in the strictest form, then, there is both a place and a demand for some unanalyzable quality of greatness and contagion. We might add that a strict formal pattern is likely to be a hindrance to a minor craftsman, but a stimulation to genius. The elaborate symmetry of Dante's *Commedia* is a case in point. And we may do well to join precept to example by remembering Théophile Gautier's insistence that the artist does his best work when struggling with recalcitrant materials.[1]

What, then, is this redoubtable form? Actually, it is not so complicated as it might seem. It is fairly easy to grasp with a little attentive listening, though it is difficult to describe clearly. Like various large musical forms, it is simply an expansion of ABA form, but each section has its own prescribed structure. Also, it is based very largely on a single theme, or "subject," and is written in a contrapuntal style. In other words, each voice * has a melodic line of its own, and is to be listened to separately as well as in combination with the others. This is the way in which a contrapuntal style differs from a "homophonic" style—like that of *Swanee River*—in which a single melody is supported by a background of chords.

On the basis of its ABA form, the fugue is divided into three sections: the exposition, middle section (development), and final section. The exposition begins with the announcement of the subject, or theme, in a single voice, unaccompanied. When the subject has been thus given out, a different voice enters and repeats it,† usually either a fifth higher or a fourth lower, while the first voice goes on with contrapuntal material of its own. If this contrapuntal material is regularly repeated each time by the voice which has just had the subject, it is known as a counter-subject; but if there is no counter-subject this material may differ with each occurrence of the subject or answer. After the entrance of the subject and answer there may be a brief episode, which is illogically called a codetta. Then the third voice will enter with the subject and will have as counterpoint the counter-subject in the second voice and free material in the first. This will be followed by the fourth voice with the answer, against the counter-subject in the third voice and free material in the first and second. After this (assuming that we are dealing with a four-part fugue) the exposition is complete, though it may be followed by a counter exposition (a version of the exposition which gives the subject to voices which formerly had the answer, and vice versa). It will be noticed that the exposition shows a steady increase in complication throughout, beginning with one voice, solo, and adding the others one at a time.

* In this sense of the word, a "voice" may be human or instrumental. Thus a string quartet consists of four "voices," one for each instrument.

† This repetition is known as the "answer." Such distinctions as that between a "real" answer (an exact repetition of the subject in the new key) and a "tonal" answer (a slight modification of the subject) can have no literary application, and hence, in the interest of simplicity, are omitted from the general description of the form.

The middle section gives the composer a good deal more freedom than does the exposition. It is formed of episodes alternating with "middle entries" of subject, one such entry being required in the middle section, and almost any number being possible. The middle section is in varied keys and allows complete independence in the combination, modification, and invention of subject, counter-subject, new contrapuntal material, and episodes.

The final section returns to the keys of the exposition. It very frequently uses a "stretto"—a passage in which one voice takes up the subject before another has finished it: if a fugue were written on the theme of *Three Blind Mice,* the round itself would be the *stretto.* Also, the final section often has, just before the conclusion, a "pedal-point" —a single note sustained for a considerable length of time against the independent movements of the other voices. Up to this point the entire treatment has been contrapuntal, but now the voices usually abandon their separate motion and finish off with a block of chords in the original key.

So much for the general pattern of the fugue—a pattern which combines freedom and restriction in a remarkable way. "The great variety of possible treatments of the subject-matter makes the fugue highly flexible; and the great coherence which can result from the use of these few essential materials makes it at the same time the most completely logical and unified of musical forms." [2]

For rather obvious reasons, the literary fugue has seldom been attempted. The form is essentially contrapuntal, and, as we have already seen, real counterpoint is impossible in literature. The extensive repetition demanded by the economy of materials presents another problem. Thus the author who sets out to write a verbal fugue has Gautier's recalcitrant materials with a vengeance.

Nevertheless, there is one really brilliant example of the fugue in literature. De Quincey's *The English Mail-Coach* [3] consists of three sections, the last of which is entitled *Dream-Fugue.* [4] The first section contains two essays: *The Glory of Motion* is self-explanatory, and *Going down with Victory* describes De Quincey's experiences as a student at Oxford during the Napoleonic Wars. He used to ride the mail-coaches when, elaborately caparisoned and decorated with flowers, they spread the news of a victory throughout the land.

The second section, *The Vision of Sudden Death,* describes an accident on one particular journey. The driver of the coach was asleep, and so was the guard. The coach, tearing down the wrong side of the road, entered "an avenue, straight as an arrow, six hundred yards, perhaps, in length; and the umbrageous trees, which rose in a regular line from either side, meeting high overhead, gave to it the character of a cathedral aisle." In this avenue was a light carriage containing two lovers preoccupied with their own affairs. De Quincey watched in fascinated horror as the coach bore down on them. After vainly trying to wake the driver and the guard, he finally managed to shout and to be heard by the man in the carriage just in time for the latter, by a tremendous effort, to rouse his horse to a leap which almost cleared the path of the coach, so that it only grazed the carriage and spun it about in the road. As the coach thundered on, he turned and looked back on the startled hysteria of the woman in the carriage. "The moments were numbered; the strife was finished; the vision was closed. In the twinkling of an eye, our flying horses had carried us to the termination of the umbrageous aisle; at right angles we wheeled into our former direction; the turn of the road carried the scene out of my eyes in an instant, and swept it into my dreams for ever."

The *Dream-Fugue* tells how this event dominated his dreams, and its object is to secure for this sequence of dreams the grandeur and the effect of variety in unity given by the musical fugue. Most commentators have brushed aside the title of this section with some meaningless comment, but De Quincey's knowledge of music and his interest in it, together with his passion for intellectual analysis, make it reasonable to suppose that his title was something more than a fanciful name.[5] Actually, De Quincey's method of producing the musical effect was to follow, as far as the limitations imposed by a different medium would permit, the structure of the musical form. He succeeded in following it far more closely than has been generally realized.

The full title of the work is *Dream-Fugue: Founded on the Preceding Theme of Sudden Death.* The practice of taking a fugue-subject from a theme which has already occurred elsewhere is common enough, and was ideally suited to De Quincey's purpose. He had to recount a series of visions all of which were derived by his sleeping mind from the incident described in *The Vision of Sudden Death.* At first thought it might seem that the theme and variations was the form best suited for the purpose, but it lacks the strict logic and the resulting inevitability of the fugue; and these were precisely the effects for which he was striving. To the possible objection that he may not have thought out the form as carefully as the following analysis will attempt to show, it may be answered that he probably considered the title of the last section a sufficient indication of the form. His explanatory notes [*] concern themselves entirely with the psychological problem of why his dreams of the accident should take on their peculiar imagery; and the question of how he has chosen the literary form in which these visions are presented is passed over in silence.

The *Dream-Fugue*, then, is an original literary use of the prelude and fugue. Since there are practically no limitations on the form of the prelude, De Quincey uses it as a pause for a rhetorical apostrophe to the "passion of sudden death"—an apostrophe headed by the musical direction *Tumultuosissimamente*. This section simply serves as a connecting link between the accident itself and the fugue of dreams to which it gave rise.

The greatest problem confronting De Quincey was that of suggesting the simultaneous voices of the fugue, and his solution of this difficulty helps to emphasize the transmuting power of dreams. His subject is not a group of words, but rather a group of ideas: speed, urgency, and a girl in danger of sudden death. These ideas remain constant, while the varying settings and details perform the function of the shifting contrapuntal accompaniment. [*]

After a brief prelude, the fugue proper begins with Section I of the *Dream-Fugue*. Here we have a group of dancers on a ship covered with midsummer decorations. Their craft runs under the bows of the larger ship on which the author is stationed, and vanishes. The writer is particularly concerned about one of the dancers, "the unknown lady from the dreadful vision." " 'Where are the lovely women that danced beneath the awning of flowers and clustering corymbi? Whither have fled the noble young men that danced with *them*?' Answer there was none." A few more lines, however, serve to introduce the answer. [†]

Section II gives an answer, in both the musical and the general sense of the word. The dancers' ship reappears in the distance on a sea which has suddenly become stormy. It comes on at terrific speed until it is again almost under the bows of the observer's ship; then it suddenly veers off and disappears rapidly into the distance. The girl stands high in the rigging. "There she stood, with hair dishevelled, one

---

[*] The schematic diagram on page 157 will be found helpful in reading the following discussion.

[†] The detailed setting of Section I might be taken as implying counterpoint along with this first statement of the theme. The problem here was insoluble, for a bare statement would have made Section I disproportionately short. As it is, the first three sections are of very nearly equal length. The use of detail sacrifices a minor consideration of form to the more important necessity for proper proportion.

hand clutched amongst the tackling—rising, sinking, fluttering, trembling, praying; there for leagues I saw her as she stood. . . ." This series of participles, constant in form, but varying in words, is one of the principal structural elements of the piece. It had already been used in the original description of the accident and in the prelude to the *Dream-Fugue*. In the fugue itself, it is absent from only one statement of the subject after Section I. Thus it appears with the statement of the answer by the second voice, and generally accompanies the subject and answer thereafter. In other words, it is a regular counter-subject. By the device of having the subject identified by its content, and the counter-subject by its form, De Quincey keeps the two separate, and manages to achieve something roughly suggestive of counterpoint.

The subject and answer of the first two sections form a completed unit; and Section III has, as would be expected, a reappearance of the subject in a different setting, and with the accompaniment of the participial counter-subject. In this vision a girl runs along the shore and is engulfed in quicksands. At this point it is interesting to look back at the opening lines of the first three sections:

> I. "Lo, it is summer—almighty summer! The everlasting
>   gates of life and summer are thrown open wide. . . ."
> II. "I looked to the weather side, and the summer had departed.
>   The sea was rocking, and shaken with gathering wrath."
> III. "Sweet funeral bells from some incalculable distance,
>   wailing over the dead that die before the dawn. . . ."

The first and third give an atmosphere of tranquillity, and are further connected by De Quincey's habitual association of the ideas of summer and death; the second is a contrasting storm-scene. Was he consciously trying to suggest the contrast in key between the subject (I and III) and the answer (II)?

It will be noticed that, whereas the first two sections have only one paragraph each, the third has two. Its short final paragraph is the episode which concludes the exposition. It is derived from material used earlier in the same section, and it leads directly into the middle section of the fugue.

This middle part begins with Section IV, and is constructed exactly as it should be. The news of Waterloo and victory, the coach carrying that news, the cathedral seen in the distance and rapidly approached and entered—all these are presentations of material closely connected with the subject; but there is a definite departure from the set statements of this subject found in the exposition. In the middle section we expect at least one direct restatement of the subject in addition to this episodic material; hence we look for another vision of sudden death. We are not disappointed. After a considerable interval the girl of the visions, now an infant, appears directly in the path of the coach, which is thundering up the aisle of the vast cathedral. There is a moment of suspense, and then, just as death seems certain, she vanishes. After a dramatic pause, she reappears as a full-grown woman, on an altar of alabaster, within the cathedral and yet among the clouds. On one side of her is dimly seen the shadow of the angel of death, and on the other her better angel prays for her. What we have here is simply a recurrence of the subject and answer, the counter-subject appearing with the answer only. It will be observed that the answer always saves the victim from the immediate peril presented in the subject, but keeps the idea of further danger. In the single instance where fugue-form does not demand an answer (Section III), the girl goes on to her fate.

The form of this middle section is not so easy to follow in detail as that of the exposition. It would seem that perhaps De Quincey had some difficulties with it, and was satisfied (reasonably enough) with the general scheme, without trying to imitate music too closely. Certainly almost anything connected with the subject and fitting into place would be satisfactory in the earlier part, and the subject and answer are definitely used. The stone trumpeter who comes to life is something of a problem from the point of view of form, though his dream development from the guard's horn is satisfactorily explained in De Quincey's note. A number of explanations of his position in the fugue might be devised, but none would be so obviously right as to justify its presentation here. In Section V we shall see that, towards the end of the fugue, De Quincey relied more and more on actual descriptions of sound. He did not abandon the imitation of musical form, but the use of the trumpeter, organ, and chorus in the last section show the addition of another type of musical suggestion to strengthen the climax.

The final section of the fugue begins with Section V, and the division is clearly indicated by the opening sentence: "Then was completed the passion of the mighty fugue." This conclusion is a summary of what has preceded, and a comment on it, offering no detailed new vision of sudden death, but presenting the idea in a general form along with the counter-subject. The musical suggestions come into conflict with the musical form in some places, as in the "columns of heart-shattering music" from the organ. These "columns" certainly seem to suggest the concluding chords, yet they occur early in the section. However, as in the middle section of the fugue, the principal structural features are clearly discernible. The two long sentences with which the composition ends have a weight and a repetition of phrases that may be an attempt at suggesting a pedal. This is followed by a summary of the visions which is an unmistakable *stretto*: mentioning the preceding dreams of sudden death in a series of phrases secures the foreshortening and telescoping effect of the *stretto* (which I have italicized in the passage quoted below), although it is obviously impossible to make the phrases actually overlap. After this *stretto,* the rest of the sentence goes on briefly to the peace and unity of the final chords. It is worth while to quote these last two sentences in full:

As brothers we moved together; to the dawn that advanced, to the stars that fled; rendering thanks to God in the highest—that, having hid His face through one generation behind thick clouds of War, once again was ascending, from the Campo Santo of Waterloo was ascending, in the visions of Peace; rendering thanks for thee, young girl! whom having overshadowed with His ineffable passion of death, suddenly did God relent, suffered thy angel to turn aside His arm, and even in thee, sister unknown! shown to me for a moment only to be hidden forever, found an occasion to glorify His goodness. A thousand times, amongst the phantoms of sleep, have I seen thee entering the gates of the golden dawn, with the secret word riding before thee, with the armies of the grave behind thee,—seen thee sinking, rising, raving, despairing; a thousand times in the worlds of sleep have seen thee followed by God's angel *through storms, through desert seas, through the darkness of quicksands, through dreams and the dreadful revelations that are in dreams;* only that at the last, with one sling of His victorious arm, He might snatch thee back from ruin, and might emblazon in thy deliverance the endless resurrections of His love!

The accompanying chart presents graphically the relationship between this literary fugue and the musical form.[7] Each of the three lines represents one of the voices of the fugue. A solid line represents the subject, S, or the answer, S(A). Long dashes are used for the countersubject, CS, and short dashes for free material. The indications above the lines refer to the musical form, and those below to De Quincey's work. Those structural elements which cannot be assigned to an individual voice are written above the entire group for the music, and below it for the prose. A few questionable elements may be noted. It is certainly unusual for one voice to give the subject twice in the course of a single *stretto,* but the reference to "dreams and the dreadful revelations that are in dreams" is needed to make the point that the dreams given are only specimens from the series which extends end-

Chart for Dream-Fugue

EXPOSITION

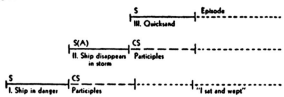

S _____ | Episode
III. Quicksand · - - - - - - - - - - - - - - -

S(A) _____ | CS _ _ _ _ _ _ _ |
II. Ship disappears | Participles · · · · · · · · · · · · · · · · ·
in storm

S _____ | CS _ _ _ _ _ |
I. Ship in danger | Participles · · · · · · · · · · · · "I sat and wept"

MIDDLE SECTION

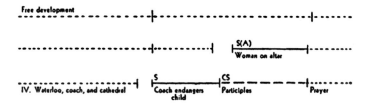

Free development
- - - - - - - - - - - - - |- - - - - - - - - - - - - - - - - - |- - - - - -

· · · · · · · · · · · · · · · · · |-· · · · · · · -| S(A) _____ |- - - - - - - -
Woman on altar

- - - · · · · · · · · · · · · · · -| S _____ | CS _ _ _ _ _ |
IV. Waterloo, coach, and cathedral | Coach endangers | Participles · · · · · · · · Prayer
child

FINAL SECTION

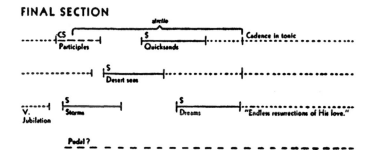

stretto

· · · · · · | CS _ _ _ | | S _____ | · · · · · · · · Cadence in tonic · · · · · · · · ·
Participles | Quicksands

· · · · · · · · · · · · · · · -| S _____ |· · · · · · · · · · |· · · · · · · · · · · - -
Desert seas

· - - - -| S _____ | | S _____ |· ·
V. | Storms | Dreams | "Endless resurrections of His love."
Jubilation

Pedal? -

lessly through the infinite time and space of the opium dream. Literally, of course, it is a reference to the cathedral vision and the
revelation with which the fugue closes. The suggestion of a pedal involves the idea of an extra voice, but nevertheless the rhetoric of the
last sentences seems to have the purpose of a pedal. Since in literature
the use of several voices can be at best only suggested, there is no
reason for objecting to this extra voice, or falling back on the idea of
an accompanied fugue.

A comparison of the first published version of the *Dream-Fugue* [8]
with the final version made for the collected edition gives further proof
of De Quincey's striving for musical form. There is evidence that this
first version had not been sent to the press hastily (as were many of
De Quincey's articles), and that it had undergone careful rewriting. [9]
However, he was obviously not satisfied with the *Edinburgh Magazine*
version, for he revised it carefully. The changes made in the first four
sections during this last revision are slight, and have no bearing upon
the form of the fugue. Section V, on the other hand, was radically
altered, largely by omissions. It was reduced to about three fifths of its
original length, and the excisions sacrificed some of De Quincey's
favorite symbols, such as the Pariah, to the exigencies of form. The
omitted portions contain primarily a speech of De Quincey's, some
standard recollections of childhood, a voice from heaven, and an implication that the coach itself is in flight from something. A premature
consolation which is not a part of the subject (musically speaking) is
also removed, as is a phrase of the *stretto*, "through fugues and the
persecution of fugues." This phrase required deletion, as the girl was
not pursued through fugues, but through many incidents which built up
into fugues of dreams in the author's mind. Since there should be very
little new material in the final section of a fugue, these omissions improve the form. It appears, then, that De Quincey was well aware of
the formal difficulties in the last section, that he was still not contented
with it when he was satisfied with the rest of the composition, and
that he reduced the extraneous elements as far as possible.

Summing up the discussion, we may say that De Quincey's musical
knowledge and interest suggested to him the use of fugal form, and that
he applied this form with surprising accuracy and effectiveness, but
was sufficiently conscious of the differences between the media of music
and literature not to press the analogy so far as to damage his work.
The end in view was the presentation of a series of dreams with all

their agonies and exaltations, and the approximation to fugue-form was adopted as the most efficient means for such a presentation.

It must be noted that De Quincey had two specific advantages over most writers who might be tempted to write verbal fugues. In the first place, a succession of dreams made ideal subject-matter, since it allowed the repeated use of the same general subject with different accompanying circumstances. It would be difficult to find any other topic which would so readily lend itself to this type of treatment. In the second place, De Quincey had already perfected his own peculiar style over a period of more than twenty years before writing the *Dream-Fugue*. This intricately ornate style, with its parallelisms, its climaxes, its parentheses, its elaborate and weighty periods, sometimes falls very flat when De Quincey is dealing with trivialities or forced attempts at the comic, but it is a perfect medium for those purposes for which he really devised it. Furthermore, though the exact analogies defy specific analysis, its general texture is strongly suggestive of music, and particularly of contrapuntal music. It is a style that has something in common with the manner of Milton and of Sir Thomas Browne. Since we associate the organ more than any other single instrument with contrapuntal music and the fugue, it is perhaps no accident that two writers have independently made the same association with the style of these men. Tennyson's reference to Milton as a "God-gifted organ-voice of England" [10] is famous, and one of the standard histories of English literature employs the same comparison in an attempt to characterize the ornate prose of Sir Thomas Browne.[11] De Quincey's similar style uses the same suggestive power for reinforcement of the associations set up by his title, his form, and his actual musical references (including the organ) in the last section.

Considering these special circumstances, it is not surprising to find that De Quincey's use of the fugue as a literary form is rather an isolated phenomenon. A few poets have described the form without attempting to imitate it—Milton did this in a highly concentrated passage [12] which De Quincey significantly quoted as a motto for his own fugue, and Browning did it more extensively in *Master Hughues* (a name shamelessly invented to rhyme with *fugues*) *of Saxe-Gotha*.[13] A few writers [14] have pretended to follow the form without making any real attempt to do so.

More exact and interesting than these is James Joyce's fugato section [15] in *Ulysses*. In this scene in a Dublin pub there are recurrences and combinations of themes which are clearly based on the fugue, but so far as I have been able to determine there is no working out of the complete musical pattern. Also (and this is perhaps more important), the cumulative excitement of the fugue, which De Quincey so perfectly captured, is entirely lacking. If this chapter really be a fugue, it is certainly an academic one.

CHAPTER XIV

Sonata Form

THE term "sonata form" is somewhat confusing, for it applies in a general way to a work in several movements, but its specific application is to the structure of a single movement. We may define a sonata as a work in several movements, at least one of which (usually the first) must be in sonata form. For this reason the term "first movement form" is sometimes used as a synonym of "sonata form." Also, it must be understood that though the form is named for the sonata, it is used in various other compositions which are named according to the medium of performance. The commoner of these are:

sonata	for one or two instruments only
string trio, quartet, etc.	for strings, the standard quartet being written for two violins, viola, and 'cello
X quintet	for string quartet plus one other instrument (X): thus a piano quintet is written for string quartet and piano
concerto	for solo instrument with full orchestra
symphony	for full orchestra.

Numerous other uses of the form, such as the woodwind octet, the double concerto (for *two* solo instruments plus orchestra), and the string quartet concerto (for string quartet of soloists plus orchestra) are occasionally found.

It can be seen from this brief listing that since sonata form includes most large works of instrumental music in several movements, it is far the most important of the larger structures. The usual sequence of movements in the symphony is a first movement in fairly rapid tempo, a slow second movement, a minuet or scherzo for the third movement, and a fast finale. Any movement may be in sonata form, but forms which we have already considered are very likely to occur: for example, the slow movement is frequently a theme and variations, the minuet may be simple ABA form or some slight elaboration of it, and the last movement is frequently a rondo. Apart from the use of a sequence of different movements, the only new thing from a formal point of view is therefore the typical sonata, or first-movement, form.

Like the fugue, this is an expanded ABA pattern divided into an exposition, a development section, and a recapitulation. It differs from the fugue in that at least large sections of it are homophonic instead of polyphonic, and in the fact that, whereas the fugue exploits the full possibilities of *one* theme, the sonata is essentially devoted to the fusion into a unified whole of two contrasting themes.

A movement in sonata form, then, will begin with the statement of the principal subject.* This subject may be of almost any length and nature, the only real requirement being that it allow ample possibilities for later development. It is followed by a second subject designed as a contrast and written in a different key. If the first subject was strongly rhythmical, the second is likely to be primarily melodic; or if the first was announced by the brass, the second may well be given out by the woodwinds. Once these two themes have been stated, the essential basis of the entire movement is established: one might paraphrase Coleridge by saying that sonata form is devoted to the reconciliation of opposite or discordant themes. The announcement of these two subjects will usually be followed by a brief section devoted to a considerably less important closing subject. At this point the exposition is really complete, but conventionally and theoretically the entire section is repeated. As a matter of fact, the tendency nowadays is to ignore the repeat-marks found in most of the earlier scores and to go on immediately into the development section.

This middle section is even freer than that of the fugue. It allows for varied treatment in distant keys of any material presented by the exposition, and it may even include new material. There is really no restriction on the composer except that he exploit the possibilities of his themes and that he have a final cadence (usually a brilliant cadenza in the concerto) leading back to the original key of the movement and thus introducing the recapitulation.

This last section is exactly what its name implies—the final A section of the vastly expanded ABA form. It repeats the first, second, and

---

* Any definition of a form allowing such wide possibilities must naturally be schematic. For this reason non-essential possibilities are not noted here. For example, a movement may and often does begin with an introduction which precedes the principal subject and is used only sparingly, if at all, in later parts of the movement. Possibilities of this sort are omitted for the sake of clarity, since they are not parts of the essential idea of the form. As a scholastic philosopher would say, they are accident rather than substance.

closing subjects, putting them all in the tonic key this time in order to achieve an effect of finality. This repetition, like that of the simple ABA form, does not have to be exact and literal, but it must be unmistakable and must give the effect of repetition rather than of further development. Such further possibilities as the repetition of the entire development and recapitulation and the use of a coda are non-essentials. Reducing sonata form to its simplest terms, we may summarily describe it as the statement of a first subject, a contrasting second subject, and a closing subject; the development of this thematic material; and finally its restatement.

During the past century a number of poets have been attracted by the idea of writing verbal sonatas or symphonies, and they have produced a good many works including the words *sonata* or *symphony* in their titles. However, even in the history of music these words have senses not connected with the form which has just been described, and their popular uses are still extremely vague; hence it is clear that many poets writing "symphonies" have either no idea of what the musical form is or no intention of following it. It seems very unlikely that Gautier understood the musical implications of his title when he wrote the celebrated *Symphonie en blanc majeur*.[1] The very idea of a symphony in white major—the work itself being a poem—involves such a combination of arts and media that they cannot all be adequately represented, and as a matter of fact there is hardly any musical analogy or suggestion beyond the title. If the intention of writing in sonata form ever entered Gautier's mind it must have been quickly abandoned, for he actually wrote eighteen four-line stanzas very effectively calling up the imagery of manifold whiteness, but having no relationship whatsoever to any musical form. And the word *sonata* has even less meaning when Lamartine remarks, in a note on the writing of one of his poems:[2]

I still wrote from time to time, but as a poet rather than as a man. In this state of mind I wrote the *Préludes*. It was a sonata in poetry. I had become a more expert artist; I played with my instrument.[*]

Whatever meaning this may have as regards the general spirit, tone, or effect of the poems, it is clearly too vague a use of the word to have any relationship to the musical structure, and the poems themselves bear out this supposition. It is hardly necessary to cite further examples to show that a good many poets have called works sonatas or symphonies

[*] J'écrivais encore de temps en temps, mais comme poète, non plus comme homme. J'écrivais les *Préludes* dans cette disposition d'esprit. C'était une sonate de poésie. J'étais devenu plus habile artiste; je jouais avec mon instrument.

simply because those words have for them only the vague suggestion of something impressive and agreeable to hear.

Many poems, however, show by division into movements, use of titles like *scherzo* or *minuet* for different movements, musical indications of tempo or tonality, and various other such devices that they are supposed to be written on plans paralleling those of musical compositions in sonata form. Tristram Shandy regarded this sort of thing as a harmless humor when Yorick applied it to his sermons:

What Yorick could mean by the words *lentamente,—tenute,—grave,*—and sometimes *adagio,*—as applied to theological compositions, and with which he has characterized some of these sermons, I dare not venture to guess.—I am more puzzled still upon finding *a l'octava alta!* upon one;—*Con strepito* upon the back of another;—*Siciliana* upon a third;—*Alla capella* upon a fourth;—*Con l'arco* upon this;—*Senza l'arco* upon that.—All I know is, that they are musical terms, and have a meaning;—and as he was a musical man, I will make no doubt, but that by some quaint application of such metaphors to the compositions in hand, they impressed very distinct ideas of their several characters upon his fancy,— whatever they may do upon that of others.[3]

Like many another innovator, Yorick simply had the misfortune to be about a century ahead of his time: *Tristram Shandy* came out during the 1760's; during the early part of the next century Tieck and Hoffmann were in full cry on the trail of such novelties, and by the 1890's W. E. Henley was heading the sections of his *London Voluntaries* [4] with directions which differ from Yorick's only in the use of more accurate Italian. Since that time musical directions loosely attached to poems have proliferated to such an extent that one can hardly pick up a magazine of verse * without encountering them. Purely mechanical though differentiation of movements and use of musical directions may be, they do give some indication of how far an author may have intended to carry his musical analogy. We can know, for example, that an author who writes a verse "symphony" with only one movement is hardly attempting the musical form, but we may assume that one who divides his work into movements with plausible indications of tempo and tonality is making a somewhat more exact attempt at creating a verbal analogy. Here also, however, vagueness is frequent enough; hence the following discussion will limit itself to poems which make some effort to use the musical form.

Any serious attempt to do this is fraught with great difficulties. Most important is the inevitable problem of repetition. Even if the

* One of the recent arrivals in this field is itself entitled *Furioso.*

poet, following the tendencies of modern composers and performers, refuses to repeat the development section, he still has to let it recur in his recapitulation, and since the form is larger than the simple ABA form, the poet will be confronted with the same problem as in that form, but the obligation to repeat a larger section will make his problem even more serious. Tonality is another obstacle, for the contrast of key between the first and second subjects and the use of distant keys in the development section are both essential to the musical structure, but we have already noted that literature has no real equivalent for them. Therefore it can only imply relationships of tonality in the general use of contrast.

Development also offers a serious difficulty because of the greater limitation on variation and repetition in literature and because the normal development of literature is a matter of content rather than of form. The impossibility of sharply separating these may make this statement sound vague, but the distinction is nonetheless real. This fact can easily be seen when we consider that a musical development is rounded off by a return to something closely resembling the original statement. In a play, though, where the development is one of action, character, and situation—elements entirely external to the language through which they are presented—such a return is impossible. Once the dramatist has allowed Ophelia to drown or Gloucester to be blinded, that step in his "development" is irrevocable and any return to an earlier situation becomes impossible. It is not merely an idle figure to say that musical development is circular, but literary development is linear. From this basic difference arise many of the problems of the poet who seeks to ape the composer. Also, the problem of simultaneity arises in the attempt to develop any literary theme according to musical principles, though it is not so embarrassing in the development of a sonata as it is in a contrapuntal form like the fugue.

Another difficulty is entirely of the poets' choosing. Conrad Aiken, John Gould Fletcher, Grace Hazard Conkling, John Todhunter, Henry Van Dyke, Arsène Houssaye, Mme. Merens-Melmer, A. E. G. Legge, and Richard Plattensteiner are all authors of poems making some attempts at sonata form. With the exception of Aiken and Legge, however, they all fail to realize the scope and dignity of this form. They seem to think of a symphony as something to be tossed off during an idle weekend, and to associate it with the lyric instead of with the more ambitious literary forms, such as the tragedy and the epic. A leisurely reading of almost any of their "symphonic" poems will require between two and five minutes—a very short time in which to reproduce either the form or the effect of a musical performance lasting between twenty minutes and an hour. It is noteworthy that many kinds of suggestion are employed in these poems to produce the musical illusion, but the use of musical form is among the least of these. Some of the poems contain recognizable movements using the simple ABA form or the theme and variations, but since these have already been considered we must focus our attention on the first movements, or on any others which clearly attempt to use sonata form. In music the first movement usually lasts longer than the second or third, but the reverse is true in these poems. Thus Richard Plattensteiner writes a poem in symphonic form (*Ein symphonisches Gedicht*[5]) with a first movement of only three lines! Worse still, in two[6] of his poems written about actual musical compositions in sonata form he simply omits the first movement entirely. As a matter of fact, in none of his twenty-one poems based on sonata form do we find a single movement which accurately follows that structural plan, and there is only one[7] which effectively suggests it.

How far do poets usually manage to follow sonata form? The first movement of Grace Hazard Conkling's *Symphony of a Mexican Garden*[8] may be taken as a typical example. The poem is preceded by a brief dedication to Mozart, but its indications of tempo and tonality are exactly those of Beethoven's *Seventh Symphony*. The first movement accordingly has two clearly separated sections:

THE GARDEN

In A Major

Poco sostenuto

The laving tide of inarticulate air
Breaks here in flowers as the sea in foam,
But with no satin lisp of falling wave;
The odor-laden winds are very still.
An unimagined music here exhales
In uncurled petal, dreamy bud half-furled,
And variations of thin vivid leaf:
Symphonic beauty that some god forgot.
If form could waken into lyric sound,
This flock of irises like poising birds
Would feel song at their slender feathered throats,
And pour into a gray-winged aria
Their wrinkled silver finger-marked with pearl.

That flight of ivory roses high along
The airy azure of the larkspur spires
Would be a fugue to puzzle nightingales
With too evasive rapture, phrase on phrase.
Where the hibiscus flares would cymbals clash,
And the black cypress like a deep bassoon
Would hum a clouded amber melody.

But all across the trudging ragged chords
That are the tangled grasses in the heat,
The mariposa lilies fluttering
Like trills upon some archangelic flute,
The roses and carnations and divine
Small violets that voice the vanished god,
There is the lure of passion-poignant tone
Not flower-of-pomegranate (that finds the heart
As stubborn oboes do) can breathe in air,
Nor poppies, nor keen lime, nor orange-bloom.

What zone of wonder in the ardent dusk
Of trees that yearn and cannot understand,
Vibrates as to the golden shepherd horn
That stirs some great *adagio* with its cry
And will not let it rest?

                  O tender trees,
Your orchid, like a shepherdess of dreams,
Calls home her whitest dream from following
Elusive laughter of the unmindful god!

Vivace

The iris people dance
Like any nimble faun:
To rhythmic radiance
They foot it in the dawn.
They dance and have no heed
Of crystal-dripping flute
Or chuckling river-reed;
Their music hovers mute.
The dawn lights flutter by
All noiseless, but they know!
Such children of the sky
Can hear the darkness go.
But does the morning play
Whatever they demand,
Or amber-barred bourré
Or silver saraband?

It is interesting to compare the general musical suggestion here with the specific elements of musical form. Though the general idea is that of a symphony, the actual forms mentioned are the aria, the fugue, and two of the regular dance-suite forms—the bourré and the saraband. Other, non-formal musical associations are called up by such words as variations, melody, chords, trills, tone, and *adagio*. Beyond this there is some play at making an equivalence between various flowers and the instruments of the orchestra—an elaborate confusion of the senses involving not only the common association between sound and color, but further associations of scent and shape as well. Thus an aria would come from the throats of the irises; the flaring hibiscus corresponds to the sound of cymbals; the black cypress is a deep bassoon; the grass (being background) represents chords; fluttering mariposa lilies suggest trilling flutes; the pomegranate blossoms have an effect analogous to that of oboes; and the general atmosphere produced by some undefinable combination of trees and twilight calls to mind the tones of the horn. There is plenty of suggestion, then, to support the general hypothesis, "if form could waken into lyric sound," on which the poem is based.

But how far is this suggestion reinforced by any formal correspondence between the poem and the musical structure? Hardly at all. Of the elaborate musical pattern we find only two ninths. We can be so specific because the exposition is, of course, the first third of a movement in sonata form, and that exposition consists of a first subject, a contrasting second subject, and a closing subject. The poem includes only the first two thirds of the exposition: it states a first subject and a contrasting second subject which is clearly distinguished in verse-form, content, and mood. Beyond that it does not go.* And this stopping-point is typical of a great many attempts at the sonata or symphony in words: one repeatedly finds examples in which an author simply states two contrasting themes and lets it go at that. It is impossible to tell whether any of the other movements of this poem are supposed to be in sonata form, but we can be certain that none approximates to the form any more closely than the first. The second

* The dedication to Mozart seems to preclude the possibility that there was any intention of using Beethoven's *Seventh Symphony* as a pattern for the poem, though the exact correspondence of tempi and tonalities would be a strange coincidence. At any rate, if that symphony was supposed to be a model for the poem, the form is followed even less than on the interpretation given above. In the symphony the *Poco sostenuto* is an introduction, and the whole of the regular sonata-form is contained in the *Vivace*. If the poem sought to parallel this, it did not even state two contrasting themes for the sonata-form proper.

movement ("The Pool") consists of three ten-line stanzas of identical form, all devoted to establishing a connection between the atmosphere around the pool and the forest and garden divinities of classical mythology. The third movement ("The Birds") consists of two sections in different metrical forms, the first dealing with the birds themselves, and the second (much shorter) identifying flowers with birds by speaking of the song of the orange-tree. This movement is thus an exact formal counterpart of the first. And the fourth movement ("To the Moon") consists of five six-line stanzas on a single theme.

Considering this poem as typical, we see that there is really nothing suggestive of sonata form in its structure. It is true that two movements do go so far as to state two contrasting themes, but the closing theme (admittedly of less importance) and the whole processes of development and recapitulation are ignored. If the statement of such themes could be considered as a poetic version of sonata form, almost any Petrarchan sonnet could be the first movement of a sonata.

The verse "symphonies" of John Gould Fletcher offer another good example. Fletcher wrote a good many of these, most of them employing the color motive which is already familiar to us through Gautier and the poem which we have just been considering. Since the influence of French poetry is mentioned in a preface to these works, the extensive use of Gautier's idea is probably no accident. In such poems as *Blue Symphony, Green Symphony, White Symphony,* and *Violet Symphony,*[*] however, the only suggestion of the musical form lies in the division into movements. In fact, Fletcher's own statement on this point would hardly lead us to expect anything more:

I have called my works 'Symphonies,' when they are really dramas of the soul, and hence, in them I have used color for verity, for ornament, for drama, for its inherent beauty, and for intensifying the form of the emotion that each of these poems is intended to evoke.[10]

So much for the positive statement as to the intention of these poems. Fletcher is even more specific on the negative side. In defending the poems against certain criticisms he denies the use of any set form:

The charge against the form is less easily rebutted; but I have always felt it more important for a poet to create his form according to the state of his feelings and the condition of his material, than to borrow one ready-made and to attempt to squeeze his feelings into it.[11]

This statement certainly rules out any attempt to borrow a musical structure for the poems. And elsewhere in the same preface we find statements showing that the musical analogies which led Fletcher to call his poems "symphonies" are vague, floating ideas rather than any strict parallelism. "I have written many works in the symphonic form of four or five contrasted movements," he remarks. But we have seen that the essential structure of sonata form (and hence of symphonic form as well) is that *within* one or more of these movements.

There is also a remark that his earlier poetry was largely a matter of moods, but "since then I have tended increasingly to hold that poetry is also thought, and that thought and emotion play the part in poetry of counterpoint and melody in the works of musical composers." One cannot be sure exactly what this means. If *counterpoint* is here used as the name for a type of musical texture, then the analogy would seem to imply that, just as the existence of simultaneous melodies produces counterpoint, the existence of simultaneous emotions will produce thought. Or if—and this seems somewhat more likely—*counterpoint* is used as the name for one or more voices contrapuntally accompanying some principal voice, the meaning will be that emotion is the leading part of poetry, and that thought is an accompaniment having its independent interest and at the same time playing with and against the emotion. Yet neither of these interpretations can be considered binding, and it seems highly probable that no strict analogy of relationships is intended.

Fletcher has written some "symphonies" which are independent of the symbolism of color. *Sand and Spray: A Sea-Symphony* [12] uses Italian indications of tempo and is divided into four named movements, the second and third of which are entitled "Variations," and are subdivided into six and five sections respectively. Here again, however, the musical analogy is not kept in the way that the title might suggest. The second movement, for example, does not consist of *a* theme followed by five variations, but rather of six more or less independent sections, *each* of which is a small set of variations on a different theme. The fifth of these, "Steamers," has already been quoted as an example of the form.* Individual parts of this and other "symphonies" of Fletcher contain other forms and devices clearly suggested by music: the first two (sets of) variations of the third movement of *Sand and Spray* are simple ABA forms. As far as sonata form is concerned, however, it is clear that Fletcher does not follow it even as far as do the poems already considered.

The clearest attempts at poetic use of sonata form are poems de-

* See p. 130.

scribing or interpreting musical works having this structure. John Todhunter's *Beethoven's "Sonata Appassionata"* [18] is a good specimen which I have analyzed in detail elsewhere; [14] hence a general account of the poem will be sufficient here. In one sense Todhunter does not attempt to imitate the musical form. Each movement, for example, has its own unchanging poetic stanza. But since his poem is at the same time a description of the music and an interpretation of it as a moral allegory, the content necessarily follows the thematic material and arrangement of the music as far as possible. In the exposition this can be done in great detail: each theme is characterized and personified, and thus the verse follows the music bar by bar. As soon as the development section is reached, however, the complications of the music become such that the verse cannot reproduce them, and the poet is reduced to a brief general statement of intensification and confusion: "Fiercer the fight grows, louder shrieks the blast," etc. The recapitulation is dealt with much more briefly than the exposition, and in far more general terms.

This poem, then, serves to reinforce the conclusions we have already reached. Even when the poet sets out with a clear determination to make sonata form the basis of his poem, he finds that his poetic version cannot really go beyond the exposition. Furthermore, Todhunter seems to tire of the attempt and to feel that this extraneous form is a hindrance to his own intentions as a (fourth-rate) poet. This fact is clearly seen by considering the three movements in order. Without necessarily attributing the generality to any weariness on the author's part, we can understand why the development section of the first movement could not be treated in as much detail as the exposition. But the second movement (a theme and variations) is less accurate and detailed than was the first; and the third movement deals almost entirely in generalities. Other poems of this same type, by various poets, show the same tendency.

Before leaving the shorter poems based on sonata form we may look briefly at Sidney Lanier's *The Symphony*. [15] This work is particularly interesting because we know that the poet had an exact and competent knowledge of symphonic form and that he had devoted a good deal of careful thought to the problems of musico-literary aesthetics. Two of Lanier's favorite ideas are combined in the poem, the musical interest and the attack on commercialism. He describes a performance, and at the same time interprets into words the themes of his instruments, these words constituting the sociological jeremiad. The first subject is introduced by the violins and then taken up by all the string section. After this a beautifully described bridge-passage leads into the second subject, which is assigned to Lanier's own instrument, the flute. So far everything is clear enough, but at this point we lose track of the structure of the music, and we never quite find it again. A "thrilling calm" follows the conclusion of the second subject, and after "a little breeze among the reeds" the clarinet takes the lead, to be followed, in order, by the horn, oboe, and bassoons. Between these solos are brief indications that the other instruments are not idle: we hear of "the thick of the melodious fray" and "sea-lashings of commingling tunes." The solos seem to be something like a set of variations, but if they are thus understood the clearly described exposition at the beginning is left dangling. On the other hand, there is a reference to life as a "sea-fugue writ from east to west," and this, together with the "sea-lashings of commingling tunes," might well imply an extended fugato passage, if not a complete fugue. In fact, after the introduction of the first two themes the structure is so vague that it is impossible even to be sure whether the poem represents a single movement or an entire symphony. Lanier's initial plan of translating into words the sentiments of the different instruments and characterizing them by their utterances forced him to represent the performance as primarily a series of solos; but one cannot help feeling that, with his knowledge of music and the love with which he describes it, he would have followed out his symphony more clearly if he had felt that it was possible to do so without making poetic sacrifices which would more than offset the gain in the musical analogy.

As for the more ambitious poetic attempts at symphonic form, A. E. G. Legge's *A Symphony* [16] really differs from the examples already cited only in the fact that its length—forty-seven pages—puts it on a scale more like that of the sonata or symphony. Beyond this, only its division into movements and the approximation to rondo-form in the scherzo bear out in any way the implications of the title: the first, second, and fourth movements simply present a logical argument containing some use of contrast, but entirely independent of musical forms. Conrad Aiken's "symphonies" in verse are also on a large scale, and are extraordinarily interesting as examples of the successful application of various musical techniques to the writing of poetry. For this reason they will be reserved for discussion later, and for our present purposes it is sufficient to remark that they are not—and do not pretend to be—poetic uses of sonata form.

Up to this point we have been considering sonata form alone, as it appears (or fails to appear) in single movements. The attempt to write a poetic sonata or symphony also raises the problem of the relationship between movements. The lack of tonality in poetry is again an obstacle, but the use of different poetic forms, subjects, and general effects can overcome it. Sometimes other devices are used: Plattensteiner begins each movement of one poem [17] with a strongly alliterated passage, but gives each of these passages a different dominating sound. All things considered, the poets may well be forgiven a certain confusion as to the relationships between movements when we consider the fact that there is wide divergence among composers on this same point. The tendency of earlier works in sonata form is to have the movements connected only as a system of tonalities, tempi, and moods, with no relationship of thematic material. A later development apparently resulted from a feeling that the work should be more clearly a single thing rather than a sequence of separate compositions, and thus we find that in Beethoven's *Fifth* and Brahms' *Second* (to cite only two examples from the symphony) a good deal of the material of all four movements is derived from or subtly related to the opening notes, which thus become a sort of motto for the entire work. The next step had been prepared for in the introduction to the finale of Beethoven's *Ninth Symphony*, or even earlier, in the last two movements of his *Fifth*. With the assistance of the "idée fixe" of Berlioz and the practice of Schumann in his symphonies, it finally became well established towards the end of the nineteenth century. Its ultimate development was the "cyclical" form, in which themes were freely carried over from one movement to another. César Franck's sonata for violin and piano and his *D Minor Symphony* are familiar and excellent examples of this type of structure. Except for the impossible duplication of tonalities, the poets have followed the composers rather well on the whole matter of the relationship between movements, and we find in their works, just as in music, the three possibilities already mentioned. Naturally, these shade into one another by imperceptible degrees, but, broadly speaking, the movements of a literary sonata may be independent except for general relationships of mood, they may all rely on different phases of one basic idea, or they may be closely interrelated in their subject matter and even quote from one another. This last practice, however, seems to be simply a following of what would be the normal tendency in poetry rather than any conscious imitation of the cyclical form in music.

The great majority of the literati who have been attracted to sonata form have been poets or versifiers, but there have been experiments in prose as well. Particularly interesting is the gallant and little-known effort of Paul-Émile Cadilhac to write symphonic novels. During the early 1920's he published two [18] of them, and was reported [19] to be working on a third (which I have not seen). The second of these, *La pastorale*,* is prefaced by a manifesto explaining the author's theory of the symphonic novel. This preface is too long to quote in full, but it will be worth while to translate some selected passages from it:

> Themes are the basis for a symphonic novel. Musically, themes are the dominating ideas of a work—its framework. There are three sorts of themes. The first are very general, have a symbolic value, and are fugally treated (in *La pastorale*, Love, Madness, and Death at grips with the passions and Life). Those of the second sort describe the same landscapes and the same settings at different times of the day and the year, and correspond to the theme and variations of the musician. . . . Those of the third sort are true Leitmotivs peculiar to the persons whom they characterize.
>
> . . . The symphonic novel will create a musical atmosphere by the use of images, comparisons, and words borrowed from the musical vocabulary. It will pay great attention to sonorities and sounds, and it will not scorn imitative harmonies.
>
> . . . This book uses all rhythms and creates actual measures. But it does this warily: a style too metrical, especially if it is monotonously rhythmical, runs the risk of shattering the illusion by which the novel lives.
>
> In music there are scale-forms and tonalities: major and minor modes; keys of G, of C, of D, etc. Literature also has them: an idea can be translated into major or minor, and the tenses—present, perfect, past—are real keys. Most writers of narrative write in only one tonality. Alphonse Daudet is perhaps the only one who uses in the same chapter, on the same page, even in the same paragraph, the three tenses of narration. This is what the author of a symphonic novel should do.
>
> The problems of harmony and orchestration remain. There lay the difficulty. One cannot, as in music, write several sounds to hear simultaneously. . . . But I submit that description by enumeration—a succession of little harmonic touches welded together—achieves the effect of chords played as arpeggios. One can go even farther. One can develop a number of different themes simultaneously. To be specific, one can bring forward, in the same chapter and sometimes on the same page, different intrigues, descriptions, and dialogues. . . .
>
> And orchestration? How is a writer to give the effect of different instruments. By writing a novel which is not of one type only, but is by turns realistic, . . . lyrical, epic, ironical, descriptive, fantastic—even analytical. . . .

* This is not to be confused with André Gide's *La symphonie pastorale* (a novelette), which preceded it by some five years. Gide's story has a performance of Beethoven's *Sixth* ("Pastoral") *Symphony* used incidentally, but there is no attempt at symphonic form in the novelette, which is a rather feeble story about a preacher and

This general exposition of the theory is followed by a brief outline of the structure of the novel—an outline showing considerable familiarity with the structure of Beethoven's symphonies. (This novel is not an attempt at a literary transposition of the *Pastoral Symphony*. It gets its name from the fact that it deals with country life, and Cadilhac tells us that the last movement contains a funeral march inspired by that in the *Eroica*.) The first movement "is not divided into three sections, as in the classical symphony"—and thus does not attempt sonata form—"but into four." These divisions of dawn, morning, midday, and evening are thus a reduced parallel to the four movements, with their settings in summer, autumn, winter, and spring. The second movement, we are told, is framed between an introduction and a coda, and is written in the imperfect tense. The scherzo has a first section and a trio—but the old problem of the ABA form reappears, and there is no return to the first section. Finally, the last movement contains a funeral march and an *Allegretto*, the latter written in a major mode and in the present tense in order to symbolise the triumph of life.

After all this explanation, Cadilhac adds, with becoming modesty:

These are some of the principles by which I have been guided. I do not make any pretensions to having succeeded. I had to create a technique, and although the work was exciting, it was an arduous task. I claim only the credit for having attempted it.

But what of the novel itself? Unfortunately, we cannot give its author more credit than he demanded. The experiment is extremely interesting as an experiment, but the work is not very forceful as a novel. Furthermore, as might have been suspected from the discussions of harmony and orchestration in the manifesto, the musical analogies are severely strained. It is probable that anyone who read the work without seeing the preface or the musical headings of the movements (if that were possible) would consider it merely a none-too-coherent-run-of-the-mill novel. Nevertheless, a few reservations must be made. The *Eroica* funeral-march of the last movement contains a fantastic allegorical vision of Love, Madness, Death, and Life, each with its own chorus (suggested, we are told, by the finale of Beethoven's *Ninth*). This vision does achieve something of a symphonic effect of combination and working out of themes. There are other touches here and there

a blind girl. The title is merely a pun on the *pastor*. The same pun will work in English, but it is not compulsory.

which succeed fairly well, but they do not lie in the direction of reproducing sonata form. Rather, they employ general principles of musical development on a larger scale than that of most of the poetry attempting to do the same thing.

It is interesting to note here that Otto Ludwig developed a rather similar musical theory under the influence of which he wrote plays of some distinction. *Der Erbförster* [20] is the best of these. But the looseness of the musical and literary analogies is well shown by the fact that, whereas Cadilhac spoke of the symphonic novel, Ludwig called his form the contrapuntal drama. Furthermore, one [21] of Ludwig's critics analyses *Der Erbförster* in terms of symphonic development, after explaining his contrapuntal theory. Obviously, if counterpoint and thematic development are the same thing in literature, they are not very close parallels to the musical processes which go by the same names.

Wherever we find literary attempts at sonata form, then, we are driven to the same conclusions. Whether the short poem, the long poem, the novel, or the drama is chosen as the medium, certain very general analogies can be worked out easily. But they are so general that they involve only processes which have been independently established in literature already. And as soon as the author tries to go beyond these elements which the two arts have in common—as soon as he tries to make a literary form which shall parallel the musical pattern with any exactness—he becomes inextricably entangled. When this point is reached, he may do any one of three things. He may simply abandon the attempt at parallelism with music, and go off on his own tack as a writer. This is the solution of Grace Hazard Conkling and Sidney Lanier. He may try to stay with the musical form, but be forced so to adapt it that it becomes almost unrecognizable, as do Todhunter and Plattensteiner. Finally, he may carry the parallelism as far as his medium will allow, and then try, by means entirely outside of his work —like Cadilhac's manifesto—to improve the parallelism by forcing analogies where none really exist.

In conclusion, one other question must be considered. Though sonata form has haunted a good many writers, we do not find the unquestionably great among their number. And even among the authors who have attempted it, those of the greatest ability—like Lanier, Fletcher, and Ludwig—have used it as a hint and a starting point more than as a pattern to be rigorously followed. How are these facts to be explained? Perhaps the writer who has great powers within himself is not driven to rely on the novelty of some external pattern. Perhaps a superior literary judgment simply rejects strict sonata form as an unpromising literary medium, and hence does not even attempt it. But there is a third and interesting possibility. Perhaps it is merely accident that no writer of first rank has concerned himself with the problem. If this be true, we may some day have a work which is at the same time a great piece of literature and a consistent literary application of sonata form.* To prove that this is not an entirely fantastic possibility, we need only remember that if De Quincey had happened to be killed in a wreck between a mail coach and a carriage on a certain straight stretch of English road, we should now be deciding that the fugue offers even less opportunity for the writer than does the sonata.

---

* We do have a great novelette which might be thus described. See the account of Thomas Mann's *Tonio Kröger*, pp. 212–217.

CHAPTER XV

The Musical Development of Symbols: Whitman

THE attempts of poets during the past century to use musical forms were useful for our inquiry because they could be clearly isolated, and hence offered a rather strictly defined problem for investigation. It would be a great mistake, however, to assume that the influence of music on poetry has been limited to such overt adaptations. The chapters which follow will deal with less tangible influences and parallels.

We have frequently had occasion to note the difficulties of repetition or variation in literature on any extensive scale and to observe that these difficulties apply with particular force to any literary attempts at development of material by processes analogous to those of music. Extensive symbolism is the best solution which has been found, and it is not uncommon for a poet speaking through symbols to approximate closely to the methods and effects of music. However, we cannot assume musical influence in such cases unless there is clear external evidence for its existence: the natural poetic methods of handling symbols resemble musical development, and even musically ignorant poets have, on occasion, produced close musical analogies by a heightening of these methods.

Walt Whitman is a good case in point. He must have been practically a musical illiterate, for his references to music are of a uniform and magnificent banality: "The conductor beats time for his band and all the performers follow him,"—"The jay in the woods never studied the gamut, yet trills pretty well to me,"—"With music strong I come, with my cornets and my drums,"—

> I heard the violoncello, ('tis the young man's heart's complaint,)
> I hear the key'd cornet, it glides quickly in through my ears,
> It shakes mad-sweet pangs through my belly and breast.
> I hear the chorus, it is a grand opera,
> Ah this indeed is music—this suits me.[1]

178

Even as a poet Whitman seems generally to have been remarkably
insensitive to the possibilities (and dangers) of sound. His own characterization of his poems as a "barbaric yawp" [2] is a masterpiece of un-
derstatement for such a line as "See, dearest mother, the letter says
Pete will soon be better." [3] Furthermore, the great bulk of his poetry
is weakened by a formlessness which would seem to arise from an utter
lack of architectonic ability. All things considered, Whitman seems offhand to offer little promise of illumination on the musical possibilities
of poetry.

Nevertheless, in a few poems of medium length he attained a firm
structure and real poetic distinction by a treatment of symbols closely
parallel to the musical development of themes. In the darkness of his
musical ignorance we can only grope for an explanation. The fact that
such poems as *Crossing Brooklyn Ferry* and *When Lilacs Last in the
Dooryard Bloom'd* confine themselves to a single and limited subject
instead of magniloquently embracing the universe probably contributed
considerably to their coherence. Furthermore, the second of these poems
was the product of deeply felt personal experience,[4] and thus may well
have unconsciously shaped itself in the mind of a man who seldom took
the trouble consciously to organize his work. Whatever the explanation
may be, only the poem itself concerns us here. In spite of its length,
it must be quoted in full if we are to follow the development of
symbols on which its entire effect depends.

WHEN LILACS LAST IN THE DOORYARD BLOOM'D

1

When lilacs last in the dooryard bloom'd,
And the great star early droop'd in the western sky in the night,
I mourn'd, and yet shall mourn with ever-returning spring.

Ever-returning spring, trinity sure to me you bring,
5 Lilac blooming perennial and drooping star in the west,
And thought of him I love.

2

O powerful western fallen star!
O shades of night—O moody, tearful night!
O great star disappear'd—O the black murk that hides the star!
10 O cruel hands that hold me powerless—O helpless soul of me!
O harsh surrounding cloud that will not free my soul.

3

In the dooryard fronting an old farm-house near the white-wash'd palings,
Stands the lilac-bush tall-growing with heart-shaped leaves of rich green,
With many a pointed blossom rising delicate, with the perfume strong I
    love,
15 With every leaf a miracle—and from this bush in the dooryard,
With delicate-color'd blossoms and heart-shaped leaves of rich green,
A sprig with its flower I break.

4

In the swamp in secluded recesses,
A shy and hidden bird is warbling a song.

20 Solitary the thrush,
The hermit withdrawn to himself, avoiding the settlements,
Sings by himself a song.

Song of the bleeding throat,
Death's outlet song of life, (for well dear brother I know,
25 If thou wast not granted to sing thou would'st surely die.)

5

Over the breast of the spring, the land, amid cities,
Amid lanes and through old woods, where lately the violets peep'd from
    the ground, spotting the gray débris,
Amid the grass in the fields each side of the lanes, passing the endless
    grass,
Passing the yellow-spear'd wheat, every grain from its shroud in the dark-
    brown fields uprisen,
30 Passing the apple-tree blows of white and pink in the orchards,
Carrying a corpse to where it shall rest in the grave,
Night and day journeys a coffin.

6

Coffin that passes through lanes and streets,
Through day and night with the great cloud darkening the land,
35 With the pomp of the inloop'd flags with the cities draped in black,
With the show of the states themselves as of crape-veil'd women standing,
With processions long and winding and the flambeaus of the night,
With the countless torches lit, with the silent sea of faces and the unbared
    heads,
With the waiting depot, the arriving coffin, and the sombre faces,
40 With dirges through the night, with the thousand voices rising strong and
    solemn,
With all the mournful voices of the dirges pour'd around the coffin,
The dim-lit churches and the shuddering organs—where amid these you
    journey,

With the tolling tolling bells' perpetual clang,
Here, coffin that slowly passes,
45 I give you my sprig of lilac.

7

(Nor for you, for one alone,
Blossoms and branches green to coffins all I bring,
For fresh as the morning, thus would I chant a song for you O sane and
    sacred death.

All over bouquets of roses,
50 O death, I cover you over with roses and early lilies,
But mostly and now the lilac that blooms the first,
Copious I break, I break the sprigs from the bushes,
With loaded arms I come, pouring for you,
For you and the coffins all of you O death.)

8

55 O western orb sailing the heaven,
Now I know what you must have meant as a month since I walk'd,
As I walk'd in silence the transparent shadowy night,
As I saw you had something to tell as you bent to me night after night,
As you droop'd from the sky low down as if to my side, (while the other
    stars all look'd on,)
60 As we wander'd together the solemn night, (for something I know not
    what kept me from sleep,)
As the night advanced, and I saw on the rim of the west how full you
    were of woe,
As I stood on the rising ground in the breeze in the cool transparent night,
As I watch'd where you pass'd and was lost in the netherward black of
    the night,
As my soul in its trouble dissatisfied sank, as where you sad orb,
65 Concluded, dropt in the night, and was gone.

9

Sing on there in the swamp,
O singer bashful and tender, I hear your notes, I hear your call,
I hear, I come presently, I understand you,
But a moment I linger, for the lustrous star has detain'd me,
70 The star my departing comrade holds and detains me.

10

O how shall I warble myself for the dead one there I loved?
And how shall I deck my song for the large sweet soul that has gone?
And what shall my perfume be for the grave of him I love?

Sea-winds blown from east and west,
75 Blown from the Eastern sea and blown from the Western sea, till there on
    the prairies meeting,

These and with these and the breath of my chant,
I'll perfume the grave of him I love.

11

O what shall I hang on the chamber walls?
And what shall the pictures be that I hang on the walls,
80 To adorn the burial-house of him I love?

Pictures of growing spring and farms and homes,
With the Fourth-month eve at sundown, and the gray smoke lucid and
bright,
With floods of the yellow gold of the gorgeous, indolent, sinking sun,
burning, expanding the air,
With the fresh sweet herbage under foot, and the pale green leaves of the
trees prolific,
85 In the distance the flowing glaze, the breast of the river, with a wind-
dapple here and there,
With ranging hills on the banks, with many a line against the sky, and
shadows,
And the city at hand with dwellings so dense, and stacks of chimneys,
And all the scenes of life and the workshops, and the workmen homeward
returning.

12

Lo, body and soul—this land,
90 My own Manhattan with spires, and the sparkling and hurrying tides, and
the ships,
The varied and ample land, the South and the North in the light, Ohio's
shores and flashing Missouri,
And ever the far-spreading prairies cover'd with grass and corn.

Lo, the most excellent sun so calm and haughty,
The violet and purple morn with just-felt breezes,
95 The gentle soft-born measureless light,
The miracle spreading bathing all, the fulfill'd noon,
The coming eve delicious, the welcome night and the stars,
Over my cities shining all, enveloping man and land.

13

Sing on, sing on you gray-brown bird,
100 Sing from the swamps, the recesses, pour your chant from the bushes,
Limitless out of the dusk, out of the cedars and pines.

Sing on dearest brother, warble your reedy song,
Loud human song, with voice of uttermost woe.

O liquid and free and tender!
105 O wild and loose to my soul—O wondrous singer!

You only I hear—yet the star holds me, (but will soon depart,)
Yet the lilac with mastering odor holds me.

14

Now while I sat in the day and look'd forth,
In the close of the day with its light and the fields of spring, and the
farmers preparing their crops,
110 In the large unconscious scenery of my land with its lakes and forests,
In the heavenly aerial beauty, (after the perturbed winds and the storms,)
Under the arching heavens of the afternoon swift passing, and the voices
of children and women,
The many-moving sea-tides, and I saw the ships how they sail'd,
And the summer approaching with richness, and the fields all busy with
labor,
115 And the infinite separate houses, how they all went on, each with its meals
and minutia of daily usages,
And the streets how their throbbings throbb'd, and the cities pent—lo,
then and there,
Falling upon them all and among them all, enveloping me with the rest,
Appear'd the cloud, appear'd the long black trail,
And I knew death, its thought, and the sacred knowledge of death.

120 Then with the knowledge of death as walking one side of me,
And the thought of death close-walking the other side of me,
And I in the middle as with companions, and as holding the hands of
companions,
I fled forth to the hiding receiving night that talks not,
Down to the shores of the water, the path by the swamp in the dimness,
125 To the solemn shadowy cedars and ghostly pines so still.

And the singer so shy to the rest receiv'd me,
The gray-brown bird I know receiv'd us comrades three,
And he sang the carol of death, and a verse for him I love.

From deep secluded recesses,
130 From the fragrant cedars and the ghostly pines so still,
Came the carol of the bird.

And the charm of the carol rapt me,
As I held as if by their hands my comrades in the night,
And the voice of my spirit tallied the song of the bird.

135 *Come lovely and soothing death,*
Undulate around the world, serenely arriving, arriving,
In the day, in the night, to all, to each,
Sooner or later delicate death.

Prais'd be the fathomless universe,
140 *For life and joy, and for objects and knowledge curious,*
    And for love, sweet love—but praise! praise! praise!
    For the sure-enwinding arms of cool-enfolding death.

    Dark mother always gliding near with soft feet,
    Have none chanted for thee a chant of fullest welcome?
145 *Then I chant it for thee, I glorify thee above all,*
    I bring thee a song that when thou must indeed come, come unfalteringly.

    Approach strong deliveress,
    When it is so, when thou hast taken them, I joyously sing the dead,
    Lost in the loving floating ocean of thee,
150 *Laved in the flood of thy bliss O death.*

    From me to thee glad serenades,
    Dances for thee I propose saluting thee, adornments and feastings for thee,
    And the sights of the open landscape and the high-spread sky are fitting,
    And life and the fields, and the huge and thoughtful night.

155 *The night in silence under many a star,*
    The ocean shore and the husky whispering wave whose voice I know,
    And the soul turning to thee O vast and well-veil'd death,
    And the body gratefully nestling close to thee.

    Over the tree-tops I float thee a song,
160 *Over the rising and sinking waves, over the myriad fields and the prairies*
      wide,
    Over the dense-pack'd cities all and the teeming wharves and ways,
    I float this carol with joy, with joy to thee O death.

15

    To the tally of my soul,
    Loud and strong kept up the gray-brown bird,
165 With pure deliberate notes spreading filling the night.
    Loud in the pines and cedars dim,
    Clear in the freshness moist and swamp-perfume,
    And I with my comrades there in the night.

    While my sight that was bound in my eyes unclosed,
170 As to long panoramas of visions.

    And I saw askant the armies,
    I saw as in noiseless dreams hundreds of battle-flags,
    Borne through the smoke of the battles and pierc'd with missiles I saw
      them,
    And carried hither and yon through the smoke, and torn and bloody,

175 And at last but a few shreds left on the staffs, (and all in silence,)
     And the staffs all splinter'd and broken.

     I saw battle-corpses, myriads of them,
     And the white skeletons of young men, I saw them,
     I saw the débris and débris of all the slain soldiers of the war,
180 But I saw they were not as was thought,
     They themselves were fully at rest, they suffer'd not,
     The living remain'd and suffer'd, the mother suffer'd,
     And the wife and the child and the musing comrade suffer'd,
     And the armies that remain'd suffer'd.

                              16

185 Passing the visions, passing the night,
     Passing, unloosing the hold of my comrades' hands,
     Passing the song of the hermit bird and the tallying song of my soul,
     Victorious song, death's outlet song, yet varying ever-altering song,
     As low and wailing, yet clear the notes, rising and falling, flooding the
         night,
190 Sadly sinking and fainting, as warning and warning, and yet again bursting
         with joy,
     Covering the earth and filling the spread of the heaven,
     As that powerful psalm in the night I heard from recesses,
     Passing, I leave thee lilac with heart-shaped leaves,
     I leave thee there in the dooryard, blooming, returning with spring.

195 I cease from my song for thee,
     From my gaze on thee in the west, fronting the west, communing with thee,
     O comrade lustrous with silver face in the night.
     Yet each to keep and all, retrievements out of the night,
     The song, the wondrous chant of the gray-brown bird,
200 And the tallying chant, the echo arous'd in my soul,
     With the lustrous and drooping star with the countenance full of woe,
     With the holders holding my hand nearing the call of the bird,
     Comrades mine and I in the midst, and their memory ever to keep, for the
         dead I loved so well,
     For the sweetest, wisest soul of all my days and lands—and this for his
         dear sake,
205 Lilac and star and bird twined with the chant of my soul,
     There in the fragrant pines and the cedars dusk and dim.

Even a casual reading of this poem shows that the entire effect is
dependent on the three principal symbols of lilac, star, and bird; and
that these symbols are constantly varied in application and combined
both with each other and with various subsidiary symbols and ideas.
A detailed examination will reveal how such an excellent and comparatively long poetic work is evolved out of such slight materials. But be-

fore beginning a consideration of the structure of the poem we may note that this symbolic treatment has the remarkable effect of universalizing the theme. The personal and historical considerations may add a certain amount of interest, but that interest is not of an essential nature. Lincoln's death on April 15 explains the choice of symbols: Venus is a conspicuous evening star; the lilacs are in bloom in Brooklyn; and the spring singing of the hermit thrush is at its height. But these facts are all unessential, for the first introduction of the symbols makes the association clear. Furthermore, Lincoln is never named in the poem, and—though Whitman would doubtless resent such a statement—he is hardly essential to it. This is true because the poem itself conveys the broader idea of grief for the death of a great man on whom the destiny of a nation hangs.

It is common knowledge that Beethoven originally dedicated his *Eroica* to Napoleon (as an apostle of freedom rather than as a conqueror), but when Napoleon assumed the title of Emperor, Beethoven tore up the title-page. The work was finally called "Heroic Symphony, composed to celebrate the memory of a great man." * And it has been significantly pointed out that Beethoven did not need to change a note of the music: what would do for Napoleon would do equally well for the general idea of greatness. The same principle applies to Whitman's celebration of Lincoln. Though the specific nature of such literary symbols as the lilac and the hermit thrush aids a local application, the poem is really "composed to celebrate the memory of a great man" and is universal in its application. By avoiding direct statement it goes far beyond a provincial interest in the Civil War and the war president. The poem does contain a few particularities, but, broadly speaking, it could be applied to Lee, or to the Napoleon for whom the *Eroica* was written (and who was only a *memory* when the work was published) or to Thomas à Becket with almost equal fittingness. When we consider the deliberate local particularity of the great bulk of Whitman's work this fact is startling. The explanation, however, is obvious: by using symbolic themes developed in what is essentially a musical way, Whitman achieved the universality of great music rather than the particularity of the ordinary type of *in memoriam* verse.

An examination of the poem will make the musical nature of its development clear. Section 1 introduces the lilac and star, and associates them with past and future mourning. Already, then, the real sub-

---

* SINFONIA EROICA, composta per festeggiare il sovvenire di un grand' Uomo. . . .

ject is announced—not the death of Lincoln, as we are in the habit of loosely saying, but the undying grief for the death of a great man. The fourth line announces the trinity which forms the structural basis of the poem, but for the moment it does not make all the symbols specific. The lilac and the "drooping star in the west" are mentioned again, but the third element is an abstraction, the "thought of him I love," which is not yet given symbolic form. The principal theme of the last movement of the *Eroica* is not announced immediately, but its way is prepared by the use of a motive which later serves as its accompaniment. In an analogous way the poet here prepares for the later introduction of the third of his symbols, the bird.

Section 2 develops the recently introduced symbol of the star. By associating it with night, referring to it as "fallen" and "disappear'd," hidden by black murk, Whitman establishes the idea of grief for departed brilliance and prepares for the later specific references to death. Likewise, in the last two lines, he reiterates the fact that the real topic is his own grief rather than the blotting out of the star.

In Section 3 he returns to the lilac and develops the physical aspect of the symbol by a description of its setting, leaves, flowers, and perfume. The echo of the "thought of him I love" (line 6) heard in "the perfume strong I love" (line 14) goes beyond a mere playing with words: it establishes a more direct connection between the thought of Lincoln and the odor of the flower. We shall see that this particular little verbal formula is later used several times for a similar purpose. The repetition of parts of the description within Section 3 ("heart-shaped leaves of rich green") does not have, for the moment, any such structural purpose, but is made for its own sake. The last line of the section extends the purpose of the symbol in its account of breaking off a sprig, but since this statement is a preparation for a later union of ideas, it is deliberately left hanging at this point.

Section 4 is entirely devoted to the announcement of the third of the principal themes, the hermit thrush singing alone in the swamp. His song is associated immediately with death and characterized as "Death's outlet song of life."

The three principal themes have now been introduced. Though Whitman is certainly following no musical model and is probably unaware of the analogy, we might say that the exposition has been completed, and the development is about to begin. A composer writing in any of the larger forms must consider not only the beauty or effectiveness of his themes in their original statements, but also their possibilities of development. What opportunities do Whitman's symbols present? Being physical objects, they have attributes perceptible to the senses as well as to abstract thought. As a matter of fact, most of their symbolic development is achieved by associating their various sensuous attributes with abstract concepts. Therefore a variety of sensuous attributes will permit a variety of developments. Considering the symbols from this standpoint, we see that they are carefully selected. The lilac has the color of leaf and flower, the pattern of heart-shaped leaves and pointed blossoms, and an intangible, all-enveloping perfume. The star has its light against darkness (both of night in general and of the obscuring cloud), and it also has motion of a slow and stately type which can be interpreted as either drooping or beckoning. And the bird has his own color, his setting in the swamp with its dim trees and its perfume, and, above all, his song. These various attributes of the symbols include the primary senses and, together with associations of their settings and of abstractions for which they come to stand, allow for rich development.

Section 5 includes the first direct mention of Lincoln's funeral, but the coffin is mentioned only at the end of a periodic sentence. Before this there is a series of visual images of plants, woods, and fields—images which suggest the lilac and the bird without containing any direct reference to them.

Section 6 is built on the same plan. It is ostensibly a continuation of the description of the funeral procession, but its allusions to the symbols are more direct than those of the preceding section. The "great cloud darkening the land" not only connects with "the cities draped in black"; it also goes back to "the black murk that hides the star" (line 9). Similarly the "flambeaus of the night" make an association with the star itself, while the "dirges through the night" suggest the song of the bird. Also, the dominant background of night is an intensification of the dimness of the swamp and the setting of the drooping star. And finally the lilac sprig broken off for no particular reason (as far as one could tell when it was mentioned at the end of Section 3) is placed on the coffin. Thus Section 6 connects the star and the bird with the funeral procession by concealed allusions, and closes with a direct linking of the lilac and the coffin.

In Section 7 this association is generalized. The lilac is not merely for the coffin of Lincoln, but for all coffins. Even more than for the dead it is for "sane and sacred death." This association, very necessary in later parts of the poem, is repeated and elaborated in the second division of the section. This section also contains the first appearance of a pure abstraction, the concept of death. Its reality in this poem—as compared with its artificiality in many literary works—is due to the fact that the abstraction is not thrown at the reader, but is *developed* by a combination of simple physical objects: the flower is broken—it is destined for a coffin—not for this coffin only, but for those of all the dead—and hence for death itself. Since the abstraction is built up within the poem, the author's attitude towards it can be developed at the same time, and thus there is nothing of the ordinary personification as a monster or a grim reaper. From the very first mention we have the poet (like the bird) chanting sane and sacred death and wishing to sing a song for him.

Section 8 is devoted to an intensive development of the star theme. It makes a direct connection between the previously mentioned woe and drooping of the star and the death of Lincoln. The star is also associated with the poet's earlier feeling of foreboding, and its appearance is made into a prophecy. Also, the idea of night, both as a background for the star and as a subsidiary symbol of death and grief in itself, is closely associated with that of the star. The very word *night* is reiterated in emphatic positions so that it sets the tone of the entire passage.

The next section effects a union between the themes of bird and star. This fusion is presented by a union of sense impressions enabling both symbols to be simultaneously present, for the poet hears the call of the bird as a summons, but waits to watch "the star of my departing comrade." The song of the thrush has already been something of a solace for death, and that symbolism is later to be more fully developed, but the declining star has been associated with foreboding and grief. This combination of the two symbols into a single scene, with one detaining and the other calling, thus takes on a philosophical significance: the poet hears in the distance the theoretically known idea that death is sane and sacred—is, as the bird says specifically in a later passage (line 135) "lovely and soothing death." But at the time of the death itself (the sinking of the star) this abstract consolation is powerless to draw him from his grief. "Philosophy easily overcomes past and future sorrows, but present sorrows overcome philosophy." *

Since the three principal symbols have now received sufficient

---

* La philosophie triomphe aisément des maux passés et des maux à venir, mais les maux présents triomphent d'elle.

(La Rochefoucauld, Maxim 22)

development and interconnection for the time being, the next three sections form an interlude in which they are kept before the reader only by occasional allusions. Sections 10 and 11 are carefully balanced within themselves and against each other. The shift of subject leads now to a direct statement of the author's personal feeling—a statement more specific than that presented through the symbols, but still reinforced by them. The transition is clearly marked at the beginning of Section 10: the bird has been singing of the dead, but "how shall I *warble* myself of the dead one there I loved?" (Note the return of the "him I love" formula in these two sections.) The real question of Section 10 involves the perfuming of the grave and thus makes a connection with the lilac laid on the coffin, but the answer expands its meaning, for not only—not merely—the lilac, but the sea-winds sweeping across the continent and this poem itself shall be memorials.

Section 11, with its biblical question and answer, affords a close parallel. The song of praise and the perfume of memory are intangibles, but what shall the pictures be to adorn the burial-house? They shall be all objects and seasons of nature and civilization, including (to expand and connect with the earlier symbols) the pale green leaves and "floods of yellow gold of the gorgeous, indolent, sinking sun." This last figure is a transposition to a totally different mood and symbolism of the theme of the sinking star.

In Section 12 the same line of development is continued: all the land is praised, both for itself and (by implication) as a continuing memorial to the man who stood by it in its hour of need. The second part of the section is particularly remarkable in that its pictures run through the course of a day (with what seem to be reminiscences of Eve's morning song to Adam), thus making time itself into a visibly apprehended thing. Furthermore, by this very process the sun, which was developed from the symbol of the star in the previous section, is now resumed in the form in which it was there left, and is skilfully modulated back into its normal form and setting.

Section 13 returns emphatically to the bird, whose song is destined for extensive development in the next section. The verbal return to the opening of Section 9 reestablishes the continuity of the bird's song after the author's own chant of his hero and his country. At this point it is well to note that, as the symbols are interwoven into a closer texture, the free verse tends to fall into regular patterns. The questions in Sections 10 and 11 were strongly metrical, and the second part of

Section 12 was comparatively regular. Now, with lines 100 and 101, we get a regular and highly effective elegiac couplet:

> Sing from the swamps, the recesses, pour your chant from the bushes,
> Limitless out of the dusk, out of the cedars and pines.

The tendency towards regular metrical forms continues throughout the remainder of the poem,* and this passage is echoed, both in subject and in meter, at the conclusion. The bird's song is now specifically identified with the human song of woe, for the idea of comfort is to be fully developed in the next section. We have a momentary return to the exact combination of symbols used at the end of Section 9 (except that the star is about to depart), with the addition of the odor of the lilac. Here the three symbols can be simultaneously presented and perceived because each is presented to a different sense: the poet can watch the star while he hears the song of the bird and is surrounded by the mastering odor of the lilac.

Section 14, by far the longest division of the poem, makes specific the idea towards which the interrelated symbols have been converging. It does this by telling straight through, in symbolical form, the poet's reaction to the death of Lincoln. As Whitman looked out in his imagination over the whole of the country, with its various scenery and different pursuits, the black cloud of death appeared, not over the star this time, but over the whole of the nation, and with the fact of death came its thought and its sacred knowledge. Like two comrades they went with the poet when he fled in his grief to "the hiding receiving night, that talks not." The thought of death seems to be a personified representation of the involuntary grief which accompanies death; whereas the knowledge of death is that perception of its true meaning which is expressed fully in the song of the bird. The bird here becomes not only himself, but also the voice of nature in its comforting power, receiving the poet (with his thought and knowledge of death), and making explicit to him his own latent thought: "And the voice of my spirit tallied the song of the bird" (line 134). This thought is a song praising death as a soothing, delivering power, and lines 151–158 make it clear that all nature is represented in the song of the bird. In

---

* For a few examples, note the dactylic hexameters of lines 119 and 124 (the latter being the first line of another elegiac couplet) and the iambic pentameters of lines 118 and 155, as well as the final couplet. Notice also that the elegiac couplet form of three of the references to the swamp with its dim cedars and pines helps to point out the repetitions of the three.

these lines, as also in the poet's flight to the night for comfort, the symbol of night undergoes a transformation parallel to that of death itself. We have already noted that night, the cloud, and darkness have formed a group of subsidiary symbols connected with the idea of death. Since the day described in Section 12 and ending with "the welcome night and the stars," this value of night has been shifting, along with the parallel idea of death, to one of peace and majesty, to the picture in line 154 of "huge and thoughtful night."

This transformation is continued in Section 15 with a return to the poet standing in the night, hearing the song of the bird and realizing that it is also the song of his own soul. As he stands there with his allegorical comrades the idea which the bird's song has expressed about Lincoln's death expands (exactly as did the significance of the lilac laid on the coffin) to an acceptance of death in general. And here, for the first time, there is a reference to the particular circumstances of Lincoln's presidency. The realization, the "knowledge of death" in the song of the bird, extends to all the slain of the war as a vision of its carnage unfolds before the poet. "My sight that was bound in my eyes unclosed," and through the experience of Lincoln's death he received comfort for all the hosts of the slain. Finally, a reconciliation between the thought and the knowledge of death is made by the realization that grief and suffering remain with the living (in their thought of the death of others), but death itself is a deliverer to those who come to know it.

This central section of the poem has been presented through one of the leading symbols as the song of the bird, but otherwise it has been an interlude employing its own symbolic characters and visions. What now remains is to return to the leading symbols, which have been greatly enriched by the episode. This is briefly and effectively done in the coda, Section 16. The phrases are frequently reminiscent of those in the opening sections of the poem, as, passing the visions, the night, the comrades, the song of the bird and his answering soul (for moments of full insight, like other things, become memories)—passing all these, the poet leaves the lilac where he found it, "in the dooryard, blooming, returning with spring." There is a summary of the principal themes and most of the subsidiary ones, the chant of the poet's soul now taking its place as a fully developed motive parallel to the three main ones, and all these things are memories, "retrievements out of the night." Here, in its last appearance, the multiple symbol of night reaches a new meaning which is a fusion of all the others. It has represented the general idea of death, the pall of grief over the land, the literal setting of the star, and the revelation of the bird. Now it embraces all these meanings simultaneously and comes to signify the total experience, from which the poet emerges with the four symbols, now combined into a single line to end the poem with the memory of that experience:

> Lilac and star and bird twined with the chant of my soul,
> There in the fragrant pines and the cedars dusk and dim.

One is tempted to speak of exposition, development, recapitulation, first and second subjects, etc., in connection with this poem. By yielding to that temptation one might easily make out some procrustean adaptation of sonata form, or of the rondo, or even of a large ABA form. The very fact, however, that there would be such a choice is sufficient proof that any identification of the structure of this poem with a musical form would be a falsification. On the other hand, some relationship with music is obvious. There is no single passage, no individual treatment of a symbol which is not in keeping with established and independent literary practise, but the degree to which these devices are employed and the fact that the entire poem depends on them for its success are, to say the least, unusual in literary works.

Finally, then, we must classify Whitman's elegy as a poem not based on any specific musical form and probably not written with any musical analogy in mind, but nevertheless conforming to certain general structural principles which are more musical than literary. The essential plan is that of three symbols separately introduced, developed both singly and in every sort of combination (with the addition of subsidiary symbols and of a fourth one of major importance—"the tallying chant of my soul"—derived from the interplay of the first three), and finally restated in much their original form, but with a great enrichment resulting from their intermediate relationships. This is clearly the circular structure of the typical musical composition rather than the linear development of the literary work. Furthermore, the principle (though not the structure itself) is that of sonata form: statement of related but contrasting themes, development of these themes, and recapitulation of them in much their original form.

Also, the effect lies in the development of these themes. Anyone called on to give a summary of the logical content of the poem will find himself considerably embarrassed. One cannot say what the poem is "about" except that it is about the symbols themselves and their interrelationships—including the various treatments of the idea of death as one of these symbols. And no verbal summary can represent the material of the poem except in these terms. It is clearly inadequate to say that the poem is "about" the death of Lincoln, or death in general, except in the same way that Beethoven's *Fifth Symphony* is—if we take the old yarn seriously—about fate. The real subject of the poem is the complex and beautiful interrelationship in the author's mind by which a number of hitherto insignificant things have come to symbolize a complex experience. It is really about its symbols and their development, precisely as the Beethoven symphony is really about its themes and their interrelationships. Thus this poem approaches far more closely than do most literary works to that condition which Schopenhauer and Pater describe as the particular glory of music—the inseparability of form and content.

CHAPTER XVI

The Poetry of Conrad Aiken

PROBABLY no poet has been more concerned with music than Conrad Aiken, or has used it more fruitfully. The interest is visible even in the titles of his poems, where we find nocturnes, tone-poems, variations, dissonants, and symphonies. He describes himself as groping for musical effects from the beginning of his poetic career, and though he has tended to become more metaphysical during the past decade, the influence can still be seen in even such traditional and fixed types as his sonnet sequence, and, to a lesser extent, the *Brownstone Eclogues*. Nevertheless, the principal musical techniques and approaches had been worked out on their most impressive scale before the *Selected Poems* of 1929, and hence we shall concern ourselves primarily with the poems contained in that volume.

Many poets have used titles containing (frequently false) musical implications, and many have been fond of musical references and intricately developed symbols. Aiken's peculiarity does not lie in any one single aspect of the musical influence, but in its extent, richness, and cohesion. The formal arrangement of a good deal of his poetry is based on musical principles rather than on the more widely accepted poetic ones. His symbols are developed and combined in ways analogous to the composer's handling of themes. He has given us, here and there, enough information about the theoretical basis of his work to make it clear that the musical analogies are deliberately and skilfully cultivated. And, finally, this poetry based on music is alive with musical references which reinforce both the implications of its structure and a philosophy in which music is that epitome of the individual and the universe which it was to Schopenhauer.

From the purely formal point of view, Aiken makes extensive and intricate use of the general principles of repetition, variation, and contrast, though he never attempts exact poetic equivalents of the larger musical structures. Frequently, however, we find ABA forms, and these

forms often overlap or enclose one another. Thus four of the long poems
—*Senlin, The Pilgrimage of Festus, The House of Dust,* and *The Jig of
Forslin*—devote an appreciable part of their last sections to repetition,
either exact or with slight variation, of material from the first sections.
Forslin offers a good example of the complication created by an extension of this principle. The poem as a whole contains the ABA
structure just mentioned. But Part IV is also an ABA structure, as is
at least one still smaller subdivision, Section iii of Part V. In *Senlin*
also we find this type of organization on a smaller scale: the first four
sections have the typical musical structure of AABA (a complete form
in itself); but the A section is used twice, with new material between
the recurrences, at the end of the poem. This habit of returning to the
beginning for the end is as common in Aiken's poetry as it is in music,[1]
and the source of the device is clearly shown when he has Music, speaking as a character, refer to the

> weak hand that touched, strong hand that held, weak hand
>   that touched;
> eyes that forgetting saw, and saw recalling,
> and saw again forgetting; memory moving
> from wonder to disaster, and to wonder. . . .[2]

Another favorite musical device is parallelism carried to such a
point that one passage is clearly a variation on another. Occasionally,
as in some of the "Variations," this technique is used for its own sake
and thus resembles the musical theme and variations.[3] More frequently,
however, as in the larger musical forms, the variation occurs at some
distance from the original version as part of a larger pattern. It may
take the form of a shift in meter, tense, imagery, tone—almost any
kind of change, so long as the original passage is still clearly recognizable. A good example occurs in *Senlin,* where the morning-song[4] contains the quatrain:

> There are houses hanging above the stars
> And stars hung under a sea . . .
> And a sun far off in a shell of silence
> Dapples my walls for me . . .

Eight pages later[5] the passage is varied to

> There are houses hanging above the stars,
> And stars hung under a sea:
> And a wind from the long blue vault of time
> Waves my curtains for me . . .

Variations of this sort are among the most conspicuous structural elements of Aiken's poetry.

Another favorite device, partaking of both repetition and variation, is something of an approximation to the rondo form of music. It consists of two themes which are consistently alternated. In spite of the fact that Aiken speaks of developing such juxtapositions in an attempt to find a poetic equivalent of counterpoint, the device is really parallel to the musical practice of alternation between contrasting themes, strings and woodwinds, loud and soft, etc. One of the most striking examples of this method, a passage alternating between the thoughts of an old man and a young girl living in apartments one above the other, was originally published as a separate poem entitled "A Counterpoint," though it was later incorporated into *The House of Dust*.[6] Another conspicuous example [7] is based on the interplay between the suggestions of the music which a man hears at a concert and the chatter of his companion. Out of numerous other instances of this method we may select the morning-song of *Senlin* [8] as probably the most effective. The two alternating themes are Senlin (his actions and thoughts) and the world outside his window. The first of these, however, is in itself compound and achieves its effect by an alternation between the trivial acts with which the day begins and the sense of the vastness and beauty of the universe which occupies his mind. The first two sections (quoted on p. 142) show the interplay of these themes. This alternation is kept up throughout one section of the poem, not with mechanical regularity, for such regularity kills the very effect which the device is designed to produce, but with sufficient consistency and rapidity to give the intended sense of the simultaneity of these diverse elements in Senlin's consciousness.

The border-line between these formal devices of repetition and variation and the development of recurrent symbols is a real one, even though it cannot be exactly located. Up to this point we have dealt with formal elements, but it now becomes necessary to deal with content. In Aiken's longer poems a great deal of attention is given to the development of what, for lack of a better name, we may call symbols or themes. Perhaps the latter is really the better term, since these themes do not symbolize anything in the sense in which Hester Prynne's scarlet letter symbolizes her burden of guilt. Rather, a theme is intended to evoke a state of mind by presenting imagery suggestive of that state. And in this way they are far more like musical themes than like the ordinary subjects of poetry. We may well question whether the primary purpose of a theme in music is to evoke a specific state of mind, but the theme is certainly a thing in itself, both sensuously and intellectually satisfying, and independent of any criteria of objective truth. Its chief function is to be developed so that its own inherent possibilities and its relationships with other themes will be fully exploited. Except that words necessarily have external reference—a fact which Aiken is sometimes inclined to lament—and that there is an external portraying of a state of mind, however indefinable and tenuous, Aiken's themes are essentially like those of the composer.

Their development, then, proceeds along musical lines, with endless modification and combination. A theme already established may be merely suggested in a word or two; a casual phrase may be returned to and expanded until it becomes a full-fledged theme in its own right; two or more themes may be fused to form a single indivisible unit. The anthologists have isolated, for their own purposes, certain sections of Aiken's longer poems in precisely the same way that collections of parlor-music often print merely the statement of a theme from a symphony: the processes are the same, and the nature and extent of the loss are the same.

It is impossible to describe the effect of this technique adequately, but its methods can be shown. Perhaps it will be well to begin with such a short and simple example as *Evensong.*° A girl looked out of her window at twilight, and we are given her train of thoughts and her state of mind, with a background of the sights and sounds which she experienced. "She looked into the west with a young and infinite pity." In the next line the last words are repeated as "a young and wistful pity," and thus one of the recurrent themes of the poem is established. As twilight came on there were slight occasional sounds, such as the murmur of leaves, "and then the hush swept back." As it grew darker, lights were turned on, and the leaves casually mentioned a moment ago are now described in some detail as, wet after rain, they glistened with the street-lights shining up through them. Looking out on this, she felt "a young, and wise, and infinite pity" for the girl without a lover, and went from this feeling into a blending of memories of love with a sense of "tragic peacefulness." She wondered: "Would her lover, then, grow old sooner than she . . . ?" Would he lose interest in the light through the leaves, and the twilight? And her first question came back into her mind. A neighbor sang a child to sleep, and the song was singularly poignant. Because it came up through the leaves of the tree?

Or because, as she looked out, she "thought of all the mothers with a young and infinite pity?" The child went to sleep; "the hush swept back." If it were not raining, she thought, there would be a full moon, and the lovers would be in the park—she herself might be going there. Would she grow old and lose interest in love in the park and the latest ways of putting up one's hair? But would her lover grow old sooner than she? And yet, as she watched the city and the wet leaves, once again

> It seemed as if all evenings were the same;
> As if all evenings came,
> Despite her smile at thinking of a kiss,
> With just such tragic peacefulness as this;
> With just such hint of loneliness or pain,
> The perfect quiet that comes after rain.

Short as this poem is, and general as this account of its themes has had to be, something of their development, repetition, variation, and interplay can be seen. The longer poems are infinitely more complex. I have just abandoned an attempt to make a detailed analysis of the themes in *The Jig of Forslin*. The thing cannot be done. One soon reaches the point where, say, the underwater imagery merges with so many other things that it is impossible to say whether we have one theme or five. Is listening to rain on the roof a reappearance of this theme, or not? And what of the chance (?) occurrence of a word like *eddy* or *flow?* The problem suggests one critic's remark [10] about the omnipresent three-note figure which opens the *Second Symphony* of Brahms: "Presently we see it, even where it is not, as when the sun is in our eyes." Other themes present the same difficulties. Nevertheless, a few examples will illustrate the complexity, if not the subtlety, of the thematic development in *Forslin*.

The first section—slightly less than two pages—introduces five separate themes destined for development in later stages of the work. First comes the motive of twilight, as Forslin sits in his room and his dreams come back to him. But dream and reality merge, and the figure which illustrates the uncertainty in his own mind is the first appearance of the pervasive underwater imagery:

> Now, as one who stands
> In the aquarium's gloom, by ghostly sands,
> Watching the glide of fish beneath pale bubbles,—

> The bubbles quietly streaming
> Cool and white and green . . . poured in silver . . .
> He did not know if this were wake or dreaming;
> But thought to lean, reach out his hands, and swim.

Among other things, he remembered having "stepped in from a blare of sunlight/Over the watery threshold to this gloom"; and this sudden change from light to darkness (or from darkness to light) appears later in various guises. He also remembered music weaving its patterns and opening doors for him—a theme perhaps even more fruitful than the underwater imagery, and frequently combined with it. The idea of music in general is immediately transformed into one of its favorite forms, the music of the café or cabaret. But before this happens the clash of cymbals is compared to "a voice that swore of murder." This hint is taken up a few lines later as Forslin thinks how he sits there in his room: in the world outside, people were dancing and making love, "And the murderers chose their knives." Thus, very unobtrusively, is introduced the theme of the knife-murderer, which is later gradually built up into one of the principal motives. And finally the first section closes with a slightly varied repetition of the lines about the aquarium.

The second section is a single page, but Aiken manages, with the greatest air of casual effortlessness, to introduce into it every one of the five themes stated in the first section, to give a bit more elaboration to some of them (the knife-murderer, for example) and to make the first combination of the two most important ones:

> Deep music now, with lap and flow,
> Green music streaked with gleams and bubbles of light,
> Bears me softly away.

The third section—almost the only piece of "straight" narrative in the poem—goes back to tell who Forslin is and what he is doing there meditating in his room as evening falls. Beyond this point, detailed analysis is impossible. New themes appear, one of them a striking image of a bird falling, seen against the sheer side of a tower. Familiar themes are hinted at, combined, reinterpreted. Familiar phrases are reechoed. The twilight theme is merged with those of music and the aquarium in one passage: [11]

> This is as if, in the going of twilight,
> When skies are pale and stars are cold,
> Dew should rise from the grass in little bubbles,
> And tinkle in music among green leaves.

And near the end of the poem there is a passage of summary in which every phrase evokes associations elaborately built up by earlier treatment of the themes which are here merely mentioned:

> Who am I? Am I he that loved and murdered?
> Who walked in sunlight, heard a music playing?
> Or saw a pigeon tumbling down a wall?
> Someone drowned in the cold floods of my heart.
> Someone fell to a net—I saw him fall.[12]

Though the fact has no bearing on the aesthetic qualities of any single work, it is interesting to note that several of these themes are favorites of Aiken's and occur in a number of his poems of the "symphony" type. So standard do some of them become that in *Time in the Rock* [13] Aiken himself rejects them as so well worn that they are no longer adequate for his purposes:

> But no, the familiar symbol, as that the
> curtain lifts on a current of air, the rain
> drips at the window, the green leaves seen in the
> lamplight are bright against the darkness, these
> will no longer serve your appetite, you must have
> something fresh, something sharp—

But they were good symbols while they lasted, and they achieved remarkable effects in a number of distinguished poems. In the "symphonies" as a group they were employed in much the manner that has already been described for *Forslin*, except that in some later ones (*The House of Dust* and *Senlin*, for example) the transitions between different sections are made smoother and less startling.

What is ultimately the point of all this manipulation of forms and themes? In itself it might seem like a harmless enough kind of solitaire for anyone who happened to find it amusing, but hardly a thing to present to the public as literature. The general answer to these objections is that certain things can be communicated only by devious means, and that these happen to be precisely the things which Aiken wishes to communicate. In an article [14] contributed to *Poetry* in 1919 (ostensibly a review of his own *The Charnel Rose*) he developed at some length the theory on which these works were written, admitting that his views on the subject were not clear at first, since theory has to be developed through practice. He confesses to "some complex which has always given me a strong bias towards an architectural structure in poetry analogous to that of music," and briefly traces his efforts to achieve this structure until "finally in *Forslin* and *Senlin* it achieved something like a logical outcome."

What I had from the outset been somewhat doubtfully hankering for was some way of getting contrapuntal effects in poetry—the effects of contrasting and conflicting tones and themes, a kind of underlying simultaneity in dissimilarity. It seemed to me that by using a large medium, dividing it into several main parts, and subdividing these parts into short movements in various veins and forms, this was rendered possible. I do not wish to press the musical analogies too closely. I am aware that the word symphony, as a musical term, has a very definite meaning, and I am aware that it is only with considerable license that I use the term for such poems as *Senlin* and *Forslin.* . . . But the effect obtained is, very roughly, that of the symphony or symphonic poem.

Each section of the poem is colored by what has gone before and, retrospectively, by what is to follow; hence a section repeated will not be exactly the same thing that it was on its first appearance. Furthermore, contrasting tones ("emotion-masses") build up their effects in precisely the same way as contrasting forms. This all leads to an evocative poetry "of which the chief characteristic is its elusiveness, its fleetingness, and its richness in the shimmering overtones of hint and suggestion." In fact, "It is a prestidigitation in which the juggler's bottles or balls are a little too apt, unfortunately, to be altogether invisible."

It remains, finally, to point out the profound danger of the method I have been outlining: the danger, I mean, that one's use of implication will go too far, and that one will cheat the natural human appetite for something solid and palpable. One cannot, truly, dine—at least every evening—on, as Eliot would remark, "smells of steaks in passage-ways." One must provide for one's symphony a sufficiently powerful and pervasive underlying idea—and, above all, make it sufficiently apparent. Whether the time will come when we shall be satisfied with implication for its own sake, no one, of course, can guess.

This is a well-considered and mild enough statement from the inventor and practitioner of a theory, and objectors will find that Aiken has forestalled them on almost every point. There is, however, one question which it does not raise.

Why did Aiken wish to develop this fleeting and evocative form of poetry? Because he wished to deal, not with the relationships between the individual and other persons or his physical or social environment, but with what goes on in the individual himself. The problem of personal identity, the impossibility of fully communicating anything, the simultaneous complications of thought and feeling—these are the problems which fascinate him. These elusive things can never be stated; but there is a chance that they may be gradually formed in a reader's mind by an indirection comparable to the phenomena themselves. What the metaphysicals set out to do for the consciously thinking mind Aiken wishes to do for the feeling mind, especially in a state of reverie. Once again, his own statement is conclusive. In his novel *Blue Voyage* the rather autobiographical hero Demarest writes a long letter to Cynthia, who has apparently decided to have nothing more to do with him. The letter begins with long accounts of childhood experiences of its author, but is never finished. A second letter,[16] designed to replace this one, tells about the first:

> A long, sentimental reminiscence of my childhood! Yes, I actually believed for a moment that by some such circumferential snare as that I might trap you, bring you within my range, sting, and poison you with the subtle-sweet poison of a shared experience and consciousness. That again is highly characteristic of me. It is precisely the sort of thing I am always trying to do in my writing—to present my unhappy reader with a wide-ranged chaos,—of actions and reactions, thoughts, memories and feelings,—in the vain hope that at the end he will see that the whole thing represents only *one moment, one feeling, one person.* A raging, trumpeting jungle of associations, and then I announce at the end of it, with a gesture of despair, "This is I!"

Or, equally well, this is Forslin, who lived in poverty ten years in order to learn to throw one billiard ball into the air and catch and hold it balanced on another billiard ball; who has performed the feat for the first time in vaudeville and received no applause because it looked too easy; who has decided to kill himself with gas; and who now wanders in his own jungle of associations.

All the verse "symphonies" of Aiken have a similar purpose, and the verse strives to achieve a fluidity by which it can respond to every shift of tone or imagery. The basic form of most of these poems is irregularly rhymed verse employing considerable metrical freedom— an intermediate form which can (and does) pass with ease either to such fixed forms as regularly rhymed quatrains, or to free verse. It is an ideal medium for this purpose. A rigidly followed verse-form cannot give the required fluidity: that is why the attempt at symphonic arrangement in the "fifteen hundred more or less impeccable octosyllabic couplets" of *Earth Triumphant* had to be "exceedingly rudimentary," and why *Disenchantment: a Tone Poem* could not go much further. On the other hand, imposing form on this type of material is a difficult process at best; hence it is foolish to reject the aid offered by the recurrent patterns of verse. A comparison of the loose prose of Mrs. Bloom's famous sewer of consciousness (or of Demarest's thoughts, influenced by Mrs. Bloom, in *Blue Voyage*) with the verse of *Forslin, Senlin,* or *Festus,* leaves no doubt as to the superiority of the latter form.

We can now begin to understand Aiken's artistic preoccupation with musical effects, and our understanding will be aided by a consideration of some of his references to music. Throughout his poetry it is a recurrent theme, not as a superficial ornament, but as an inherent characteristic of his thought. His world is remarkably auditory—so much so that abstractions usually present themselves in audible form, as in the repeated references to "the horns of glory." Not content with the music of the dance or of the café, he is always hearing strange and solemn music imprisoned in walls and floors, or rising from the depths of earth or sea.

But the music actually heard, even in imagination, forms only a small part of Aiken's musical references. More often, music is a symbolic way of presenting the otherwise inexpressible complications of human thoughts, dreams, even relationships and daily lives. Music and literature are the only arts of movement, and literature can really present only one thing at a time. But music, with its different instruments, its cross-rhythms, its contrapuntal complications, can and does present *simultaneously* a number of different things which are both independent of each other and interrelated. One theory of musical aesthetics is based on the thesis that the laws of musical development are identical with those of human thought.[16] This is certainly Aiken's point of view, and thus we see why, with all his writing about music, he has so very few references to specific composers or works: he does not want the particularity of a specific composition, but rather the generality of the nature of music.

Readers of Aiken's poetry will remember countless passages in which music is symbolically used to represent the complexities of human consciousness, but it may be worth while to select a few of the most striking ones for quotation. In *Meditation on a June Evening* [17] the thought of a loved one develops musically in the mind:

> My thoughts turn back to you,
> Like tired music in a tired brain
> Seeking solution in the worn refrain;
> It returns, it returns,
> It climbs and falls, struggles, disintegrates,
> Is querulous, resentful, states, restates;
> But always, like one haunted, comes again
> To that one phrase of pain;

> And that one phrase, you know as well as I,
> Is the remembered pallor of your face;
> And a certain silence, and a certain sky,
> And a certain place.

The main section of Forslin's thoughts is introduced by a statement that

> Things mused upon are, in the mind, like music,
> They flow, they have a rhythm, they close and open,
> And sweetly return upon themselves in rhyme.
> Against the darkness they are woven,
> They are lost for a little, and laugh again,
> They fall or climb.[18]

Not only the individual's secret thoughts, but the relationships between individuals are essentially musical patterns:

> We are like music, each voice of it pursuing
> A golden separate dream, remote, persistent,
> Climbing to fire, receding to hoarse despair.
> What do you whisper, brother? What do you tell me?
> We pass each other, are lost, and do not care.[19]

But beyond this representation of thought and daily life, music opens up other vistas. Aiken frequently comments on the poverty of language and its inability to express the subtleties which he seeks. That is why, in most of his poetry, "we deal in juxtapositions." [20] When words fail, he turns to music; in fact, anything which words cannot adequately express—love and passion, for instance—*is* music.[21] In his later manner, after the period of the "symphonies," Aiken devotes a fine lyric [22] to this difference in the capacities of musical and literary expression:

> Music will more nimbly move
> than quick wit can order word
> words can point or speaking prove
> but music heard
>
> How with successions it can take
> time in change and change in time
> and all reorder, all remake
> with no recourse to rhyme!
>
> . . .
>
> But verse can never say these things;
> only in music may be heard
> the subtle touching of such strings,
> never in word.

Thus the unanswerable problems of the universe can be hinted at only by musical comparisons, for music is in itself a complete and parallel universe. At the conclusion of the speech made by Music in *The Coming Forth by Day of Osiris Jones* [23] we have a clear statement on this point:

> O death, in shape of change, in shape of time,
> in flash of leaf and murmur, delighting god
> whose godhead is a vapour, whose delight
> is icicles in summer, and arbutus
> under the snowdrift, and the river flowing
> westward among the reeds and flying birds
> beyond the obelisks and hieroglyphs—
> whisper of whence and why, question in darkness
> answered in silence, but such silence, angel,
> as answers only gods who seek for gods—
> rejoice, for we are come to such a world
> as no thought sounded.

But this explanation of the ultimate is illusory. When Festus tries to explore human knowledge, "it occurs to him that the possibility of knowledge is itself limited: that knowledge is perhaps so conditioned by the conditions of the knower that it can have little but a relative value." [24] Once again, a musical figure carries the idea. While Festus and the Old Man who represents his *alter ego* are discussing the problems of knowledge they hear a solemn, haunting music which may perhaps be the ultimate expression of the universe.[25] Yet they are forced to realize that

> It is a music
> Of mortal origin and fleshly texture.
> Who knows if to god's ears it may be only
> A scream of pain?

As they draw nearer, they see that it is played by an orchestra of butchers.

> Thus ends our pilgrimage! We come at last,
> Here, in the twilight forests of our minds,
> To this black dream.

Thinking to explore knowledge itself, they have explored only their own mind: whatever man may understand or know about the nature of things is ultimately only his own thought, and the music of the spheres is thus necessarily only the still, sad music of humanity.

Thus we return to music as a symbol of the intricacies of the human consciousness. Frequently in Aiken's poetry there is mention of music muttering behind closed doors, and clearly heard only on those rare occasions when a door is momentarily opened. A long section of *The House of Dust*[26] is devoted to an elaboration and explanation of this symbol. We can quote only a brief part of it here:

> Once, on a sun-bright morning,
> I walked in a certain hallway, trying to find
> A certain door: I found one, tried it, opened,
> And there in a spacious chamber, brightly lighted,
> A hundred men played music, loudly, swiftly,
> While one tall woman sent her voice above them
> In powerful sweetness. . . . Closing the door
> I heard it die behind me, fade to whisper,—
> And walked in a quiet hallway as before.
> Just such a glimpse, as through that opened door,
> Is all we know of those we call our friends. . . .
> We hear a sudden music, see a playing
> Of ordered thoughts—and all again is silence.
> The music, we suppose, (as in ourselves)
> Goes on forever there, behind shut doors,—
> As it continues after our departure,
> So, we divine, it played before we came . . .
> What do you know of me, or I of you? . . .
> Little enough. . . . We set these doors ajar
> Only for chosen movements of the music. . . .

This, then, is the music which haunts Aiken, the music which he so extensively describes and imitates in his verse symphonies. Until fairly recently, the great aim of his poetry was to open those doors, admit us to the room, and let us hear whole concerts of this fleeting, elusive music of the mind. The very nature of the undertaking made complete success impossible, but by means of a musical symbolism and musical techniques Aiken has succeeded farther than anyone else who has made the attempt.

CHAPTER XVII

Fiction and the Leitmotiv

For fairly obvious reasons, music has exerted considerably more influence on poetry than on prose fiction. By its very nature, poetry demands a constant attention to problems of sound, and thus is likely to suggest musical analogies to its creators. Also, except for narrative poetry (in which musical influence is slight) poetry demands the conscious search for form to a much greater degree than does fiction. Even if we ignore the great mass of fiction which is really a commodity on the market rather than a type of literature, the fact still remains that any narrative tends to become a framework in itself and to impose the form of its own characters, incidents, and relationships on the work which presents it. The writer must, of course, invent or select his narrative in the first place, but this process rarely involves the conscious preoccupation with more or less abstract form which usually falls to the lot of the poet.

Even more important is the distinction in scale between most fiction and most music. We have already noted that the poets who attempt sonata form usually work on a much smaller scale than do composers employing the same medium. The reverse is true of fiction, which, except in the short story, usually exceeds the ambitious musical work in length. The colossal type of novel which has been in vogue during the past decade has accentuated this difference. The short novelette is comparable to the symphony in its proportions and scale, but it has never been a widely cultivated form in the English-speaking countries. As a very broad generalization, we may say that there are two general literary types, the short and concentrated, and the long and diffuse. Novels and, to a lesser extent, dramas tend to fall into the latter classification.

It has been noted that one of the baffling characteristics of Wagner's music, to a person whose standards have been formed on symphonic literature, is its slowness of development, but this slowness simply keeps the music in step with the normal pace of the drama which it accompanies. By habit, Wagner mastered this type of stately composition on a grand scale and learned to practise it even in purely instrumental works.

> In short, the *Siegfried Idyll* succeeds where practically every "Symphonic Poem," from those of Liszt onwards, fails. It is a piece of purely instrumental music, quite twice the size of any well-constructed movement of a classical symphony, and yet forming a perfectly coherent and self-explaining musical scheme. Its length, its manner of slowly building up broad melodies out of constantly repeated single phrases, and the extreme deliberation with which it displays them stage by stage in combination, are features of style that have nothing to do with diffuseness. . . .[1]

Wagner's music is, then, almost the only music constructed on the same scale as the larger genres of literature, and, like the very few truly great literary works, it achieves this vastness with a sense of inevitability and even economy of means.

In the light of these facts it is natural to assume that Wagner will be of more use to the writers of fiction than will other composers, and the facts will bear out this assumption. The principal musical influence on the novel, and even the novelette, has been the adoption of methods of construction developed by Wagner.

Other music has, of course, been of occasional and sporadic importance. Cadilhac's efforts in the direction of the symphonic novel were largely inspired by the symphonies of Beethoven. A host of writers with a passion for music have brought it into their novels as subject matter: even the famous "musical" works of E. T. A. Hoffmann hardly achieved more than this. And this writing *about* music shows the influence of music on literature to exactly the same extent that Lamb's *Dissertation on Roast Pig* shows the influence of cookery.

A more interesting experiment was made by Aldous Huxley in *Point Counter Point*. The title, a literal translation of the *punctum contra punctum*, or "note against note," of the early theorists, gives a fair indication of what the novel sets out to do. The plan is, briefly, one of complication, sudden shifts of subject and tone, and the playing off of incident against incident. Part of the complication, including the idea of having one of the characters an author who determines to write the book in which he appears, seems to be borrowed from one of Gide's novels. Perhaps it will be as well to let the notebooks of Philip Quarles, Huxley's fictitious author, describe the method:

The musicalization of fiction. Not in the symbolist way, by subordinating sense to sound. [. . .] But on a large scale, in the construction. The changes of moods, the abrupt transitions. (Majesty alternating with a joke, for example, in the first movement of the B flat major Quartet. [. . .]) More interesting still, the modulations, not merely from one key to another, but from mood to mood. A theme is stated, then developed, pushed out of shape, imperceptibly deformed, until, though still recognizably the same, it has become quite different. In sets of variations the process is carried a step further. Those incredible Diabelli variations, for example. The whole range of thought and feeling, yet all in organic relation to a ridiculous little waltz tune. Get this into a novel. How? The abrupt transitions are easy enough. All you need is a sufficiency of characters and parallel, contrapuntal plots. While Jones is murdering a wife, Smith is wheeling the perambulator in the park. You alternate the themes. More interesting, the modulations and variations are also more difficult. A novelist modulates by reduplicating situations and characters. He shows several people falling in love, or dying or praying in different ways—dissimilars solving the same problem.[2]

This is an exact description of the technique of the book. While Spandrell and Illidge are murdering Everard Webley in Philip Quarles' house, Philip is arriving at his parents' home to untangle the absurd situation of his fatuous and socially prominent father, whose pregnant secretary is threatening to tell all. In the affair between cheerfully amoral Lucy Tantamount and gloomily passionate Walter Bidlake we have a fine example of dissimilars solving the same problem, and the method is carried on in the tentative infidelities of Elinor and Philip, Mr. Quarles' pompous seduction (with full cooperation) of Gladys, and Burlap's *seductio ad absurdum* of Beatrice. The same principle is worked out in the deaths of Little Philip, of Webley, and of Spandrell, and the approaching death of old John Bidlake. Finally, the screeching parrot that interrupts a passionate scene between Walter and Lucy is probably a lineal descendant of the joke in the B flat major Quartet.

Early in *Point Counter Point* Philip Quarles suggests another possibility which is also mentioned further on in the passage just quoted: the author can assume various points of view about the characters and events of his story, shifting from the cynical to the sentimental, from the religious to the physiological. It is perhaps unfortunate that Huxley did not attempt this technique. As the novel stands it is a brilliant piece of work, but somewhat too ingenious, too much of a *jeu d'esprit*. The contrasts and parallelisms are cleverly managed, but the machinery is too obvious. The essential theory, of course, is Aiken's method of juxtaposition except that, by having real characters and events instead of a succession in the mind, Huxley does give a sense of continuity: an action which has been left off halfway is being continued while a new one is described. In a literal sense he thus comes closer to counterpoint than does Aiken, but the suggestion of the musical analogy is not nearly so effective. Furthermore, for all its brilliance and ingenuity, *Point Counter Point* seems to have been a blind alley and to have made no contribution to the technique of fiction.

Wagner did make such a contribution in the Leitmotiv, and writers of fiction have only begun to exploit its possibilities. In a way this device has been known since the dawn of literature, and there is a certain amount of justification for considering the regular Homeric combination of an epithet with a noun—"the many-voiced sea," "the hollow ships," "Dawn, the rosy-fingered"—as a Leitmotiv. Similarly, one critic [3] finds that the device was used,—to some extent, well before the time of Wagner and, later, independently of his influence, by such writers as Goethe and Dickens. Sometimes, as in Goethe's *Wahlver-wandtschaften*, the motives have been organic, but more frequently they have been mechanical repetitions of some descriptive or character-izing trait, like Mr. Micawber's constant statement that he is "waiting for something to turn up." There is no reason to think that such repeti-tions as this, or as the constantly repeated phrases of the folk-tale, owe anything to musical influence or are real parallels to musical devices. With the rise of Wagner, however, a number of writers felt a distinct musical influence and deliberately began to base some of their effects on Wagnerian music. Thus there are genuine Leitmotivs here and there in Zola, and the imitation of Wagner is unmistakable in the scene in *Le ventre de Paris* which describes the shifting, blending, clashing stenches of a cheese-shop in terms of Wagnerian orchestration.

A genuine Leitmotiv in literature is hard to define, for its existence is determined more by its use than by its nature. One might say that it is a verbal formula which is deliberately repeated, which is easily recognized at each recurrence, and which serves, by means of this recog-nition, to link the context in which the repetition occurs with earlier contexts in which the motive has appeared. (It will be noted that this definition, written entirely for the literary use of the Leitmotiv, will apply equally well to the musical use if we merely change *verbal* to *musical*.) Perhaps we should add that in both music and literature the Leitmotiv has to be comparatively short and must have a program-matic association—must refer to something beyond the tones or words which it contains.

Both d'Annunzio and Thomas Mann, different as they are in other respects, have come strongly under the influence of Wagner. Both have spoken of him with admiration, and by a striking coincidence (for it seems to be nothing more) both have written books which use *Tristan und Isolde*, played by one of a pair of lovers to the other from a piano score, as the climax and key. It is not surprising, then, to find that both have cultivated the use of the Leitmotiv, on Wagnerian principles, so extensively that critical studies of its use by each have been published.[4]

D'Annunzio's novel *Trionfo della Morte* (*The Triumph of Death*) illustrates very well his use of Leitmotivs. It is the story of a man and his mistress, Giorgio being something of a Hamlet-type (though a sensualist withal), and the mistress being a "prezioso strumento di voluttà" and little more. From the very opening chapter, in which they walk in the Pincio gardens and arrive at the parapet just after a man has killed himself by leaping off, Giorgio is haunted by the fascination of death. This early suicide becomes one recurring theme. Another is the recollection of the lover's uncle, who had also killed himself. A number of other motives are employed, such as the sound of men at work ramming down paving-blocks in the streets, Giorgio's mother's agonized question "*For whom* do you forsake me?" and the music (described in rather Wagnerian terms) of the sea. These themes serve to hold together the various episodes of the story, but they have an even more important purpose in keeping before the reader the state of mind of the man—the hypnotic fascination of suicide—which is a steady undercurrent and is the real subject of the book. Finally, after playing *Tristan* for Ippolita, Giorgio takes her for a walk by the sea, lures her to the top of a cliff, suddenly seizes her, and leaps off.

D'Annunzio's preface leaves no doubt as to the deliberateness or the ultimate source of his method. It speaks of the intention of representing the inner life of a character rather than merely a series of external events, of writing "a plastic and symphonic prose, rich in images and music." More specifically still, it says that the contemporary psychological analyst has, in the Italian vocabulary, "musical elements so varied and effective as to be able to compete with the great Wagnerian orchestra in suggesting what only Music can suggest to the modern soul." *

Thomas Mann's use of the Leitmotiv is more skilful and extensive

---

* ". . . elementi musicali così varii e così efficaci da poter gareggiare con la grande orchestra wagneriana nel suggerire ci che soltanto la Musica può suggerire all'anima moderna."

than d'Annunzio's, and worthy of more detailed treatment. Perhaps it
is best seen in *Tonio Kröger*, of which Mann himself writes:

> Here probably I first learned to employ music as a shaping influence in my
> art. The conception of epic prose-composition as a weaving of themes, as a
> musical complex of associations, I later on largely employed in *The Magic
> Mountain*. Only that there the verbal leitmotiv is no longer, as in *Buddenbrooks*,
> employed in the representation of form alone, but has taken on a less mechanical,
> more musical character, and endeavors to mirror the emotion and idea.[5]

The later developments here mentioned are interesting, but the germ
of all of them is contained in *Tonio Kröger*, and this novelette is far
more convenient for purposes of illustration than are the vast novels.[6]

Tonio Kröger, the son of a good bourgeois north-German father and
a happy-go-lucky, musical Italian mother, has, during his adolescence,
two attachments. The first is to Hans Hansen, a schoolmate who likes
Tonio in a way, but shares none of his literary interests—who is oblig-
ing enough to promise to read *Don Carlos* because of Tonio's enthusiasm about it, but never does. Hans is really interested in his riding
lessons and his books about horses. A description of a walk taken by
the two after school one afternoon indicates their relationship. After
this comes Tonio's first love, for Ingeborg Holm, "the blonde Inge."
She is a feminine counterpart of Hans—gay, self-confident, a complete
extravert. Magdalena Vermehren watches Tonio with dreamy admiration, but not Inge—she laughs at him for an awkward mistake in
dancing-class, and he retires, abashed, to stand in the darkened hall
outside and vainly hope that she will miss him and come to him. He
promises himself that he will be true to her, whatever she may think
of him, but as time passes he is shocked to find that love passes and
such faithfulness is impossible.

Tonio's father dies, the house and business are sold, his mother
marries an Italian virtuoso and disappears from his life, and he leaves
his provincial home town in high scorn. When we next meet him he has
achieved considerable reputation as a writer. He visits Lisaweta
Iwanowna in her studio, and she stops her painting to have tea with
him. He does most of the talking, disburdening himself of a long series
of reflections. Artistic genius is not a gift, but a curse. The artist must
calculate his effects coldbloodedly, and thus must shut himself off from
ordinary human warmth of feeling. He is a man apart, always wanting
to mingle with his fellows as one of them, but never succeeding. In
fact, art is probably an escape from some failing as a human being,
and the artistic temperament is highly suspect. After all this, Lisaweta

gives him her answer: he himself is simply a bourgeois on the wrong path. —Some time later, Tonio again visits Lisaweta and tells her that he is setting out to visit Denmark, traveling by way of his—he almost says "home," but changes to "starting point."

He stops by his home town very briefly, but long enough to look at Ingeborg's old house, to repeat the walk taken with Hans years before, to visit his old home and find that it is now a public library, and to be detained on suspicion at his hotel and almost arrested as a swindler. (After telling Lisaweta about a criminal banker who was an excellent writer, he had drawn the conclusion that no honest banker *could* be an artist.) Then he went on to Denmark, where he soon settled down in a seaside resort. Here he witnessed a dance held by a group of excursionists. He stood in the darkened passageway and watched longingly while two youngsters remarkably like Hans and Ingeborg enjoyed themselves. A dreamy-eyed, awkward girl (Magdalena!) slipped and fell; Tonio helped her to a chair, looked once more at Hans and Inge, and went to his room. "From below floated up to him, muffled and soothing, the sweet, trivial waltz-time of life."

He sat down and wrote to Lisaweta—not a narrative, but a general statement. He sees that he is a mixture of his father's bourgeois nature and his mother's artistic temperament. "I stand between two worlds but am at home in neither, and this makes it rather difficult for me. You artists call me a bourgeois, and the bourgeoisie want to arrest me —I don't know which group wounds me more." But he goes on to say that he accepts the mixture, that if anything can make a poet out of a mere man of letters, it is precisely this attachment to the human, the living, and the ordinary. "Do not scold me for this love," he writes, and (seeing now for himself what the author had seen in him as he returned from his walk with Hans years before) he concludes: "Longing is in it, and sorrowful envy, and a tiny bit of scorn, and an utter, pure happiness." *

This summary of the action is sufficient for our purposes, though many details have necessarily been omitted. Before examining the use of the Leitmotiv, we should notice that the structure is clearly sonata form, the four paragraphs of the summary including respectively the exposition, development, recapitulation, and coda. The exposition states separately the two themes of Hans and Inge. The development is devoted largely to the conversations with Lisaweta, in which the signifi-

---

* "Sehnsucht ist darin und schwermütiger Neid und ein klein wenig Verachtung und eine ganze keusche Seligkeit."

cance of these themes for Tonio's character and life is worked out. The recapitulation is devoted to Tonio's journey, though with the addition of some new episodes. Nevertheless, in the return to Tonio's home town, the childhood recollections, and the repetition of the walk with Hans we clearly have the recapitulation of the first subject; and (after a brief account of the intervening days) in the dance at the inn, even including the accident on the dance floor, we have the second. Finally, the letter to Lisaweta is a coda which sums up the whole thing.

The fact that a work based on sonata form can be an excellent example of the literary use of the Leitmotiv shows that musical analogies in literature are never exact. Yet the combination, strange as it seems from a purely musical point of view, solves very effectively the problem of repetition. To repeat exactly the opening chapters would have been both tedious and pointless, for the significance of the mature Tonio's visit to his home and his stay in Denmark lies in the fact that he now sees from a different point of view the experiences of his childhood. Nevertheless, the repetition is close when he relives these experiences, and the basic identity must be clearly shown. This is achieved by the repetition of short passages like the conclusion of the letter to Lisaweta. In the same way, the description of the blonde dancer at the seaside resort repeats phrases from the description which introduced Ingeborg Holm. When Tonio repeats the walk taken with Hans in his childhood, Mann repeats his account of that walk in essentially the same words, but with appropriate slight differences: "Then he left the promenade along the wall not far from the station, saw a train puff by in clumsy haste, amused himself by counting the cars, and looked at the man who sat on top of the last one." As children, Tonio and Hans had waved to this man.

These passages which are repeated in order to call attention to the essential unity of superficially different experiences are necessarily somewhat long. It may even be questioned whether they should be classified as Leitmotivs at all, for, because of the nature of the story, each of them is repeated only once. There can be no such question about certain shorter phrases which occur more often. Three of these, all connected in one way or another with Tonio's good philistine of a father, will show the method. The first is, to all appearances, merely a physical description: the father was "a tall, carefully dressed man with thoughtful blue eyes, who always wore a wild flower in his buttonhole." This formula is repeated when Mann speaks of the father's death; and when Tonio, a literary man of note, lives in large cities, but finds no joy of heart there, it is suggested that perhaps his heredity from this identically-described father is responsible. Finally, when Tonio revisits his home (now a library), he thinks of his father in these same terms. Through these repetitions the motive gradually comes to stand for the bourgeois element both in the father and in Tonio. Its ramifications are seen, for example, when Lisaweta tells Tonio to sit down on a trunk in her studio, if he is not too afraid for his "patrician garments"; and he replies that as far as possible the artist ought to dress and act like a respectable person. (A similar description of "his dark and fiery mother, who played the piano and mandolin so beautifully" likewise comes to be a representation of the artistic side of his nature.)

The other two motives derived from the father both originate in an early passage which tells how young Tonio found his father's scolding of his artistic vagaries "more proper and respectable" than his mother's tendency to reward or ignore them. The boy went on to think (obviously quoting a lecture from his father), "We are not gypsies in green carts, but substantial people. . . ." This gypsy-theme returns when Tonio, startled by Hans' repugnance for his foreign Christian name, thinks that there is always something different about him which makes him not quite acceptable to his fellows. It returns again, when he recoils from the escapades of Bohemian life. It appears for the last time when he considers revealing his identity to the police in order to prove that he is no swindler, no gypsy in a green cart.

From this same original passage is derived another motive, that of finding "quite as it should be" (*sehr in der Ordnung*) the attitude of the everyday world towards art and the artist. The exact verbal formula does not appear until later, but the connection with his secret approval of his father's condemnation in this passage is clear from the fact that its first two appearances (when he first returns to his home town, and later when he visits the house itself) are connected with the recollection of his father's lectures. The third use is in connection with the bourgeois distrust shown in the suspicions of the police.

Other important motives include the reference to the living heart (used five times) to summarize the world of warm and natural human relationships; and the contrasting reference to device and effect (*Pointe und Wirkung*) for the coldblooded calculation of the deliberate artist. Minor motives abound: books about horses, for example, not only refer to Hans Hansen's literary interests, but come to represent the general way of life of the sound extravert who has no need of literature. But a full listing of such motives would extend to inordinate length without contributing any new principles.

Various critics have attempted to classify literary Leitmotivs, but the results are not very convincing. The failure is not surprising, for the device is essentially a method of economy by which a short expression comes to stand for and to recall to the reader's mind an entire and frequently complex idea, character, or situation. Because of its very economy, then, a motive will frequently accomplish several different things at the same time. Since the classifications are based primarily on the use to which a motive is put, they necessarily fall to pieces in cases of multiple significance. One suggested grouping, for example, distinguishes between characterizing and structural motives, and in some very simple cases the distinction can be made. In *Tonio Kröger,* however, such a classification is meaningless. The description of Tonio's father is, from one point of view, purely a motive of characterization. Nevertheless, it is structural in that it connects one side of Tonio's own character with his father, and it is structural in an even more mechanical way when, as Tonio sits in that part of the library which used to be his own room, he thinks that another part now occupies the place where he sat at his father's deathbed. In this instance, the character of the father is hardly in question, and the purpose of the repeated characterization is simply to connect this visit more directly with Tonio's earlier life. Any really effective use of the literary Leitmotiv will similarly defy classification because of its multiple relevance.

The recent development of the Leitmotiv as a literary device is an example of reciprocal interaction between literature and music. The English *riding coat* was borrowed into French (with the Gallicized spelling and pronunciation) as *redingote,* and English has recently borrowed this form of the word back, Anglicizing the pronunciation and using it for something quite different from a riding coat. A similar interchange has taken place in the case of the Leitmotiv. As we have already seen, the musicians created it by imitating language—by giving an external significance to a group of sounds. But this group of sounds was, in most cases, longer and more impressive than a single ordinary word. Above all, it attracted attention to itself in a way that a single word cannot imitate except in such very rare cases as Macbeth's "this hand will rather/The multitudinous seas *incarnadine.*" And since it thus attracted attention and called for recognition, it lent itself to a variety of uses in the handling of plot, characterization, and idea demanded by the programmatic music in which it was used. Seeing its usefulness, the writers then borrowed it back by creating, in imitation of it, a *phrase* which would be easily recognizable and could be employed in a similar way. They are still exploring its possibilities and finding new uses for it. Thus music would not have developed the Leitmotiv without certain antecedent suggestions from literature, and literature would not have developed it to anything resembling its present use without the example of music.

CHAPTER XVIII

Literary Types in Music

FOR several chapters now we have been considering the influence of musical forms and techniques on literature. We have seen that this influence has been extensive, but somewhat sporadic. It has been of real force primarily during the past century and has affected a number of writers and forms, but has been largely isolated or confined to small groups of writers. Certainly we cannot say that music has wrought any real change in literature as a whole.

We turn now to the converse problem—the influence of literature on music. In this field we shall find something of an opposite situation: extensive changes in instrumental music have resulted from literary influences and the attempt of composers to invade fields which have been generally considered the province of the literary artist. Though other matters will necessarily be considered, the principal change has been the development of program music—the tendency of composers to abandon the identity of form and content peculiar to absolute music and to deal with subjects external to the music itself.

Before taking up this larger topic, however, we must see to what extent literary types have influenced musical forms.

We have already noted that the larger forms of musical composition have far more clearly defined structural patterns than have the larger literary types. For that reason imitations of musical forms were largely confined to short literary works, which allow far more formalism in their arrangement than do the larger types. But the literary types which, like the sonnet and the ballade, have fixed structural patterns could hardly be expected to influence music, since the musical forms are already more elaborate structures based on the same principles. On the other hand, the larger literary types are structurally free. The novel is the dominant literary form of our age, but even when we include considerations of medium, length, and content we cannot give any really adequate definition of it. Fifty years ago we might have said that it was a fairly long narrative in prose. Now, however, we have novels in verse, and we also have novels which are so largely devoted to analyses of character, situation, or the stream of consciousness that they can be called narratives only by courtesy. The difference between the novelette and the novel is primarily one of length, but that length is very vaguely defined. In general it might be concluded that the novelette is of such length that it is supposed to be read at a single sitting, whereas the novel—in spite of the favorite cliché of those book reviewers who are not literary critics *—is not. The important thing to notice is that none of these tentative definitions has been able to make any statement about the actual structure of the work.

It is not to be expected, then, that literature should have supplied composers with new forms. Yet we can see a certain attempt to get suggestions from literature in the proliferation of titles using the names of literary rather than musical types. Among the piano solos of Edward MacDowell, for example, we find legends, idylls, poems, a novelette, stories, an epilogue, fireside tales, and fairy tales. Similar lists could be drawn up for a number of composers, and even though we must realize that in many cases these names are merely fanciful, their very existence shows a preoccupation with literature and literary forms. It is necessary, however, to separate the mere use of such a title (doubtless thought up, in many cases, only after the composition had been finished) from any genuine influence exerted by literature on the music itself. In order to do this, we must attempt to answer two questions: (1) What sort of influence have literary analogies exerted on musical form? and (2) How extensive has their influence been?

Literary suggestion has really not so much created new forms, in the strict sense of the word, as it has conferred a certain amount of freedom from what many composers were coming to regard as the tyranny of the old forms. Though many literary works are written in set forms which prescribe certain relationships of subject matter and material, such works actually constitute only a very small proportion of the total literary output. And here it becomes necessary to make a distinction. Any poem will necessarily be in some metrical form—will be either in free verse or in some particular meter, will be in stanzas or not in stanzas, will be rhymed in some particular pattern, freely

* I recently saw an advertisement of a mammoth novel which was described in the heading as "1100 pages of entertainment." In the next paragraph the prospective purchaser was given a guarantee that if he once picked up the book he would be unable to put it down until he had read every word. The large sale of this book must, I suppose, be taken as a conclusive proof that people do not believe advertisements.

rhymed, or unrhymed. Thus we are accustomed to speak of blank verse (unrhymed iambic pentameter) as a poetic "form." There is no inherent objection to this practice, but it is likely to be confusing when one is dealing with the relationships between music and literature. In this sense of the word, a composer must also have a predetermined form. He must write atonally or else in some specific key or combination of keys; he must write in free rhythms or in some definite musical time; he must (except in the earliest days of instrumental music) write for some particular medium of voice or instrument. As we use the term "form" in music, however, it has nothing to do with these necessary choices. It refers to the patterns of relationship between themes and keys. Thus the fugue is a musical form, but 4/4 time in C major is not. To avoid confusion it will be well to use the term in the same sense when we apply it to literature. Thus we will say that the Italian sonnet is a form because of its prescribed relationship between octave and sestet, but not because of its meter or rhyme-scheme, and that blank verse and Spenserian stanza are not forms at all.

In this sense, then, we can say that the great majority of literary works have no set forms, but have individual forms depending upon the exigencies of the poet's subject and materials. And the chief formal influence of literature on music has been the achievement of a similar freedom for the composer. A very brief historical consideration will show how essential literary influence was to this musical freedom. Working by itself music could easily have developed new forms which would have become established and obligatory, just as sonata form was developed in the eighteenth century. But as long as the majority of music continued to be absolute, form and content continued to be indistinguishable; and hence it would have been nonsense to say that the composer should work out his form according to the exigencies of his subject matter. With the wide spread of program music, however, composers did actually make a separation. And once the composer had a subject outside of his themes and their relationships, he began to find the preconceived forms far more embarrassing than they had ever been before. The story of Mazeppa or of the Sorcerer's Apprentice can be told only in its own terms, and there is little chance of finding attractive subjects for program music which *happen* also to fit the established musical forms. Hence the revolt against these forms was led by the writers of program music, and program music, as we shall see later, is the direct impact of literature on instrumental composition. The great structural freedom enjoyed by the present-day composer can

therefore be very largely attributed to literary influence rather than to
any purely musical evolution.

In addition to this general freedom, which now profoundly affects
even the writing of the traditional musical forms, there are two really
new types of musical compositions (*not* forms, in the sense in which
we have agreed to use the term) which owe their origin to literary influence.

The first of these types is what Mr. Ernest Newman [1] has named
the small poem in music. He comments on the fact that music has, in
general, nothing corresponding to the perfect small lyric. In literature
from Sappho and the *Greek Anthology* to the Imagists and A. E. Housman we find very short poems of a lyrical or aphoristic nature (or frequently a mixture of the two) which are not ambitious efforts, but
are perfect within their clearly accepted limitations. These poems—
the carved gems and ivory miniatures of their art—are to be found in
every period and school of literary activity. We naturally expect them
to be produced under the influence of the polish and restraint of
classicism and by writers who, like Jonson, Herrick, Landor, and Housman, are under strong classical influence. But we find them also in the
folk poetry of the Middle Ages, in lyrics encased in some of the most
wooden of the neo-classical plays—in fact, almost anywhere that we
choose to look.

> O western wind, when wilt thou blow
> That the small rain down can rain?
> Christ, that my love were in my arms
> And I in my bed again! [2]

Thus wrote some unknown lover at some unknown time before the
Renaissance in England. And at the end of a letter in Latin apparently
written during the twelfth century, an unknown girl added a postscript
in her own tongue: *

> Dû bist mîn, ich bin dîn:
> des solt dû gewis sîn.
> Dû bist beslozzen
> in mînem herzen;
> verlorn ist das slüzzelîn:
> dû muost immer drinne sîn. [3]

Examples might be quoted indefinitely, but every reader may as well
be left to think of his own favorites. Our point for the moment is that

* You are mine, I am yours: you can be sure of that. You are locked in my heart;
the key is lost: you must stay there forever.

the very short poem is a permanent literary type depending on extreme limitation to one very small subject and perfect expression of it. Frequently there is a mixture of sentiment and humor, but irony, bitter satire, and even near-nonsense are also possibilities. Really, there is no restriction on the type except a strict limitation of both the scope and the length of the poem. Nor can we really restrict the type to poetry: the proverbs of Solomon and the maxims of La Rochefoucauld will have to be included, as well as some of the remarks of Dr. Johnson.

Only recently has a parallel form been developed in music. Earlier composers seem to have felt that music demanded a certain duration, a certain amount of formal framework and deliberation, if it was to make any impression at all. Mr. Newman suggests thirty bars or a single page of ordinary music as convenient limits to place on this new musical type, but admits that both are arbitrary. Perhaps forty seconds' playing-time would be a more reasonable limit, if we must try to set one, for after all the real length of a piece of music is its duration rather than its bar-lines or typography. Mr. Newman also demands that the pieces belonging to this type be something beyond pure music —something beyond a pattern of sounds. They are not to have specific programs, but rather to be poetic in that they are definitely suggestive of moods. On this count he rules out some of Schumann's little pieces. As examples of the sort of thing he wishes to include he cites a few of Chopin's *Preludes,* defining the second, fourth, sixth, ninth, and twentieth as "the really poetic ones." The exact characteristics of the type are most clearly summed up in a description of a number of little pieces of Scriabin which are cited as examples:

> Practically all of the twenty-two that I have selected are undeniably poetic, and have something of what I can only call the aphoristic about them. They obey a poetic rather than a simply musical *ordonnance;* they plunge into the very heart of their subject without preamble; they often end with a kind of query or an aposiopesis, and they have throughout the air of having set out to say something very definite, which they say in the fewest possible notes, every one of which plays a vital part in the story; and having said what it set out to say, the poem ends without rhetoric, without trimmings, without flourishes, without any of music's usual attempt to make an effective formal exit from the stage.[4]

We need not necessarily restrict the field quite so severely as Mr. Newman does, but it is significant that he demands an unspoken programmatic mood. The implication is that poetry has served as the direct suggestion to the composers of such works, which are thus sharply differentiated from the short preludes of Bach or various other brief compositions which have a purely musical interest. For our purposes the short piano pieces of Schumann and MacDowell, with their more explicit programs explained in titles, could be included in the "small poem" along with works like Schönberg's *6 Kleine Stücken* and Prokofieff's *Visions Fugitives*. It must be admitted, however, that this musical type is not yet of great importance. Both the number of its practitioners and the quantity of their production are limited, and there is no way of predicting its future. Nevertheless, it is clearly a new musical *genre* relying heavily on literary art.

Of considerably greater importance is the second musical type developed under literary influence, the symphonic poem. Liszt invented the name for a series of his own works written between 1850 and 1860, and he came as near to inventing the musical type itself as any one man ever comes to inventing a type of artistic expression. Grove's *Dictionary* supplies us with an excellent definition of Liszt's expression in the statement that "It has become a generic term used to describe orchestral works generally of large design but not according with any of the accepted categories of musical form, and having some reference to a programme more or less governing the style and course of the music." This definition makes it clear that the symphonic poem has the freedom of form characteristic of literary works, but in its origins the literary connection was far closer than that. To Liszt the original idea seems to have been the actual transposition of a poem into music, and many of his works of this type are actually based on poems by such writers as Byron, Hugo, Lamartine, and Schiller. Though some others are based on sketches and paintings, the literary impetus is predominant: eight of Liszt's thirteen symphonic poems are derived from literary works. What Liszt proposed to do in these works was to make a "transposition of art" in the approved mid-nineteenth-century manner—to take a work already created in one art and to express the same thing in another.

The idea immediately became popular, and for some seventy-five years after Liszt's first ventures the symphonic poem was one of the dominant types of orchestral composition. Also, it may be noted that the requirement of an external program continued, and that even in subject-matter there were few new developments. In all the mass of symphonic poems which have been written it is very difficult to discover one that does not have its prototype in the works of Liszt. Literary adaptations continued to form the bulk of the production, with such works as Tschaikowsky's *Hamlet* and *Romeo and Juliet*, César Franck's *Le chasseur maudit* (after a ballad of Bürger) and *Les Djinns* (on a poem by Hugo), Saint-Saëns' *Danse Macabre* (Henri Cazalis), Dukas' *L'apprenti sorcier* (Goethe), Elgar's *Falstaff*, Richard Strauss' *Don Juan* (Lenau), and several works of Sibelius based on the *Kalevala*. This list includes only a few of the more familiar ones. Other composers have used familiar legends without depending on any specific literary source. Saint-Saëns' *Rouet d'Omphale* and Strauss' *Till Eulenspiegel* may serve as examples of this practise.

Sibelius' *Finlandia* and Smetana's series including *The Moldau* are typical of the numerous nationalistic symphonic poems. They all go back to Liszt's *Hungaria*. A number of composers have tried to make transpositions from painting to music, and this attempt has produced such works as Rachmaninoff's *Die Toteninsel* and Weingartner's *Das Gefilde der Seligen* (both based on paintings of the same names by Böcklin). Their ultimate source is Liszt's *Hunnenschlacht*, a symphonic poem suggested by Wilhelm von Kaulbach's fresco in the Berlin Museum. Strauss' grappling with a philosophical concept in *Also sprach Zarathustra* has its prototype in Liszt's *Héroïde funèbre*. Finally, the symphonic poem with no announced program is to be found in Liszt's *Festklänge*, which has no indication of subject beyond its title, "Festal Sounds." It was actually written to celebrate the intended marriage between its composer and Princess Wittgenstein, together with their triumph over the hostile plots of her husband, who had blocked her attempts at divorce. (Actually, the triumph existed only in the music: she never got her divorce, and by the time of her husband's death the love between her and Liszt seems to have burnt itself out.[5]) It is naturally impossible to know how many works have been produced with only vaguely descriptive titles, but have been based directly on the private personal experiences of their composers.

Since the capabilities of the symphonic poem were so thoroughly explored by its inventor, Liszt's explanation of its principles will give an adequate understanding of the type. During the period in which the symphonic poems were written Liszt also composed two programmatic symphonies, one based on Goethe's *Faust* and the other on Dante's *Commedia*. They are not, however, in regular sonata form, and Liszt's final allegiance seems to have been given to the symphonic poem rather than to the programmatic symphony. His own statement, though unfair to "the so-called classical music," gives a complete explanation of both his reasons for developing the symphonic poem and the characteristics of this type of music: [6]

> In the so-called classical music the return and thematic development of the themes are determined by express rules, which are considered inviolable, although the composers who originated them had no other precept for them than their own imagination, and themselves made the formal dispositions which people wish now to set up as a law. In program music, on the other hand, the return, change, modification, and modulation of the motives are conditioned by their relation to a poetic idea. Here one theme does not, according to the law, call forth a second theme; here the motives are not the consequence of stereotyped approximations and contrasts of tone-colours, and the colouring as such does not condition the groupings of the ideas. All exclusively musical considerations, though they should not be neglected, have to be subordinated to the action of the given subject. Consequently action and subject of this kind of symphony demand a higher interest than the technical treatment of the musical material; and the indefinite impressions of the soul are raised into definite impressions by an expounded plan which is here taken in by the ear, similarly as a cycle of pictures is taken in by the eye. The artist who prefers this kind of art work enjoys the advantage of connecting with a poetic idea all the affections which the orchestra expresses with so much power.

The symphonic poem, then, differs from the symphony in that it is not a musical *form*, but a musical type in which each composition has its own independent form. Furthermore, it is not broken up into movements, but is played as a continuous whole; it has its changes of tempo and tonality, but these are conditioned by the subject. And when we add that its treatment of themes is generally that of Berlioz' *idée fixe* and Wagner's *Leitmotiv*, we have said all that can really be said about the structure of a musical type whose most striking characteristic is its revolt against standardized form.

Before leaving this type of music, however, we should note that this unchartered literary freedom apparently tired its beneficiaries. Richard Strauss is generally considered as the last great exponent of the symphonic poem. Like most artistic revolutionaries, he began with an apprenticeship in conventional forms. At the age of twenty-one, however, he came under the influence of Alexander Ritter, who systematically arranged his conversion to modernism. *Aus Italien* (a programmatic work composed one year later) is really a suite, though Strauss himself called it a "symphonic fantasia." He also stated explicitly that it "is the connecting link between the old and the new methods." [7] From this work through the *Sinfonia Domestica* (1904) Strauss devoted himself very largely to the composition of symphonic poems. It is impossible in a brief compass to deal accurately with the plan of these works, but one striking generalization can be made. During the first half of this eighteen-year period Strauss was very largely independent of tradition in his forms and seemed to be enjoying his new-found freedom. With *Till Eulenspiegel* (1895) a change appears. The work is, as the composer's full title emphasizes, in rondo form. One other work intervenes between this and *Don Quixote* (1897), which consists of an introduction, theme and variations, and finale. And only one work intervenes between this and the last of the important * programmatic works for orchestra, the *Sinfonia Domestica* (1904). This work, though played continuously, has four movements differing in tempo and nature. It is not in sonata form, but it does have three principal themes which are developed both in the first movement and in the rest of the work. Thus it may be regarded as something of a compromise between the freedom of the symphonic poem and the mildly rigorous form of the "cyclical" symphony. Also, the finale contains that arch-enemy of modernity and formal freedom—a double fugue. Since this work, Strauss has devoted himself largely to opera.

Too much should not be made of the separate items in this survey, but their combined effect certainly is an indication of a desire for greater formal organization of the music. Even *Ein Heldenleben* (the work between *Don Quixote* and the *Sinfonia Domestica*) has its two principal and contrasting themes for development, with a less important third subject thrown in.

There is, however, no forcing of the subject into these established forms. "It may be said with a good deal of force that in his earlier works † . . . he was preoccupied rather with the question of how much can be expressed within the limits of a given form of music, whereas in later symphonic poems his chief anxiety was to find the musical form which would best express what he had to say." [8] Thus the theme and variations of *Don Quixote* is the natural form: all that mad knight-errant's escapades are really variations on one basic theme, and the musical structure reinforces the logical one.

It is further interesting to note that, though Strauss has made no connected statement of his aesthetic views, the remarks which have

---

* Strauss actually did write some orchestral and programmatic music after the *Sinfonia Domestica*—such as the *Festive Prelude* (for a 156-piece orchestra) of 1913 and the *Alpine Symphony* of 1915. Nevertheless, his claim to attention as a composer for orchestra rests entirely on the earlier works.

† "Earlier works" here refers to the works *before* his real entrance into the field of the symphonic poem.

been collected [9] show a consistent interest in the form of the music rather than in the content of the program, or even in expression in general. He has a good deal to say about the program as merely a means of inspiring the composer to the production of new forms, and the whole matter is summarized in one statement:

> The musical poem must have hands and feet, so to speak; must be ship-shape musically considered. Let him who likes look on it merely as a musical work of art. In *Don Quixote*, for instance, I show how a man goes mad over vain imaginings. But I do not wish to compel any listener to think of Don Quixote when he hears it. He may conceive of it as absolute music if it suits him.[10]

In the end, then, we see that the symphonic poem is a type demanding formal freedom in music and based on the analogy of literature, but that its practitioners began to discover, after the first careless rapture wore off, that the old standardized forms of music which they had scornfully rejected as hindrances to free expression were at the same time great aids to effectiveness. Naturally, music has not returned to any exact following of earlier formal patterns. (No art ever returns to what it was before a revolutionary development, for even if the development itself turns out to have been a blind alley—which was hardly true in this case—it necessarily exerts a certain influence on even the reactionary works which follow it.) But in spite of all allowances and reservations, the bright ironic gods may well find amusement in the career of the man who stalked into the field of program music blowing the clarion of freedom and marched out to a double fugue.

CHAPTER XIX

Program Music: a Short Guide to the Battlefield

IT IS customary to make a distinction between "absolute" music and "program" music, and though the exact dividing line between the types is a matter of endless debate, the main difference is clear enough. A piece of absolute music is to be heard as music and nothing else. Like a piece of "abstract" or non-representational painting, its point lies in its own pattern and effects, without reference to any external subject matter. A piece of program music, on the other hand, is supposed to represent some subject matter outside itself, to be "about" something in the same way that a literary work is about some subject outside its own words. Thus when Liszt writes a symphony about Faust, when Tschaikowsky writes a work for orchestra about Napoleon in Russia, when Strauss writes a symphonic poem about the mind and adventures of Don Quixote, the result is program music.

In one sense, all vocal music is programmatic, for the words carry with them ideas outside the music, and if there is to be any connection between text and music, the music must in some way be concerned with the ideas expressed in the text. Vocal music, however, is usually excluded from discussions of program music for a very obvious reason: the text is a part of the music, presented simultaneously with it, and hence the principal problems of instrumental program music do not arise. For this reason the term *program music* is usually reserved for exclusively instrumental works or passages.

A great many of the problems which we have been considering up to this point have received comparatively little attention in the past. Those connected with program music, however, have given rise to a large and frequently acrimonious literature. Skirmishes on the subject go far back into musical history—as does the practice itself [1]—and for something upwards of a century the logomachy has raged, like an earlier Hundred Years' War, with only occasional uneasy truces between the hostile camps of absolutists and programmatists. At present it seems that a compromise has been reached, but there is no way to tell whether this represents the end of the struggle or merely another temporary truce.

At any rate, since the actual battle is not joined at the moment, we can make a brief survey of the extensive field and review the major tactical moves of both sides. And a very brief survey, like the one-day tour of the World War I battlefields which Cook's tourists used to take from Paris, is all that can be allowed here.* Also, for the present we must make our classifications on the basis of the *expressed intentions* of the composer. There is no way to prevent the adherents of program music from making out their own programs for works of an apparently absolute nature: numerous philosophical or narrative interpretations of the first movement of Beethoven's *Ninth Symphony* have appeared,[2] and only recently a "phrase for phrase interpretation" of his *Seventh Symphony* came off the presses.[3] Similarly, as Strauss realized, there is no way for the composer to force a confirmed absolutist to think of a program when he hears the music. In fact, it is frequently stated by extremists that all music is really absolute or really programmatic. For our purposes, however, Beethoven's *Sixth Symphony* is program music because he called it "Pastoral" and gave it a sketchy program, and his *Seventh* is absolute because he gave no indication of any program.

Even this classification may err in favor of the programmatic, for not all named compositions were written with their titles in mind. Schumann named his *Kinderszenen* as "hints for interpretation" *after* he had finished composing them,[4] and other composers have done the same thing.[5] Since a descriptive title is a great aid to immediate popularity, there is good reason to think that the naming of many pieces of instrumental music in recent years may be merely a profitable commercial device.[6] Furthermore, a good many programmatic titles never sanctioned by composers are abroad in the land.†

The defenders of program music have almost always felt themselves to be rebels or insurgents against a type of instrumental music already established by the practice of composers and the aesthetics of theorists. Hence their manifestos have usually been attacks on the position of

* Every attempt is made to keep the following account as unbiased as possible. But the reader is entitled to know that if the present truce breaks down and the battle must be joined again, I will be found in the camp of the absolutists.

† The names of Beethoven's "Moonlight" and "Appassionata" Sonatas, for example, were neither bestowed nor sanctioned by the composer.

the absolutists, and they have taken the defensive only in order to protect themselves against counter-attacks. Before investigating the theories of the programmatists, then, we must see the point of view which they wished to dethrone.

Naturally, the defenders of absolute music have not really had only one viewpoint, nor have they been in complete agreement about musical aesthetics—in fact, no two persons who have gone into that subject at all are in complete agreement about it. Nevertheless, the principal arguments of the opponents of program music are admirably summed up in Eduard Hanslick's treatise, *Vom Musikalisch-Schönen,*[7] or *The Beautiful in Music*. This work, first published in 1854, went through ten editions before the author's death in 1902, and has been translated into the principal European languages and frequently reprinted. All this is evidence of its importance, but the most striking proof comes from its opponents. Even today the defender of the more extreme positions of program music feels called upon to reply to Hanslick, and it is safe to conclude that a work which has called forth such a host of replies over such a long period of time has never been answered decisively. When St. Anthony of Egypt was praying in the desert, a host of devils in the form of wild beasts came and threatened him, but he looked them over calmly and observed, "If you were real, one of you would be enough."

Hanslick's main position is simple enough. Music, he says, is a self-contained art having no reference to anything outside itself. A composer deals with ideas, but these are musical ideas—themes, rhythms, etc. They are not and cannot be ideas of persons, physical objects, philosophical systems, or anything which does not exist as sound—as musical material. His point can be easily illustrated by such a form as the fugue, for in this case the fact is admitted by technical terminology: a fugue, like a poem, is about its subject, but the "subject" of a fugue is a musical theme. "The ideas which a composer represents are first and above all purely musical ideas. A specific beautiful melody appears to his mind. It is not supposed to be anything except itself."[8] We may be fooled by a title or a superscription, and made to assume a state of feeling which we falsely attribute to the music, but music cannot present any specific feeling or emotion, and to speak of "representing the indefinite" is merely a contradiction in terms.

There are only two means by which music can suggest objects or emotions. Beyond mere imitation of natural sounds (which everyone agrees to be, in itself, puerile) music can deal with objects only dynamically or symbolically. Since music is itself a dynamic art, it can, to a certain extent, imitate or suggest movement, but movement has only a vague connection with moods or emotions, and yet these are precisely what music is most frequently supposed to portray. Also, there is a slight possibility of tonal symbolism: just as certain colors are associated with certain states of mind, so tonalities, scale-forms, instruments, etc., may have their associations. But, as in the case of the colors, there will be individual differences; furthermore, we do not usually think of colors symbolically. White for innocence is a standard piece of symbolism, but not one out of a thousand times does it operate when one sees white.

Hanslick is now in a position to answer the question: What is musical beauty? And the answer is simple enough: Musical beauty is musical beauty—precisely that, and nothing more. If one is asked what is to be expressed with musical materials, the answer is: Musical ideas. "Moving patterns of sound are the content of music." [9] Perhaps this simple (and, to many persons, startling) idea is most clearly put in the statement that music "is a language which we speak and understand, but cannot translate." A specific example will illustrate this point. One is frequently asked to explain—in words—what a piece of music means. Would it not be equally reasonable to say, "I don't quite understand Milton's sonnet on his blindness. Will you please play it for me on the piano?"

This is not to say that music is entirely different from the other arts, but rather that it resembles them. "The goal of every art is to incorporate in some external work an idea in the mind of the artist. In music this idea is a tonal one, not a logical one which must first be translated into tones." [10] Thus a musician will get a far better idea of an unfamiliar composition if he is given even a simple statement of its tonal effects—if he is told, for example, that it makes too much use of tremolo and diminished seventh chords—than if he is given an elaborate poetic account of the feelings which it produced in a hearer.

Interpretations of music in terms of its composer's emotions may or may not seem to be appropriate, but they are never necessarily correct. "Aesthetic criticism knows nothing and wants to know nothing of the personal affairs or the historical environment of the composer; it will accept and believe only what the work of art *itself* says." [11] This does not mean, of course, that biography and artistic history are not legitimate subjects of investigation, but only that they are not the same thing as aesthetic criticism.

Hanslick continues with an investigation of the subjective effects of music, even its physical effects. But these also are regarded as non-essential, for they depend on the hearer more than on the work. As for the vaunted overpowering physical effect of some music, it can be generally stated that the greater this effect, the less the real value of the music. (Ravel's *Bolero* is a perfect example.) And if we praise its power to soothe and relax, we are merely considering it as a poor imitation of chloroform.

Therefore the physical ("pathological") effects are irrelevant. The man who uses music as a background for his own daydreaming—who overhears music instead of listening to it—has no aesthetic experience at all. And the waltzes of Strauss, charming music though they are, cease to be music at all as soon as people dance to them instead of listening. "Without intellectual activity there can be no aesthetic enjoyment." [12]

One point on which music does differ sharply from the other arts is the fact that it is not in any sense an imitation of nature. Natural sounds do not fit our musical scale, and a melody in nature is an extremely rare thing. (William Ellery Leonard states in *Two Lives* [13] that he once found, in a Bavarian cave, eight stalagmites which, when struck with a stone, gave out a perfect diatonic octave. But even here, there was no music of nature; the stalagmites stood "waiting the music-master of the cave," and no music came from them except by human agency.) Even natural melody is far commoner than natural harmony. Who, Hanslick inquires, has ever heard a triad or a dominant seventh chord in nature?

We are here brought face to face with the fact that music is a purely human invention without any natural prototype. Our timbres, intervals, chords, and musical forms are all pure invention, and thus music is the least imitative of the arts. As Schopenhauer observes, it is not a reproduction of the external universe, but is rather an independent and self-contained universe in which the human mind has created the materials and reduced them to order. Hanslick goes further, and says that even the natural sounds which have been musically imitated, like the cock-crow of Haydn's *Seasons* and the cuckoo, nightingale, and quail in Beethoven's *Pastoral Symphony*, can be heard either as thematic material or as imitations, but not as both. As soon as the cuckoo becomes an imitation of a bird, it ceases to be music.

Finally, Hanslick takes up the vexed question of form and content, and finds that some confusion is caused by the loose use of terms. In a long work we may easily speak of the themes as the content of the music, and of their treatment and interrelationships as the form. But if we come down to the smallest aesthetic unit of music, the theme itself, we see that the two are inseparable. If we play a theme an octave higher, or on a different instrument, or in a minor key instead of a major, have we altered its form or its content? Obviously both, in the same manner and degree. Form and content are, then, truly identical in music, and thus music can have no program—no content beyond its purely musical pattern.

This summary of Hanslick's position has necessarily been brief, and hence it has lost a good deal of its force. The contention that the impression arising from words and titles is falsely attributed to the music itself, for example, is beautifully supported by citing the erotic Italian doggerel for which Handel originally composed the music (as a madrigal) of "For unto us a child is born"—music which has been universally admired as an expression of religious triumph! Other such examples and answers to possible objections make Hanslick's treatise a formidable fortress for the absolutists.

Nor is he alone in his views. As attempts have been made to overthrow his system of musical aesthetics, support has been given by various other writers who have modified or strengthened his position. Busoni, for example, makes the impossibility of representing even certain simple and obvious things in music very clear when he asks how any composer could possibly give a musical representation of a poor but contented man.[14] The question is as ruinous as that which I heard addressed to a professor of English literature who was insisting at a great rate that any good line of poetry should be something that could be acted out. Finally a student inquired: "Professor Histrion, how would you act out 'Thou still unravished bride of quietness'?"

The principal attempts to take the fortress of absolutism have been flanking movements and raids on scattered outposts rather than frontal attacks. Since Hanslick admits that suggestive rhythms and certain symbolic musical patterns can be used for representation or suggestion of things outside the music, the defenders of the program have frequently set out to demonstrate that these devices really have far wider possibilities than Hanslick was willing to allow them.

In discussing vocal music we have already dealt with the suggestive power of rhythms; and in applying this power to such states as exhaustion and dejection, which do not necessarily involve motion, we have already overstepped the limits assigned to their usefulness by the strict absolutists. In an interesting essay on "Suggestion in Music," [13] Edward MacDowell—inveterate composer of music on poetic subjects that he was—goes a good deal further:

Neither pure tonal beauty, so-called "form," nor what is termed the intellectual side of music (the art of counterpoint, canon, and fugue), constitutes a really vital factor in music. This narrows our analysis down to two things, namely, the physical effect of musical sound, and suggestion.*

He goes on to say that the repetition and periodicity of sound can call up definite ideas, and that imitations of natural sounds (birds, wind, galloping horses, etc.) are universally intelligible. Furthermore, there are certain patterns which are partly imitative and partly suggestive, and which have also become standardized in use so that they have definite meanings.

Mendelssohn, Schumann, Wagner, Liszt [and we might add Schubert], and practically everyone who has written a spinning song, has used the same pattern to suggest the turning of a wheel. That such widely different men as Wagner and Mendelssohn should both have adopted the same pattern to suggest undulating waves is not a mere chance, but clearly shows the potency of the suggestion.*

MacDowell also discusses the symbolism of pitch. High tones suggest light, and low tones obscurity. (We may note in this connection that the very words *high* and *low,* as applied to tones, are really a related sort of symbolism.) And upward or downward motion in pitch can suggest exaltation or depression. Furthermore, there is a definite symbolism of harmony. The major or minor triad suggests repose and finality, and departures from it suggest restlessness, the degree of the feeling depending on the extent of the departure. Thus a chord foreign to the key of the music "will carry with it a sense of confusion or mystery." (It has frequently been pointed out that the sense of mystery given by the opening bars of Beethoven's *Ninth Symphony* is produced by avoiding the third degree of the scale and thus keeping the listener ignorant as to whether the key is major or minor.) The suggestion of longing produced by dissonances whose resolution is delayed belongs in this same category.

All these things extend the range of musical suggestion considerably beyond what Hanslick was willing to grant. But MacDowell has not been able to build up a case strong enough to enable him to say that the real power of music lies in its suggestive effects, and he finally gives up the problem as a mystery whose heart cannot be plucked out.

* Reprinted by permission of the publishers. Copyright 1940 by The Arthur P. Schmidt Co.

He coins the term "ideal suggestion" to describe the essential quality of great music and poetry, and concludes that it is something which defies analysis: it "cannot be ascribed to physical or mental suggestion, and certainly not to any device of counterpoint or form, in the musical acceptance of the word." This is the unanalysable entity which has appeared down the centuries as *daimon*, inspiration, and genius, and MacDowell's final accomplishment in aesthetics was simply to add another item to its list of names.

Another possibility of musical suggestion, this time by association of ideas, has been pointed out by Carl Spitteler.[16] He wrote to attack what he called "orchestral allegory," but his essay shows the power of the device. He points out the fact that we have very definite associations with certain instruments, and that a general grouping can be made on this basis. The orchestra can be divided into: (1) the religious group (trombone,* harp, organ, etc.); (2) the rejoicing group (cymbals, drums, triangle, bells, etc.); (3) the pastoral group (flute, oboe, clarinet, and bassoon); and (4) the romantic group (horns).

These associations have been set up by history and literature as well as by purely musical uses. Thus the ascription of pastoral qualities to the wood-winds goes back to the syrinx of Pan, and comes down through the practice of shepherds, the pastoral poetry of Theocritus and Vergil and their Renaissance imitators, and, finally, the scoring of composers under the influence of this association. Spitteler points to a number of instances of musically bad orchestration caused by this type of allegory. And anyone who has read much in the literature of musical "interpretation" knows how consistently the predominance of instruments of any one of these groups will control a hearer's programmatic response. A single example will suffice. Berlioz interpreted a famous passage [17] for the oboe in the *Scherzo* of Beethoven's *Ninth* as a representation of a fresh May morning, and Sir George Grove, in a historical and critical work which devotes a good deal of wrath to "unauthorized programs," tends to agree.[18]

But even when all possible allowances have been made, the programmatists will readily admit that the suggestions given by music

---

* This listing shows how purely the significance here given depends on association. In German, *die Posaune* is the trombone, but it is also the name given to that indefinite instrument which ,Gabriel is to blow on the Day of Doom. A different accident of words makes the English-speaking world associate with the *trumpet* some characteristics which the Germans attribute to the trombone.

The strings are so variously and extensively used that they have no specific associations.

without the aid of words are, at best, indefinite. Experiments of various
sorts bear out this conclusion. A number of investigators [19] have tried
to check the possibilities of conveying definite external ideas by music
alone, and their experiments, while differing in minor points, have all
used the same basic method. One or more pieces of avowed program
music are played (without any indication of title or program) to persons who are not already familiar with them, and these persons are
then asked to make their own interpretations. As would be expected,
the interpretations show a wide degree of divergence. It is particularly
interesting to note that even the literal imitations of barking dogs,
galloping horses, and singing birds—imitations which MacDowell described as universally intelligible—are frequently heard as thematic
material alone, or, if recognized as imitations, are frequently misin-
terpreted.

It is unfortunate that many of the "scientific" studies on this subject by psychologists contain blunders revealing appalling ignorance of
music on the part of investigators, and some show an utter inability to
think logically.* Nevertheless, the general results show complete agreement. The nature of these results can be seen from a very simple and
informal experiment which I once made with a class. I played recordings of six of the short orchestral selections in Saint-Saëns' *Carnaval
des animaux*, without announcing the composer's name or the titles.
Students were asked to indicate the fact if they knew the composer or
titles, or if any selection was familiar (this last on the theory that the
associations set up by a title can easily survive when the title itself is
not consciously remembered). They were asked to write down their
programmatic interpretations in so far as such interpretations existed,
but not to force anything which the music did not suggest. When the
answers came in, all that indicated previous familiarity with any selection were thrown out.

Before hearing the first three selections used ("Birds," "Fossils,"
"The Swan"), the class was told merely that each selection was sup-
posed to represent something that could be named in one or two words.
No one recognized the music of "Birds" as familiar, and five found that

* "Of the fifteen men and women selected as listeners four were Indian students,
seven were male students, two of which [sic] were not fond of music and could not
distinguish one tone from another; and eight were women. Of the latter two were
not sensitive to music, one was hysterical, one was an instructor in music, one had a
defective heart valve, and the others were fond of music."—I kindly refrain from
giving the source of this logical classification, but it comes from a standard scientific
journal.

it had no programmatic suggestion. The rest distributed their answers over a wide range: birds in forest, wind, deer in forest, chase, festival, water and Pan-pipes, storm, waterfalls, elves, mill, dawn, waves, animals in woods, fairies. Only two out of the twenty-four got the idea of birds, though several had the general suggestion of a forest and wildlife of some sort. The general idea of water was the most prevalent single interpretation, in spite of the fact that the music contains a good deal of direct imitation of bird-song.

The answers for "Fossils" showed a particularly interesting effect of association. No one came remotely near to the title of the composition. This is easily understandable, since the principal programmatic effect is secured by the use of the xylophone—in imitation of the sounds that *might* be produced by fossils *if* they were struck. The selection suggested nothing to ten students. Five interpreted it as a peasants' merrymaking, two as gaiety, and one each as puppet dance, fire, children's music-appreciation hour (not bad!), sleigh bells, orchestra, children, and rain. The extensive selection of a peasants' merrymaking is a clear case of extraneous suggestion: the class had been considering, a day or two earlier, the program and music of Beethoven's *Pastoral Symphony*, and this interpretation was obviously suggested by Beethoven's third movement.

Several recognized "The Swan," and one who did not recognize it selected the correct title. Six found no suggestion in it, and six others took it as a representation of a mood rather than a physical object. The mood seems to have been fairly consistent, though it was expressed in such varying terms as melancholy, peace and sadness, and quiet resignation. One each identified the work as love, brook, sailing (a close miss), consolation, spring, gentle breeze, love song, and evening.

These results show the wide divergence of interpretations when no verbal guide is supplied. Before hearing the next three selections ("Tortoises," "Elephant," "Kangaroo"), members of the class were told that each one represented an animal, "not necessarily a mammal." No one, however, identified the tortoises. Five left it blank; eight decided on lion, six on elephant, and one each on mule, snakes, bear, panther, and bird.

One already knew the music of "Elephant." Of the rest, six gave no answer, seven gave the correct title, six selected lion, and one each gave bear, tiger, kangaroo, and herd of horses. These two pieces gave instructive results in that they show a certain communication of the ideas of size, weight, and general ponderosity, but the particularities which distinguish a lion from an elephant, or either of these from a tortoise (Saint-Saëns presumably refers to giant tortoises) are not communicated by the music.

A similar result is shown in the interpretations of the "Kangaroo." Six found no suggestion of any animal, and other answers included four monkeys, two rabbits, one peacock, two deer, three cats, one dog, two kittens, one leopard, one panther, and one butterfly. Here again the reasoning is clear. The music can present irregularly leaping motion, and that is an attribute of most of the animals selected, but those conspicuous features which, at a glance, distinguish the kangaroo from any of the animals here named are beyond the power of music. At least—to make a more cautious interpretation of the facts—they are beyond the communicative powers of Saint-Saëns in combination with the receptive powers of this particular group of students.

A similar experiment was made with Dukas' *L'apprenti sorcier* as a test of music's narrative powers. The work is based on a ballad by Goethe dealing with a sorcerer's apprentice who has learned the charm by which his master makes an old broom come to life and wait on him. In his master's absence the apprentice decides to do a little conjuring on his own. He accordingly calls the broom to life and commands it to fetch water. The broom does so, to the delight of the apprentice at first, and to his horror when he realizes that he doesn't know the charm necessary to make it stop. When the broom does not heed his commands—and the whole house is getting full of water—he gets a hatchet and chops the unruly servant in two. There is a momentary lull, but then each half of the broom comes to life and goes to work, thus fetching twice as much water as before. The commotion and the apprentice's alarm increase until finally the sorcerer himself returns, sees the situation, and orders the broom back to its corner.

This work was presented without its title, but with the information that it told a definite story, and interpretations were called for. No one came near the story of the program. Two had the idea of a hunt for an animal, and one of a man-hunt, all three explaining the lull when the broom is cut in two as a temporary losing of the trail. Several interpreted it as a battle, fitting in various alarms and excursions as best they could. Most interpretations were variations on these two general themes of pursuit and battle, but a few said that they could hear the selection only as a piece of music and that it suggested no narrative of any kind. It is worth noting that water, in one form or another, entered into a good many of the interpretations.

After these interpretations had been written, Goethe's ballad was read, and such salient features of the music as the incantation, the broom's coming to life, the water-themes, the stroke that cuts the broom, the doubling of the water-fetching motive thereafter, and the sorcerer's final authoritative command were pointed out. Then the selection was played again, and this time it proved both easy to follow and very appropriate for its program.

These casual experiments suggest several points of interest about the whole problem of program music. They should make it abundantly clear that instrumental music without verbal assistance can suggest certain general states of mind and types of movement, but cannot adequately represent either objects or actions. Listeners who are told that a selection represents an animal are far more likely to make a correct identification than those who are told merely that it represents something. Various other evidence, such as poems written about pieces of music with suggestive titles, but without any detailed program, shows that listeners agree in their interpretations of a piece of program music exactly as far as the title takes them, and that beyond that point there is no more agreement than was found in the stories guessed at from Dukas' symphonic poem. So far as I know, no such experiment has been tried, but it would be interesting to play a detailed piece of narrative program music like this before a number of different groups to whom it was not familiar, and to give it a different title, bringing out a different element of the narrative, for each group. For example, "The Sorcerer's Apprentice" could be kept for one group, but it could also be called "The Magic Broom," "The Water-Carrier," "The Forgotten Incantation," "Water Everywhere," etc. One entirely misleading title —"Hannibal in the Alps," for instance—might prove entertaining. It is a reasonable guess that the members of each group would agree with each other as far as the suggestions of their particular title went, but would be otherwise at cross-purposes.

The two compositions chosen for my experiment also suggest a fundamental division of program music into two classes which may be called descriptive and narrative. Saint-Saëns' animals were described, but were not represented as taking part in any particular series of actions. To this same class belong far less literal pieces of program music which attempt, like Mendelssohn's *Hebrides Overture* (also known as "Fingal's Cave") to present a general scene and its characteristic atmosphere. Other possibilities of this type include the picture of a mood (as in Debussy's *Afternoon of a Faun*), a character (in Couperin's *Soeur Monique*), a picture (in various compositions based on Böcklin)—in fact, the musical representation of any object, scene, mood, or idea which is considered in a more or less permanent form rather than as a participant in a series of actions.

From one point of view, this descriptive program music is not necessarily based on literary ideas. In fact, literary description, when indulged in as an end in itself, has been condemned as an attempt of the writer to invade the field of the painter. And sometimes, as in Saint-Saëns' animals, the composer is working directly from nature. In such cases, however, he is invading what is even more obviously the domain of another art; and since he is likely to be concerned, as was Beethoven, more with the feeling of a scene than with its literal representation, we can say that he is, to a certain extent, following literature. As we saw in the works of Liszt, the inspiration of program music has been largely literary, and it is often impossible to separate the literary from the pictorial. Thus Mendelssohn wrote the *Hebrides Overture* after an actual visit to Fingal's Cave, and as an attempt to present the total experience—sight, sound, feeling, etc.—of that visit. But behind all this, and even conditioning his own experience in the cave, lay the great vogue of MacPherson's Ossianic poems. To take another example, the suggestion of the *Afternoon of a Faun* is (to me, at least) largely a blending of heat, landscape, and sensuality, but the origin of this combination is the literary experience of a similar combination in Mallarmé's poem. Thus we can say that descriptive program music is historically and practically a literary manifestation, though many individual examples have no literary connections.

Narrative program music is a more directly literary type. Music and literature, as the two temporal arts, are the only two which can attempt to represent a series of moving events or actions, and narrative is the literary form *par excellence*. Also, with a very few exceptions, narrative program music is based on literary works.

The problems of musical narration are necessarily much more difficult than those of musical description, for description is necessary preliminary to narration. Characters, objects, etc., must be identified before their actions can be represented. A composer who should undertake to compose one of Aesop's fables would have as his starting point Saint-Saëns' problem of musically representing the animals, plus all the added difficulties of indicating their specific actions. The problem of *purely* musical narration is readily seen to be insoluble, and all the evidence goes to support this view. Thus the composer of a work of narrative program music must have a fairly elaborate program presented by non-musical means. He may take a familiar literary work, and if it is familiar enough the title will possibly suffice, but only because it serves as a reference to an elaborate program already known to the audience. Or he may write his own program, or authorize someone else to do it for him. This latter course is shown by the verse-programs of two of Richard Strauss' symphonic poems: *Tod und Verklärung*,[20] by Alexander Ritter (the man who made a modern of Strauss); and *Ein Heldenleben*,[21] by Eberhard König. Again, he may, like Tschaikowsky in the *1812 Overture,* choose a familiar subject based on history rather than literature, but this practice involves the same principle as the use of a familiar literary title.

Whichever of these methods the composer chooses, he is admitting that the music alone is not sufficient to convey the narrative. Sir Donald Tovey's analysis [22] of Elgar's "symphonic study," *Falstaff,* is a fine and highly interesting piece of evidence on this point. When Tovey wrote this analysis for one of his Reid Concerts in Edinburgh, he had not seen Elgar's own interpretation. But when he reprinted his analysis he obligingly left it unchanged, and put Elgar's interpretations into footnotes so that they could be readily compared with his own. This process "gives rise to a unique opportunity for demonstrating how far a great piece of 'programme music' can be intelligible as pure music and at the same time convey the subject of the composer's illustration to other minds without the use of words." Thus the reader is given three things running parallel: Tovey's formal analysis of the work as pure music, Tovey's guesses as to its programmatic significance, and Elgar's authoritative explanations of this significance.

It is beyond the scope of this discussion to enter into this essay in detail, but several interesting conclusions present themselves. Tovey was a musician of great ability, and he knew his Elgar; hence he was in a favorable position to get as much of the program as the music can convey. In general his guesses (his own word) agree with Elgar's intentions, though there are frequent minor differences. Occasionally he is entirely wrong, even on the mood which the music is intended to convey, as when he speaks of a theme "blown up like a bladder with sighing and grief," when Elgar had intended to represent "a goodly, portly man, of a cheerful look, a pleasing eye, and a most noble carriage." In another place Tovey mistakes the King for a mood of Falstaff. Nevertheless, he has done remarkably well in getting the composer's intentions. Yet we must make a considerable reservation on the evidence given by this comparative success. After all, Falstaff is a character from drama. We know him so well that we are likely to forget that we see only about two hours out of his whole life.* Now, an ambitious symphonic study can well allude to every one of the comparatively few adventures and separate aspects of Falstaff; and it will be likely to follow the general sequence of events in the plays. Thus the problem was not really to understand a musical narrative, but to compare Shakespeare's text with Elgar's translation and identify the corresponding passages. One cannot help wondering what Tovey could have done with the program of this same music if it had been called merely *Symphonic Study for Orchestra, Op. 68.*

Our discussion has already suggested the common ground which exists between the two schools of thought about the practice of program music. The advocates of the program will admit that music without verbal aid cannot convey an external idea with any precision or certainty, and that program music is still essentially music. The absolutists, on the other hand, will admit that the following of a program may add a certain interest to the hearing of a piece of music, though they may deny that this extra interest is really musical. Thus the compromise is reached: the composer must write something which will stand on its own feet from a musical point of view, something which *can* be satisfying if considered as absolute music; but he has every right to include subject-matter outside the range of "pure" music— to attach as much or as little of a program as he desires.

Heated statements have come from both sides, like Schopenhauer's dictum that all descriptive music is rubbish. But in their milder moments both sides have long agreed on this practical solution of the difficulty. Mendelssohn wrote a great deal of program music, but when a young Frenchman put names to the unnamed numbers of the *Songs Without Words* and wrote to know whether they were correct, Mendelssohn replied in a famous letter [23] that music is not too indefinite to be put into words, but rather too definite:

If you ask me what I thought of when I was composing, I can only answer, "The song itself, just as it stands." And if I did have one or more definite words in mind while composing some of these works, I will not tell them to anyone. For a word does not mean the same thing to one person that it does to another; only a piece of music can awaken the same mood—say the same thing—in every case: a feeling which not everyone would call by the same name. . . .

If a man is a sufficiently enthusiastic hunter, a Wild Hunt and The Praise

* Tovey shrewdly guesses that *The Merry Wives of Windsor* can be ignored.

of God [these are among the suggested titles] may come to much the same thing. . . . But we would hear in it only the hunt, and no matter how much we might wrangle with him, we could get no further. The word remains ambiguous, but we would both understand the music correctly.

Will you accept this as my answer to your question? It is at least the only one that I can give, though it is only ambiguous words.

Mendelssohn's reply includes moods as a sphere of musical representation, but not words. Schumann—also a writer of a good deal of program music—tended to be inconsistent and wavering in his views on the subject. One statement, however, about one of Spohr's works with an elaborate program, sums up the matter: "If a composer holds up a program to us before the music, I say: 'First of all let us hear that you made beautiful music; afterwards we shall be glad of your program.' " [24] And that is more or less where the matter rests today among musicians and critics.

The aestheticians, however, are not men to compromise on a principle, and musical aesthetics is still divided into the two sharply separate camps of "heteronomous" (programmatic) and "autonomous" (absolute) explanations of the nature of the art. Having seen the practical compromise, we may leave the abstract question with them and wish them joy of it. As Tovey remarks on this same question, "These are hard matters and too high for me."

CHAPTER XX

Descriptive Music

WHEN a musical reactionary was inveighing against the prevalence of program music, Mendelssohn replied that since Beethoven had committed himself in the *Pastoral Symphony* it was impossible for a composer to keep clear of it.[1] There is profound historical truth in this remark. Descriptive music had, of course, been written long before the first performance of this work, in 1808. More than half a century before this time, Vivaldi had written a set of four violin concertos based on four sonnets describing the seasons,[2] and it is thought that a *Portrait musical de la nature* (c. 1784) by one Justin Heinrich Knecht influenced the program-notes—though not the music—of Beethoven's symphony. There had been other similar works too numerous to mention, but it is clear that the authority of Beethoven's example, along with the general tendencies of romanticism, made a regular practise out of what had been merely a sporadic experiment.

Furthermore, this type of experimentation seems to have been suggested by literature. In the eighteenth century a considerable group of poets writing in German discovered nature as a poetic theme and wrote vast masses of purely descriptive poetry. The nature-poetry of Brockes eventually sprawled out into nine volumes and was the basis of a poetic school which includes the works of Haller and Ewald von Kleist. Since Vivaldi died only four years before Brockes, it is probably significant that his concertos on the seasons are based, not directly on nature, but on poems dealing with nature. So far as I know no one has made any detailed study of the relationship between the descriptive nature poets and the rise of descriptive music, but it is likely that a good deal of the description of nature in earlier program music was suggested by poetry on the same subject and was written in competition with that poetry.

Beethoven's experiment in the description of nature is not only the work which established such music as a recognized and respectable type of composition. It is also a highly effective work in itself—so effective, in fact, that Grove, writing nearly ninety years later, and with the works of Berlioz, Liszt, Wagner, and Mendelssohn before him, does not hesitate to call it "the greatest piece of program music yet composed." The *Pastoral Symphony*, then, is the obvious starting-point for any discussion of descriptive music.

Before coming to the music itself, however, we will do well to consider Beethoven's intentions in composing it. His notes for the titles have survived in four different forms, the one regularly printed with the music being:

Pastoral Symphony, or a recollection of country life (more an expression of feeling than a painting).
1. *Allegro ma non troppo.* The cheerful feelings aroused by arrival in the country.
2. *Andante molto moto.* By the brook.
3. *Allegro.* Peasants' merrymaking.
4. *Allegro.* Storm.
5. *Allegretto.* Shepherds' song: joy and thanksgiving after the storm.

Among the various jottings on this subject in Beethoven's notebooks are a number of comments which throw further light on the work:

The hearers should be allowed to discover the situations.—A recollection of country life.—All painting in instrumental music, if pushed too far, is a failure. —People will not require titles in order to recognize the general intention to be more a matter of feeling than of painting in sounds.—Pastoral Symphony: no picture, but something in which the emotions are expressed which are aroused in men by the pleasure of the country, or in which some feelings of country-life are set forth.

It is clear that Beethoven went into the composition of descriptive music with several reservations. The music was not to rival painting, but was to describe or represent the feelings which the landscape produces. There is, of course, a certain amount of direct description, and even of imitation: the fourth movement certainly represents the storm itself rather than the state of mind of one experiencing a storm, and the same thing can be said of the charmingly burlesqued rustic band in the third movement. But a certain possibility of effectiveness in direct description, or "painting," is allowed, for it is only when the composer attempts to push it too far that it fails. This moderate view is in strong contrast to Schopenhauer's condemnation of the symphony on the grounds that all music that tries to paint is trash.* It is equally far from the aunts (trumpets) yelling "Just like Papa" and the uncles (trombones) shouting back "Just like Mama" in Strauss' *Sinfonia Domestica*.

Since Beethoven's opinion makes the legitimacy—in fact, the possibility—of musical painting simply a question of how far it is to be carried, the *Pastoral Symphony* itself is the best source of information as to his conclusions. In the first place, it should be noted that most of this work is highly satisfactory if heard as absolute music.† This is especially true of the first two movements. The storm and the village band are less comprehensible as pure music, but these are both suggestions of sound rather than of visible scenery. As far as the band is concerned, even Hanslick would have to admit that music is entirely capable of representing itself.

Since the indication of sounds is a minor part of program music, but is the principal element in the peasants' merry-making, storm, and song of thanksgiving, we will do well to concentrate on the first two movements of the symphony; and since there are no programmatic effects in the first movement which are not also to be found in the second, we may confine ourselves largely to the latter, the scene "By the Brook."

This movement is written in sonata form and is, with the possible exception of a brief passage almost at the end, entirely intelligible as absolute music. Nevertheless, once a hearer knows its title the programmatic suggestion is both strong and effective. The general suggestion of the out-of-doors is obtained by a number of devices. There is, for example, a good deal more repetition of short phrases over and over than is usually found in Beethoven's music. (The first movement shows this characteristic even more conspicuously than does the second.)

* Music "dem Kopfe *unmittelbar* nichts zu sagen hat und es ein Missbrauch ist, wenn man ihr dies zumutet, wie in aller *malenden* Musik geschieht, welche daher, ein für allemal, verwerflich ist; wenn gleich Haydn und Beethoven sich zu ihr verirrt haben. . . ." Stabenow, *Arthur Schopenhauer: Schriften über Musik* (Regensburg, 1922), pp. 147–148.

† George Sand's attitude towards this symphony furnishes a fine example of the indefiniteness of program music without a title. She tells of hearing the *Pastoral Symphony* once without knowing its title or program, and of inventing for herself a program based on *Paradise Lost*, with the rebel angel's last cry towards heaven represented by Beethoven's imitations of the nightingale and the quail. On a later hearing she knew Beethoven's program and found that it fitted perfectly. And elsewhere in the same book (*Lettres d'un voyageur*) she tells how beautifully and minutely this symphony recalls to her mind the landscape of Italy!

Since the sounds of nature are largely repetitions of short sequences with no musical development, this effect suggests the woods, even though the noises of nature are not literally imitated. In the same category comes the extensive use of pedals which frequently come in on weak beats of the bar: both the mild dissonance and the rhythmic casualness of these sustained notes help to suggest the independent and unorganized sounds of nature.

Also, there is an extensive use of grace-notes and trills which, as Grove remarks, "somehow suggest heat." Grace-notes frequently occur in the principal voices, but the trills are very largely confined to subordinate parts and are kept in the background. I believe that it is possible to go beyond Grove's statement and to see why this suggestion of heat is actually conveyed by such devices. The shimmering effect given to a landscape by the rising currents of warm air through which it is seen on hot days is so familiar that any such appearance immediately calls up an association of heat. The trills are, in my opinion, simply an auditory equivalent. They are kept in the background because we do not look at warm air—we look *through* it. Similarly we do not listen to these trills softly given in inconspicuous parts, but rather listen *through* them to the more arresting parts of the musical fabric. Like the visual effect, they give a certain different sensation to the object of attention, and the analogy is close enough to carry over—with the aid of the verbal directions suggesting the out-of-doors—into a suggestion of heat in the music. Grove points out that Gluck uses the same device for a similar suggestion.

So far we have seen only general effects of nature. What of the brook mentioned in the title of the movement? It similarly is a background rather than an object of primary interest. Throughout most of the movement the lower strings softly keep up a figure suggestive of running water. It begins with the opening note, and is at first presented by the second violins and violas, doubled by two muted solo 'cellos an octave lower:

Sometimes this figure is given in sixteenth-notes instead of eighths by the simple process of alternating the notes which are paired in the example above, but the theme of the brook is almost always kept in the background in some easily recognizable form.

The border between imitation and suggestion is rather vague in music, and on the basis of this theme alone we should find it impossible to say in which category the representation of the brook should be placed. Fortunately, biographical information will clear up any doubt, and at the same time throw light on Beethoven's attitude towards musical imitation. Five years before the composition of the *Pastoral Symphony*, while his hearing was still relatively good,* he jotted down in one of his notebooks the actual sound of a brook, with the notation, "The more the water, the deeper the tone":

By the time of the composition of the *Pastoral Symphony* Beethoven was probably incapable of hearing a brook at all. If he had intended to make a literal imitation he would certainly have used this earlier transcription of the sound of an actual brook. What he did, however, was to invent a figure similar enough to carry the suggestion, but musically much more interesting. Imitation for its own sake was clearly no object.

With the exception of a bit near the end of the movement, the features already described include all the programmatic effects of any importance. They can hardly be called literal in any sense, for they deal very largely in the freest sort of suggestion. So far not one word has been said about the principal themes of the movement, but since we are dealing with sonata form we know that these themes will have to carry the main burden of the musical structure. We now come face to face with the revealing fact that Beethoven's programmatic effects are all in the background and accompaniment, and his principal themes are pure music except in so far as they may be able to suggest the mood of the beholder of a peaceful natural scene. Here he is being true to his characterization of the work as "more an expression of feeling than a painting." Perhaps it would not be going too far to say that the principal themes, with their purely musical beauty, *are* the feelings of the observer, and are thus appropriately set in the almost unconsciously heard background of the actual sounds of nature which help to produce them.

* The notebook containing this sketch dates from 1803, the year after the famous "Heiligenstadt Testament" in which Beethoven laments his increasing deafness.

This observation brings us to one of the most hotly disputed points in all music—the bird-imitations just before the end of the movement. After a pause, the nightingale (flute) begins with a repeated F, which then begins to alternate more and more rapidly with a G until it leads into a trill. Just before the trill begins, however, the quail (oboe) comes in with a repeated figure consisting of a dotted sixteenth, a thirty-second, and an eighth note, all on the same D. Before the conclusion of this figure the cuckoo (clarinet) joins the other two birds with the literal imitation of a descending major third. The first violins then come in for half a bar, after which the entire performance is repeated; and then three more bars form the conclusion of the movement.

This is a bare statement of what happens, and many critics have unequivocally condemned it as a puerile trick cheapening the entire movement. Beethoven himself wanted the imitation recognized, for he wrote the names of the birds into the score. He might well have spared himself the trouble, for they are so obviously bird-calls and are so strange from a purely musical point of view that there was little chance of their failing of recognition. A few critics have objected mildly to the birds, or been indifferent to them, but in general this passage seems to bring out all the tendency to speak *ex cathedra*—a tendency which the critic always has, though he may be able to control it on most occasions. Consequently another group contends that this passage, far from being a silly stunt, is one of the greatest beauties of the symphony. Those who take this position support it by pointing to facts intentionally omitted from my earlier description of the passage. The half-measure which comes at the end of the bird-songs each time is not a pointless figure, but a very beautiful and purely musical one:

Furthermore, it is a part of the organic material of the movement, having been introduced first as an episode, and then used later as the concluding theme of the exposition. Thus its repetition at the end of the recapitulation (and hence of the movement) is called for, and it is dramatically introduced by the pause and the new material of the birds. It is also in keeping with these calls, and thus a union between the musical and the programmatic material is made just before the conclusion. Since the entire passage, including the repetition, covers only eight bars, it is casual, and hence does not place too much emphasis on the imitative element.

So runs the defense of this embattled passage. Personally (for this is a matter on which I cannot suppress the *ex cathedra*), I wish that Beethoven had left the ornithology alone. The birds always produce in me that very unpleasant sort of embarrassment which comes when one sees a loved and revered friend mildly but publicly making a fool of himself.

This one movement from Beethoven illustrates most of the methods and problems of descriptive music, but one or two further points may be shown by different examples. Mendelssohn's *Hebrides Overture* is useful for comparison on several points. Like the scene by the brook, it deals with the imagery of water and has a water-theme which is almost omnipresent, but it is much more than a background. It is the most important single theme of the overture, and therefore is treated in a variety of ways. Its very difference from Beethoven's brook-theme is illuminating from the point of view of musical representation. Both themes suggest the sound made by moving water, but here the resemblance ceases. Beethoven, dealing with a brook, wanted a soft, unobtrusive, continuous sound, and the constant murmur of accompaniment throughout the brook scene is ideal for his purpose. But Mendelssohn, portraying the stormy northern seas, required the separate noise of individual waves, each with its own breaking and ebbing. His wave-figure is ideally designed for this purpose. It is first played by bassoons and 'cellos in unison, with the violas doubling an octave higher:

The one-bar phrase keeps the separate wave-effects from running together by the fact that it must have its rest on the opening half-beat. It also allows for that endless repetition which we saw effectively used by Beethoven to give the effect of the sounds of nature.

Furthermore, it can be combined into larger units, as in bars 37–38, where the gathering and breaking of a huge wave is very clearly suggested. Here a modification of the opening figure is made, so that it can be continuous, and is taken by the flutes, oboes, and violas. The whole passage has a crescendo from pianissimo to fortissimo in the first bar, and a corresponding diminuendo in the second. Against this modified wave-theme a number of the instruments sustain chords, with the bassoons taking that strangely dissonant interval of the tritone (here E sharp to B); the violins have rapidly alternated notes including a different tritone; and the 'cellos and contrabasses have an ascending figure which alternates the interval of the octave with the harshly dissonant major seventh, while the kettledrum rumbles a long roll. All this wave-theme, dissonance, and change of volume is rather unintelligible from the standpoint of absolute music, but here, though the overture has no program beyond its title, there can be no mistaking its intention.

Other material in the work is less specifically programmatic. The second subject, "quite the greatest melody Mendelssohn ever wrote," [3] has no connection with Fingal's Cave beyond the fact that it is first given out by bassoons and 'cellos in unison, thus making an association of timbre with the opening wave-theme and keeping an effect of depth and hollowness which reinforces the suggestion of a cave.

This music was written entirely for its extra-musical expressiveness —not, as sometimes happens, as a piece of absolute music to which a program was attached. Mendelssohn visited Fingal's Cave with a friend in 1829, and wrote a letter enclosing some of the music which later became this overture: "In order to make you understand how extraordinarily the Hebrides affected me, the following came into my mind there. . . . You will excuse a short note, the more as what I can best tell you is contained in the above music." [4] Nor was the attempt to express the Hebrides merely a starting point for the composition. It was so entirely the purpose that nearly three years after the letter just quoted, when the composition was complete from a technical standpoint, Mendelssohn was not satisfied with parts of it because they did not convey the things which they were supposed to represent: "I cannot bring *The Hebrides* to a hearing here [in Paris] because I do not consider it finished as I originally wrote it. The middle section in D major is very stupid, and the whole so-called development smells more of counterpoint than of blubber, gulls, and salted cod." [5]

We note here that Mendelssohn's intention was not specifically to reproduce the cave itself, or to imitate the basalt pillars which, as his friend wrote, suggest "the inside of an immense organ, black and resounding." What he wished to do was to suggest the atmosphere, the general feeling, of the Hebrides, and the literal imitation of the sea is used only because the sea is the fundamental basis of that atmosphere. But the suggestion or reception of atmosphere is much more a matter of feeling than of intellect, and this fact brings us to an interesting development in the history of descriptive music.

In the scene by the brook Beethoven uses sonata form, but that form is hardly more than a convention; it commands nothing like the interest of, say, the first movement of his *Ninth Symphony*. And this peaceful, leisurely, somewhat drowsy music became a starting point for later writers of atmospheric pieces: "Without it," writes Schauffler, "there would have been no *Waldweben* and no *Après-midi.*" ⁶ Mendelssohn also used a fixed form for his *Hebrides Overture,* but well-handled though this form is, it is really irrelevant. It does not assist in suggesting salted cod. In order to enjoy this music, "you have only to abandon yourself to its influences, and the sensations, thoughts, and feelings that engendered it will rise up in your imagination." ⁷

This abandonment of oneself is a new and interesting development. An aesthetically mature listener does not simply abandon himself to a Bach fugue, or really to any music written before the nineteenth century: he listens to it attentively, and it involves his intellect at least as much as his emotions. The art of by-passing the intellect and making the appeal directly to the affective part of the listener's mind is a recent development known, in its extremer forms, as impressionism. And it is by hinting at this possibility that Beethoven cleared the way for the pictures of scene and mood of Wagner and Debussy.

The *Afternoon of a Faun* is a perfect example of this method carried to its limit. The ordinary English title is somewhat misleading, for it is likely to lead one to expect a narrative. Debussy actually called his work *Prélude à 'L'Après-Midi d'un Faune.'* The implications of this title are clear enough: the music is simply a prelude for Mallarmé's poem, a preliminary establishment of the languorously idle and sensuous mood of that hauntingly vague work. Clearly, then, we should look for no imitation of anything—in fact, we should not look at all, but rather should surrender ourselves casually to the composer.

At this point we are forced to violate the composer's intention, for we are concerned with the methods by which his effect is achieved. If one wants to see the wheels go 'round he must do some violence to the watch, and his only hope is not to take it apart so completely that it cannot be put back together. There is litle danger of doing this with the *Après-Midi*, for the mood of the composition is so skilfully conveyed that it is almost impossible, even with the worst intentions, to hear it and at the same time keep an analytical approach.

Musical form, in the ordinary sense of the word, is abandoned entirely. One edition of the score characterizes the work as "a sensuous pastoral rhapsody following no fixed form," and a better description could not be found. Within this freedom, however, certain principles are at work. In the first place, the pastoral character of the music depends largely on Spitteler's instrumental allegory: the woodwinds dominate the entire composition. Though the effect is in many ways different, such devices as Beethoven employed for his suggestion of heat and the sounds of nature are extensively used. Furthermore, definite effects which might demand attention from the intellect are studiously avoided. The principal theme, given out by an unaccompanied flute at the beginning, has the suggestion of nothing even so definite as an improvisation; the chromatics and relaxed rhythms suggest a flautist idly toying with his instrument, and something of the same effect is produced by many other themes and passages, particularly the frequent glissando phrases of the harps. In fact, considerable portions of this work suggest the agreeable little warming-up exercises produced by an orchestra before a concert, but happening, by some freak of chance, not to produce clashes of sound. Probably the famous Chinaman who found the tuning-up better than the concert would be enthusiastic about the *Après-Midi*.

Beyond these features there is little that can be said in explanation of its strange effectiveness, except to comment that, as usual, something —the vital thing—eludes the analyst. Anyone could easily write a composition embodying all the features of this work to which attention has been called, but he would be very likely to produce no effect beyond one of irritation.

The development of music of this type closely parallels a similar development in poetry. There is a great deal of poetry which does not command the reader's strict attention, and such work is to be found throughout the history of literature. Most of it is simply bad or tedious poetry, and the fact that it is hard to give one's undivided attention to many of the Middle English metrical romances, or to vast wastes of the later Wordsworth, is merely an indication that the authors have failed. There is, however, a totally different kind of poetry which aims at receiving only the casual, dreamy kind of attention which we give to such music as the *Afternoon of a Faun*. Such passages occur from time to time in Vergil's *Eclogues*, and there is a good deal of this type of writing in the *Faerie Queene*, but its development as a recognized type belongs to the nineteenth century. In *The Lotus Eaters* Tennyson used this method admirably for a subject which demanded it, and Swinburne used it constantly without much concern for its appropriateness. This kind of poetry has been appropriately called "hypnotic poetry." [8]

In both poetry and music pure examples of types are almost nonexistent. Hence the great body of work in both arts contains something of the intellectual and something of the hypnotic, but most poems or compositions will have a clear predominance of one or the other. For the primarily intellectual we can find such examples as the fugues of Bach, the symphonies of Brahms, the bagatelles of Tcherepnin, and most of the poetry of Dante, Donne, and T. S. Eliot. Many persons do read and hear—and, strangely enough, enjoy—these works without understanding them, but they are definitely missing the point. On the other hand, such hypnotic works as Bach's *Air for the G String* (with limitations), Debussy's *Après-Midi*, Sibelius' *Swan of Tuonela*, Tennyson's *Lotus Eaters*, and Swinburne's chorus from *Atalanta in Calydon* beginning "When the hounds of spring are on winter's traces," have little intellectual point to be missed, and hence properly induce trance rather than thought.

The neglect of this obvious distinction has led to a good deal of confusion in recent criticism of both arts. In literature a revolt against the "sentimentality" and "vagueness" of much nineteenth-century poetry has confused weak attempts at intellectual work with effective hypnotic poems, and has led to an extreme intellectualist position which sometimes comes perilously close to defining the only true poem as a complex of intricate puns. In music the revolt has not yet gone so far, but there is a great tendency to demand mathematical pattern regardless of how it sounds and to suspect works which are more beautiful than logical. A clear recognition of the existence and legitimacy of both types of work would go far towards untangling many of the confusions in contemporary criticism.

Descriptive program music has been written under strong literary influence, and most of its creators have realized from the first that it cannot represent details of scenery with any exactitude—that it must necessarily be an expression of feeling rather than a painting. And since many states of feeling are not arrived at by intellectual processes, they have quite properly emphasized the emotional appeal at the expense of the intellectual. For this reason any good piece of descriptive program music, even though it may be written in some strict form and adhere faithfully to its preconceived pattern, is almost certain to belong primarily to the hypnotic type. Unless one is engaged in geologizing or botanizing the landscape (in which case the feeling of it as landscape is lost or minimized), he gives himself up to its general effect instead of attempting to grasp all its particulars.

CHAPTER XXI

Narrative Music

WE HAVE already seen that music which tells a story presents a much greater problem than does purely descriptive music, because in order to have a story one must clearly depict both the participants and their actions. The participants require much more accurate delineation than do general scenes or moods, and they are very likely to present problems like Busoni's riddle as to how a poor but contented man is to be musically delineated. Thus its problem of description alone is more difficult. Furthermore, the delineation of characters and objects, even if successfully accomplished, presents only the *dramatis personae*. Thereafter the composer must depict a series of actions involving his characters and objects in their progressive relationships.

Historically, descriptive and narrative instrumental music seem to have originated about the same time. Niecks [1] lists as the two earliest known pieces of non-vocal program music a *Fantasia* by John Mundy (d. 1630) describing fair weather, lightning, thunder, etc., and a battle-piece by William Byrd (d. 1623), described as follows: "The march before the battle; the soldiers' summons; the march of footmen; the march of horsemen; now followeth the trumpets; the Irish march; the bagpipe and the drone; the flute and the drum; the march to the fight; here the battle be joined; the retreat; now followeth a galliard for the victory." It is clear that the first of these pieces properly belongs to descriptive music, like the storms of Beethoven's *Pastoral Symphony* and Rossini's *William Tell Overture*, though there is necessarily a certain amount of narrative in any storm, since it must have, like Aristotelian tragedy, a beginning, a middle, and an end. As far as can be judged by this outline, the battle piece also has a good deal of purely descriptive music. Niecks (who does not make our distinction between descriptive and narrative music, but applies the term "tone-painting" to both) says that "The tone-painting is chiefly to be found in 'The Battle Joined' and 'The Retreat.' No one can fail to recognize in the former the bustle and tussle of the contest, and in the latter the giving way, first slowly, then quicker and quicker, until it ends in a wild flight." This latter section, with its emphasis on a developing sequence of events, is clearly to be placed in the category of narrative.

After various other sporadic attempts at musical narrative had been made, Kuhnau began the practice on a large scale in 1700, with his *Musical Representations of Some Bible-Stories in Six Sonatas to be Played on the Clavier.** The word *stories* is an exact indication of the nature of such examples as his *Combat Between David and Goliath, David Curing Saul by Means of Music,* and *Jacob's Death and Burial.* With these works the essentials of narrative music were established, and these basic principles have not changed. A program is necessary, and each selection has a long "argument" as well as superscriptions placed over the different parts of the score to show what is being represented. David vs. Goliath, for example, is divided into eight sections: the boasting and defiance of Goliath; the terror of the Israelites and their prayers to God at sight of their terrible enemy; the courage of David, his desire to subdue the pride of the giant, and his boyish trust in God; the contest in words between David and Goliath, and the fight itself, in which Goliath is wounded in the forehead by a stone so that he falls to the ground and is slain; the flight of the Philistines, and how they are pursued by the Israelites and slain by the sword; the rejoicing of the Israelites over their victory; the praise of David, sung by the women in antiphonal choirs; the general rejoicing, expressing itself in heartfelt dancing and leaping.

Here we have all the characteristics of narrative music. The verbal program gives the main course of the action which the music is to represent, and the music itself is divided into what may properly be called paragraphs—i.e., into sections which are determined, not by musical considerations, but by the episodes of the plot. There have been tremendous developments in the expressive power of music, but the basic scheme of the musical narrative is the same in Kuhnau and in Dukas or Strauss.

Even the subject-matter is typical. Fighting, pursuit, flight, dancing, and other actions involving definite types of physical motion have always been favorite subjects of the narrative composers simply because music can represent motions with some accuracy. Almost any

* *Musikalische Vorstellungen einiger Biblischer Historien in 6 Sonaten auf dem Clavier zu spielen.*

piece of reasonably successful narrative music will depend more on overt physical actions than will the average literary narrative.

In spite of the similarity in idea between Kuhnau's *Bible Sonatas* (as they are usually called) and the storytelling music of the nineteenth and early twentieth centuries, a modern listener finds David and Goliath singularly unconvincing. Nevertheless, we cannot be sure that the work was not tremendous in the ears of Kuhnau's contemporaries. It has frequently been remarked that music wears out forms and techniques more rapidly than any other art, and the pursuit of program music in the nineteenth century led to great developments. Though the symphonies of Beethoven made some contributions to the orchestration of absolute music, we can make a generalization to the effect that the development of the orchestra and its resources, from Mozart to the present, has come about largely as a result of constant strivings to express non-musical ideas. The greatest—or at least the most spectacular—developments of the orchestra during the past century were due to the efforts of Berlioz, Wagner, and Richard Strauss, all of whom were concerned primarily with musical narrative. The extension of the orchestra adds many new possibilities of timbre for the expression of different characters, states of mind, and magnitudes of action. This last item has come to be very largely a matter of volume of sound, and our dissatisfaction with Kuhnau's fight is primarily due to a feeling that it is not loud enough to be much of a battle: the lethal stone is merely the loud "plunk" of a single note.

It is not my intention here to try to trace the historical development of musical narrative, but it has been necessary to show that the form is nearly as old as instrumental music and that its essential subjects and principles have changed very little, though the application of these principles has undergone considerable development. We turn now to a few examples in order to see how composers actually go about representing literary narratives by musical means. But when we come to select examples we are confronted by a striking fact: in spite of the long history of narrative instrumental works, not one of them is unequivocally great music. We can readily enough give them their praise as amusing, interesting, revolutionary, or ingenious, but we tend, probably unconsciously, to withhold from them the final praise of a work of art. Unless this be due merely to an unreasonable prejudice, it must be a severe stricture on the achievements of this artistic type.

Having no compulsion to consider any particular work, then, we may as well take our examples where we find them, and the more familiar they are, the better. Saint-Saëns' *Danse macabre* will be a good starting point.

This composition runs true to form in that it is based on a poem. The dance of the dead has been a favorite subject of poets and painters since the Middle Ages and is familiar to all English readers in *Tam o' Shanter*, but the particular version of it used by Saint-Saëns is a short poem by Henri Cazalis in which Death, patting his foot on a tomb, plays on his violin ("Zig et Zig et Zig"); the skeletons come out and dance in their shrouds, cracking their bones as they move; the cock crows; and they disappear in flight. The twelve lines of the poem containing this program are prefixed to the composition as a guide to the hearer.

As the music begins the clock strikes midnight—an invention of the composer not found in the program. The harp repeats the same note twelve times, with a bar of 3/4 time for each occurrence, while the horns sustain this note throughout and the upper strings come in on the fifth stroke very softly and mysteriously, holding the chord of the striking clock for four bars. After the last stroke the horns continue to sustain its pitch and the strings once again very softly play its chord. This is followed by a soft pizzicato of the 'cellos and contrabasses. All that this section does is to add to the literal imitation of the clock a sense of mystery and expectancy.

Then, suddenly and loudly, Death begins to tune his fiddle:

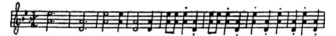

The solo violin, to which this recurrent passage is assigned, has the E-string tuned a semitone flat so that the interval A-E flat may get the full resonance of open strings, and the effect is weird and startling enough in itself. But its programmatic significance is also symbolic. This interval of the tritone, or augmented fourth, was known to mediaeval writers as the devil in music (*diabolus in musica*), and its use in ecclesiastical music was strictly forbidden. Thus its effectiveness here goes beyond its mere sound and depends to some extent on its history: as the particular musical embodiment of the devil it forms an appropriate summons to the spooks.

The greater part of the composition from this point on is devoted to the dance itself, and hence can be musically effective without any consideration of the program. The two principal themes are selected on the general musical principle of contrast. The first is tripping and lively, but with something a bit forced and unnatural about its revelry:

The second is considerably less energetic, with a touch of melancholy in its chromatic descent:

The opposition between these two themes is musically useful and interesting, but they have a programmatic significance as well. The first seems to represent the hectic merriment of the dead:

> Les squelettes blancs vont à travers l'ombre,
> Courant et sautant sous leurs grands linceuls.*

The second theme (which comes first in the poem) is a musical presentation of the melancholy and longing of these frustrate ghosts:

> Le vent d'hiver souffle, et la nuit est sombre;
> Des gémissements sortent des tilleuls.†

The greater part of the composition is made up of alternations of these two themes, the first remaining practically unchanged in spirit, and the second going through several transformations, including one rather wistfully flippant one taken by the woodwinds and harp against an ingenious triplet figure rising an octave on each beat in the strings, and with a cymbal struck softly on the second beat of each bar. The tritone tuning-theme of the solo violin comes in from time to time and separates the different sections of the work. A xylophone is used occasionally as a piece of literal immitation: the bones can be heard rattling.‡ The dance continues, with some points of high revelry and others of depression, and with musical development and combination of the main themes and occasional episodes, until finally, when it is going at

---

* "The white skeletons come through the darkness, running and leaping in their great shrouds."
† "The winter wind whistles, and the night is dark; groans and sighs are heard from among the lindens."
‡ Zig et Zig et Zig, chacun se trémousse,
On entend claquer les os des danseurs.

full blast, there is an abrupt stop, the horns (suspense, as in the opening measures) sustain an octave, and the cock crows:

After the cock-crow and the horns fade out together, a loud scurrying
begins, but gradually grows fainter. The solo violin declaims a few sad
phrases, and the whole thing then slowly dies away.

Verbal description of music is necessarily inadequate, but even this
brief resumé will suffice to show something of the elements which normally enter into narrative music. In the first place, there is a certain
amount of direct imitation to be found in the striking clock, the crowing cock, and the rattling bones. The clock depends on timbre for the
imitation and on plain counting for its programmatic significance in
setting the time as midnight. (Even here there is a certain ambiguity:
except for the verbal program the opening might just as well represent
noon, though the effects of mystery and suspense help to reinforce the
already-present idea of night.) The rattling bones depend entirely on
the timbre of the xylophone, and their effect is therefore lost in a piano
transcription. The cock-crow depends on both the timbre of the oboe
and its time and pitch relationships to suggest a familiar sound.

Next in order comes suggestion. The dance-themes and Death's
violin cannot properly be called imitation, for they are already musical
materials and it would certainly be forcing logic to contend that imitative sound is involved when a violin is used to represent a violin. The
weirdness of the tuning, however, is suggestive: an ordinary tuning
would not distinguish Death's violin from any other, but this special
tuning gives a suggestion of the eerie—of something not quite right
about the whole thing. Actually, the solo violin seems to blend the characters of Death and the Devil, and really to partake of both. The two
principal dance-themes likewise have suggestions of two moods or
aspects of this dance of the dead, each capable of its own shadings.
Other suggestions are contained in such things as the startled flight
which follows the cock-crow. This cannot be called imitation because
there is no assumption that the dead make these sounds, in the sense in
which the cock makes the sound of crowing; rather, these sounds are
used to *suggest* both the movements of the dancers in flight and, at the
same time, their state of mind.

Finally we come to uses of symbolism, which in some instances can hardly be separated from suggestion. The tuning of Death's fiddle is a useful example because its suggestive and its symbolic significance can be separated. The interval of the augmented fourth is the source of both. In so far as the listener is merely conscious of a weird sound introducing and reinforcing the idea of the evilly supernatural, musical suggestion is at work. If, however, he recognizes the *diabolus in musica* and associates the interval with its name and history, the suggestion is heightened by symbolism.

This particular type of symbolism—the use of a musical element already associated with the thing to be represented—is an interesting musical phenomenon and is more common than is generally realized. In its most obvious form it uses folk songs for local color, and numerous examples of this use are to be found in nationalistic pieces of descriptive music. Those who loudly insist that American composers should write "American" music usually cannot tell, when questioned, what they mean by American music; but any composer who thinks it worth his while to placate them can easily do so by slipping in a few bars of *Yankee Doodle* here and a snatch of *Swing Low, Sweet Chariot* there. Here the association is simply a matter of place of origin: the tune is an American tune, and therefore it symbolizes America with an admirable flexibility which allows each listener to take it for whatever he personally happens to think America is or should be. A similar symbolism is to be found in Brahms' *Academic Festival Overture*, with its use of German student songs, and in the various pieces of religious music which incorporate the Dresden Amen.

In the same way that folk-tunes are used to symbolize the general feeling and civilization of a country, national anthems may represent it as a political or military unit. There is an excellent example of such a device towards the close of Tschaikowsky's *1812 Overture*. The subject is, of course, the Russian victory over the armies of Napoleon. It is easy enough—too easy, in fact—for Tschaikovsky to give the general idea of military pomp and activity, but how is he to identify the participants and their different fates? He can write a paean of victory, but how is the music to tell *whose* victory? Music cannot specify without external aid, but tunes already associated in the public mind with the two nations will require no commentary beyond this association. Therefore the *Marseillaise* is used for the armies of France, and both the Russian hymn "God Preserve Thy People" and the *Czarist Anthem* symbolize Russia. A considerable part of the composition, devoted to a representation of the Battle of Borodino, uses the *Marseillaise* fitfully and in broken phrases. After a good deal of this sort of commotion a long series of descending scale-figures, gradually slowing down, is used (as in the *Danse macabre*) to indicate flight and exhaustion. Then the hymn comes in pompously with the idea of religious thanksgiving. (The overture was written for the consecration of a cathedral in Moscow.) A few bars later the *Czarist Anthem* enters, played in octaves, *ffff*, by half a brass band and the two bassoons, four horns, three trombones, bass trombone, tuba, violas, 'cellos, and contrabasses of the orchestra. A military theme already well established in earlier parts of the overture is played against this by the other half of the band and all the orchestral instruments that are left over, while the whole "kitchen" helps with the rhythm, not to mention a battery of artillery (also *ffff*) if the community and conductor are sturdy enough to stand it. Tschaikowsky was not the man to do things by halves.*

In spite of the theatrical nature of this hullabaloo, it does manage to achieve its purpose, and that purpose could not possibly have been achieved without the quotation of musical themes having a pre-established connection with the fates of France and Russia.

This use of musical quotations can be very clearly distinguished from the ordinary borrowing of a theme for musical purposes. When Mendelssohn uses "Old Hundred" in the finale of a trio (*Op.* 66), he is borrowing thematic material only, and the effect would be much the same if it happened to have convivial rather than religious associations. In either case, Mendelssohn would be using it as a pattern of sounds and nothing more. Tschaikowsky, on the other hand, was little concerned with the *Marseillaise* or the Russian anthem as musical materials. What they happened to sound like was almost irrelevant in comparison with what they stood for, and if their significances had happened to be reversed, he would cheerfully have broken up the anthem in order to defeat it, and then gone on to score the *Marseillaise* for band, orchestra, and artillery.

Musical quotations programmatically used are really the same thing as the Leitmotiv, the only difference being that the quotation is chosen because its significance is already established, whereas the composer must establish the significance of his Leitmotiv. The Leitmotiv

* He had written to a friend, "The overture will be very banging and noisy." (Niecks, *Programme Music*, p. 434.) There is no record to show whether the cannon were used at the first performance, but the indications of the score have been faithfully followed in some later renditions.

plays a large rôle in program music, where it can easily represent a character or idea and can be repeated or modified according to changing circumstances. In fact, historically it was developed for instrumental program music by Berlioz and Liszt at the same time that Wagner was working out its operatic applications. The only real difference between the two uses lies in the fact that the composer of opera can, by the aid of actors, plot, and scenery, establish the significance of his motives unobtrusively. The composer of instrumental program music, on the other hand, must have verbal aid. Once the meaning is established, the two types of music use the motive in the same way.

Narrative program music seems to have been carried to its ultimate point in the works of Richard Strauss, and there is considerable difference of critical opinion as to whether this point constitutes an apotheosis or a *reductio ad absurdum*. Whatever the final aesthetic judgment may be, the principal features of the works are illuminating.

Strauss greatly enlarges the orchestra, particularly by the addition of instruments which produce noises rather than tones. The reason for this practice is clear: since noises are the rule and musical tones the exception in nature, the composer who sets out to produce the sounds accompanying any sequence of actions will find noises extremely useful. Strauss employs a big rattle to join in the uproar of merriment at some of the pranks of Till Eulenspiegel; he has a literal imitation of Till's ride through the pots and pans of a stall in the market place; and he introduces a theatrical wind-machine to represent Don Quixote's ride through the air. Even more important than the addition of new noise-makers to the orchestra is the extensive use of such more or less standard ones as snare drums, cymbals, and triangles. Both these tendencies are to be seen in a good deal of the more recent absolute music also, but the principal impetus seems to have been programmatic. Sometimes noise becomes a goal sought by the composer for its own sake and rejected by the audience on equally disinterested principles.* The writer of narrative music has also been forced, by his need for special

* Deems Taylor (*Of Men and Music*, p. 83) writes of George Antheil's *Ballet mécanique*: "I forget the entire instrumentation of this work, but I do recall that the score, among other things, called for ten grand pianos, one player-piano, six xylophones, four bass drums, a couple of automobile klaxons, a fire-alarm siren, and an airplane propeller—from which you can form a rough idea of how it sounded." (Reprinted from *Of Men and Music* by permission of Simon and Schuster, Inc. Copyright 1937, by Deems Taylor.) He goes on to tell how this concatenation of cacophony called forth what is probably the most damning audience-reaction ever seen in Carnegie Hall —and the cleverest.

effects of timbre as well as his general desire for the colossal, to employ large numbers of such semi-standard instruments as fifes, piccolos, contrabassoons, bass trombones, bells, and celestas.

Yet with all these impedimenta, the narrative composer, in so far as his purpose is really the telling of a story, is dependent on the written word. The various program-notes and interpretations of the works of Strauss furnish plenty of examples. In the folk-tales about Till Eulenspiegel there is no mention of his death, but Strauss has him hanged. At first the composer refused to give any program for the work.

> It is impossible for me to furnish a program to Eulenspiegel. Were I to put into words the thoughts which its several incidents suggested to me, they would seldom suffice, and might even give rise to offence. Let me leave it, therefore, to my hearers to "crack the hard nut" which the Rogue has provided for them. [There are two themes which pervade the whole work, and the Rogue is finally hanged.] For the rest, let them guess at the musical joke which a rogue has offered them.[2]

This was all that the early commentators were told. Hence they were sure of the death, but otherwise were left to pick at random among the ninety-six "histories" of the exploits of Till. Later, however, with characteristic inconsistency Strauss gave a critic a copy of the score in which he had labeled the twenty-six sections, and it then became possible to point with confidence to his ride through the stalls of the market-place, his disguise as a priest, his shocking of the Philistines, and a number of other episodes.

Don Juan's departure from this life was not specified, and the results of this uncertainty among the commentators are interesting. Strauss' *Don Juan* is based, not on Tirso de Molina or Mozart or Byron, but on Lenau's dramatic poem. All that Strauss gave by way of program was three extracts from Lenau dealing with the abstract idea of Don Juan's career rather than with any concrete adventures, and a few sparse indications in the score. In Lenau's version of the story, Don Juan, finding that his life has become a blank emptiness, deliberately allows himself to be killed in a duel, but the passage describing this event is not among those quoted on the score. Hence there is a good deal of uncertainty among the commentators about the end of Strauss' sensualist-on-principle. Characteristic comments include:

> The fatal sword-thrust, represented by a piercing dissonant high trumpet note, is famous.[3]

> A lightning harp-glissando, like the flash of a darting rapier; a sigh in an A-minor chord into which the *f* of the trumpets pierces like a thrust—and then

a collapse. The tremolos of the strings trickle down like dripping blood; there is a muffled, wailing chord, a last ebbing of blood—and all is over.[4]

Then comes the duel, with the death scene. . . . There is a tremendous orchestral crash; there is a long and eloquent silence. A *pianissimo* chord in A minor is cut into by a piercingly dissonant trumpet F, and then there is a last sigh, a mourning dissonance and resolution (trombones) to E minor.[5]

His death in a duel is easily recognized in the music.[6]

The debauch closes in a manner indicating the hero's fate, and at last his end is announced by the trumpet.[7]

A final elemental burst of passion stops abruptly before a long pause. The end is in dismal, dying harmonies,—a mere dull sigh of emptiness, a void of joy and even of the solace of poignant grief.[8]

[The two principal themes] combine and after a mighty climax sound out a short tragic coda.[9]

These comments have been arranged in an order of increasing abstraction. We see all views from the literal one by which the trumpets' F *is* a sword thrust, through interpretations in which it simply indicates an unspecified form of death, to a point of view which treats the entire passage as purely musical material. Thus they serve as an epitome of the whole problem of narrative music. Even the interpreters who go into some detail usually take pains to point out the triviality of such analysis, and to take the final position that "With program-music . . . it is a mistake to attempt to refer the music to details. Either it coheres as music, or it does not."[10] This is merely a rewording of Schumann's famous dictum, still in force nearly a century after it was first uttered. The only real concession which aesthetic judgment can make to the demands or execution of a program is that attached by Percy Buck to his statement of the general principle: *

There is only one sane test that can be applied, at this moment, to any piece of Programme-music by an unprejudiced person. Is the music, *qua* music, satisfactory to me apart from its programme; and if not, do I, in my own individual case, think that the deficiency is made good when I apply the programme and review my verdict?[11]

And it is highly unlikely that anyone who resents the muted brass in Strauss' *Don Quixote* as music will enjoy it when he is told that it is an imitation of bleating sheep.

* From Grove's *Dictionary of Music and Musicians*. By permission of The Macmillan Company, publishers.

CHAPTER XXII

Conclusion

WE HAVE seen that music and literature have many points in common, and that they also have essential differences which no attempts at imitation of one by the other have been able to overcome. Furthermore, we have found that though there are numerous accidental differences between them—such things as music's greater rhythmical flexibility and capacity for repetition, and literature's linear development—the essential difference is the one pointed out in our original classification of the fine arts: the sounds out of which the literary work is constructed must have an external significance, and those used in music require no such meaning.

We may well inquire, however, whether this difference is really essential, or whether it is merely due to the stages of development in which we find these arts. Deems Taylor has recently pointed out [1] that the history of painting shows a steady development from illustration to abstraction, while that of music shows the opposite tendency from abstraction to illustration. We might go further, and say that painting went from the attempt to represent objects exactly as they are, through a freedom deliberately to distort them, to a school of abstraction in which patterns are created for their own interest with no representational intention whatsoever. Conversely, the general course of instrumental music has been from pure formal abstraction, through formal patterns designed at the same time to represent states of mind and feeling, to the illustration of objects and stories.

In literature no such simple line of development can be seen as in painting, and we must speak in very broad generalizations, without taking into account the numerous individual exceptions (even entire schools and periods) which disrupt the simple pattern of development. Nevertheless, the general course of literature seems to have been, like that of painting, from the literal and concrete to the abstract. This change can easily be seen within individual literatures: Homer was presumably incapable of the degree of abstraction found in *Prometheus Bound*—or, if capable of it, he was not interested in it, which comes to much the same thing. Though various ideas govern his characters, we always feel that the principal interest of the Homeric poems lies in the persons or—even more literally—in their actions. But Prometheus is a symbol rather than a person, and all his action in the play is internal. His dealings are with such personified abstractions as Strength and Force, which are given human form merely for the convenience of the dramatist and spectators.

The same thing may be seen less obviously in the development of occidental literature as a whole. The *Inferno* and *Purgatorio* are devoted almost entirely to a treatment of sin, but sin is an abstraction which Dante, going beyond the standard mediaeval allegory, does not personify. Nevertheless, his abstractions are based on a dogmatic theology and a literally conceived and minutely described cosmography. Both of these the reader is unquestioningly to accept. The further step taken by Goethe can be seen in the concluding scene of Part II of *Faust*, where the hero's soul ascends through various levels (suggestive of Dante) to the final solution of the riddle of human existence. Goethe's orderly heaven, however, is not a fact from which certain abstract conclusions follow. He made this quite clear when he explained that, in his attempt to present the metaphysical and transcendental, he took over the heaven and angels of Christian theology *as a poetic device* which would help to present the abstract thought in a concrete form.[2] Since Goethe's time the nature of the abstraction has changed, but not the general trend. Recent literature has constantly sought to present that one abstraction which includes within itself all others—the human consciousness. Like Goethe, such writers as Proust, Joyce, and Aiken have used persons and events merely as a necessary scaffolding to present the abstraction of consciousness itself.

Thus we see that, in a very general way, literature has tended to abandon the representational element and to devote itself increasingly to the presentation of abstraction. This development can be clearly seen in the works which have been mentioned, each of which was deliberately chosen as the most complete literary abstraction to be found in its period. If, as seems reasonable, these works are part of a general tendency, then it will follow that music and literature have started out as opposites and each has set as the goal of its own development the starting point of the other.

In this pursuit of abstraction, however, literature has not abandoned its essential nature, for it still seeks to represent things outside itself. The difference is that the objects of representation have become things not immediately perceptible by the senses. Literary attempts to go further than this and create an "absolute" poetry, analogous to absolute music, in which words shall be employed to make patterns of sound without reference to their conventional meanings, have never grown out of the faddist category. Similarly, as we saw in the last chapter, program music has never existed in a pure state—has never set out to represent its object, regardless of how the result may sound. As far as concreteness and abstraction are concerned, the two arts have started from opposite extremes and have both ultimately taken a middle-ground of compromise.

The great difference is that all literature of any value is based on this compromise. It must have a satisfying structural pattern of its own, and it must communicate something outside that pattern, though in keeping with it and reinforced by it. The greatest instrumental music, on the other hand, has for its main concern the patterns themselves. This statement will hold good whether we agree with the extreme absolutists that this is its only concern, or whether we decide that it also communicates disembodied ideas and moods. And even the extreme programmatists admit that the abstract pattern is the principal concern when they concede that good program music must also be intelligible on an absolute basis, for they never make the converse statement that all good music must be programmatically intelligible.

The balance between pattern and representation, then, is not so complete in music as in literature. There are two possible explanations of this situation. From a historical point of view, we must remember that instrumental music is a very young art, and even when we allow for the fact that other arts are slower in their evolution than music,[*] we still see that its course of development has been relatively short. Furthermore, only during the latter half of its history has the representation of external things been one of its primary concerns. But already the attempts at such representation have led to the development of new types, the employment of larger and more varied orchestras, and some other general changes. Is it not possible, then, that music simply has not yet had sufficient time to develop its capacities for the expression of things outside itself? The question is necessarily unanswerable and must remain so for at least the next five centuries, but the possibility should temper our judgments.

In the light of the art as we know it, however, and on philosophical grounds, it would seem that music, by its very nature, differs from literature in this respect, and that its attempts at complete compromise between form and representation must continue to be, like literary attempts at absolutism, interesting meanders which cannot alter the general course of the stream.

Notes

CHAPTER I

1. Milton, *Paradise Lost*, I, 44–47.
2. Coleridge, *The Ancient Mariner*, 289–291.
3. Dryden, *Oedipus*, IV, i.
4. Pope, *The Rape of the Lock*, III, 95–98.
5. *Poetics*, XIII, 7 (Butcher's translation).

CHAPTER II

1. Irving Babbitt, *The New Laokoon* (London, 1910), p. 182.
2. See A. W. Rimington, *Colour-Music: the Art of Mobile Colour* (London, 1912), and A. B. Klein, *Colour-Music: the Art of Light*, 2nd. ed. (London, 1930).
3. Stabenow, *Arthur Schopenhauer: Schriften über Musik* (Regensburg, 1922), pp. 112–113.
4. J. C. Squire, *Collected Parodies* (London, n.d.), p. 176.

CHAPTER III

1. W. H. Frere, *Grove's Dictionary*, Art. "Plain-Song."
2. The problem is discussed in the opening chapters of Saintsbury's *History of English Prosody*.
3. Lanier, *The Science of English Verse* (N. Y., 1901). See also J. P. Dabney, *The Musical Basis of Verse* (N. Y., 1901).
4. *Samson Agonistes*, 40–42.
5. J. C. Pope, *The Rhythm of Beowulf* (New Haven, 1941).

CHAPTER IV

1. Tennyson, *The Princess*, VII, 206–207.
2. Spenser, *Faerie Queene*, I, i, 41.
3. From the sonnet beginning, "Only until this cigarette is ended."
4. Tennyson, *Morte D'Arthur*, 186–192.
5. *Sämtliche Werke von Detlev von Liliencron* (Berlin, n.d.), VII, 51–52.
6. The opening line of "Le cor."

7. *Oxford Book of French Verse*, No. 317.
8. *Ecclesiastes*: 12:6.
9. *Kubla Khan*, line 30.
10. S. Sitwell, *The Thirteenth Caesar, and Other Poems* (London, 1924), p. 46 ff.
11. *Poetry: a Magazine of Verse*, XIV, 152–159 (June, 1919).
12. Later included in "The House of Dust," IV, iv. See Aiken, *Selected Poems* (N. Y., 1929), pp. 143–144.
13. E. V. Gordon, *An Introduction to Old Norse* (London, 1927), Introduction, xli.
14. Milton, *Samson Agonistes*, 227–230.

CHAPTER V

1. Plato, *The Laws*, II, 669 (Jowett's translation).
2. Ronsard, *Abrégé de l'art poétique françois*, Sec. 1.
3. Lanier, *Music and Poetry* (N. Y., 1898), p. 6.
4. *Ibid.*, "The Centennial Cantata," pp. 80–90.
5. This and the following references to Bridges are from his essay "On the Musical Setting of Poetry" (*Collected Essays, Papers, Etc.*, London, 1935, vol. 9) unless otherwise indicated.
6. *Collected Essays, Papers, Etc.*, 9, 77–156.
7. Combarieu, *Les rapports de la musique et de la poésie, considérées au point de vue de l'expression* (Paris, 1893), pp. 179–180.
8. *Ibid.*, Preface, xxvi.

CHAPTER VI

1. Morrison C. Boyd, *Elizabethan Music and Musical Criticism*, (Philadelphia, 1940), p. 130.
2. Charles Avison, *An Essay on Musical Expression* (London, 1753), pp. 57–59. This essay was first published in 1752. In 1753 Dr. W. Hayes anonymously published *Remarks on Mr. Avison's Essay on Musical Expression*

by way of rejoinder, and during the same year Avison republished his *Essay*, adding a reply to Hayes.
3. *Ibid.*, p. 66.

CHAPTER VII

1. Albert Schweitzer, *J. S. Bach*, tr. by Ernest Newman (London, 1935), II, 38. The first 122 pages of Vol. II contain an extraordinarily interesting discussion of the relationship between text and music in the works of Bach.
2. *Ibid.*, II, 48.
3. *Ibid.*, II, 81.
4. Erich Sorantin, *The Problem of Musical Expression* (Nashville, 1932).
5. "The Eve of St. Agnes," line 56.
6. Combarieu, *Les rapports de la musique et de la poésie*, p. 239.
7. Coleridge, *Biographia Literaria*, Ch. I.
8. *Ibid.*, Ch. XIV.
9. Cäsar Flaischeln, *Zwischenklänge: Altes und Neues* (Stuttgart, 1921), pp. 133–191. The "Silversterlied" is on p. 189.
10. See Friedrich Chrysander, "Ein Klavier-Phantasie von Karl Phillip Emanuel Bach mit nachträglich von Gerstenberg eingefügten Gesangmelodien zu zwei verschiednen Texten," *Vierteljahrsschrift für Musikwissenschaft*, 1891, pp. 1–25.
11. *Theodor Körners sämmtliche Werke*, Reclam ed., pp. 120–123.
12. Dorchain, *Poésies, 1881–1894* (Paris, 1895), pp. 267–268.
13. Alfred de Musset, "Rapelle-toi," *Poésies nouvelles* (Garnier: Paris, n.d.), pp. 196–197.
14. Leigh Hunt, *Poetical Works* (Oxford, 1923), p. 742.

CHAPTER VIII

1. Stabenow, *Arthur Schopenhauer: Schriften über Musik* (Regensburg, 1922), p. 153.
2. "An Essay of Dramatic Poesy," *Essays of John Dryden* (Ker's edition), I, 63.
3. Coleridge, *Biographia Literaria*, Ch. XIV.
4. Aristotle, *Poetics* (Butcher's translation), IX, 9.

5. *Ibid.*, IX, 10.
6. *The Poems of S. T. Coleridge* (London, 1881), p. 169.
7. Newman, *A Musical Motley* (N. Y., 1925), p. 133.
8. Berlioz, *Les soirées de l'orchestre*, Vingt et unième soirée.
9. Quoted from Hadow, "Music and Drama," *Collected Essays* (London, 1928), p. 175.
10. Mann, *Leiden und Grösse der Meister* (Berlin, 1935), p. 96.
11. Wagner, *Tristan und Isolde*, II, iii (Breitkopf & Härtel's miniature score, p. 692).

CHAPTER IX

1. See S. G. Spaeth, *Milton's Knowledge of Music* (Weimar, 1913).
2. See Irving Babbitt, *The New Laokoon: an Essay on the Confusion of the Arts* (London, 1910). The title is, of course, an allusion to Lessing's *Laokoon* (1766), which attacked the descriptive poets who tried to compete with painting.
3. See W. M. Flinders Petrie, *The Revolutions of Civilisation* (N. Y., 1922), for the general theory; and Cecil Gray, *Predicaments, or Music and the Future* (London, 1936), Ch. III, for a more extended application of this theory to music and literature.
4. Pater, "The School of Giorgione," in *The Renaissance*.
5. Schopenhauer, "Wie die Musik zu werden, ist das Ziel jeder Kunst," *Schriften über Musik*, p. 159.
6. Coleridge, *Biographia Literaria*, Ch. XIV, last paragraph.
7. H. C. Colles, Grove's *Dictionary*, Art. "Form."
8. *Judges*: 5: 27.
9. Malory, *Le Morte D'Arthur*, XXI, 5.
10. *Iliad*, VI: A 87–98   269–278 302–310
    B 244–246 248–250
    C 378–380 382–385
11. Lines 59–66.
12. Wordsworth, "To the Daisy," ll. 9–40.
13. Shelley, "To a Skylark," ll. 36–50.
14. Fitzgerald, *Rubáiyát* (4th ed.), Stanzas 68–70.

15. See my article "On Reading *Beowulf*," *Sewanee Review*, L, 78–86.
16. For the climactic use of repetition see my article on "Triumphant Repetition in Music," *Kenyon Review*, III, 52–62.

CHAPTER X

1. *Psalms*: 19: 1–2.
2. Rossetti, "Lovesight," *The House of Life*, No. 4.
3. Housman, *Last Poems*, XXXVII.

CHAPTER XI

1. Shakespeare, *Hamlet*, II, ii.
2. Milton, *Paradise Lost*, IV, 641–656.
3. *Ludwig Tiecks sämmtliche Werke* (Wien, 1818), XIII, 5–154.
4. Fletcher, *Preludes and Symphonies* (N. Y., 1930), pp. 50–51.
5. Gautier, *Émaux et camées* (Paris, 1852).
6. Conkling, *Ship's Log and Other Poems* (N. Y., 1924), pp. 131–140; Hillyer, in Untermeyer, *Modern American Poetry*.
7. Plattensteiner, *Musikalische Gedichte* (Leipzig, 1927), p. 21.
8. *Ibid.*, pp. 52–53.
9. Merens-Melmer, *Sous la signe de la musique* (Paris, 1926).
10. London, 1927.
11. Sitwell, *The One Hundred and One Harlequins* (London, 1922), p. 48 ff.

CHAPTER XII

1. Catullus, Nos. 16, 36, 52, 57.
2. *Oxford Book of Italian Verse*, No. 39.
3. "Nur wer die Sehnsucht kennt," *Oxford Book of German Verse*, No. 124.
4. *Ibid.*, No. 193.
5. *Oxford Book of French Verse*, No. 312.
6. Schelling, *A Book of Elizabethan Lyrics* (Boston, 1895), pp. 11–12.
7. *Oxford Book of French Verse*, No. 304.
8. *Oxford Book of German Verse*, No. 181.
9. Aiken, "The House of Dust," *Selected Poems* (N. Y., 1929).
10. Vialls, *Music Fancies and Other Verses* (Westminster, 1899) pp. 7–8.

11. *Ibid.*, p. 11.
12. "Tłúmaczenia Szopena," *Poesje Kornela Ujejskiego* (Lipsk, 1866).
13. See Richard Dehmel, *Aber die Liebe* (Berlin, 1907), pp. 50–56, for a German translation of this poem.
14. Johnson, *Songs of Liberty and Other Poems* (N. Y., 1897), pp. 20–23.
15. Edition of the Istituto Nazionale, *l'Orto e la prora* (Verona, 1930), p. 38.
16. *Oxford Book of English Verse*, No. 774.
17. *Oxford Book of German Verse*, No. 86.
18. See John Murray Gibbon, *Melody and the Lyric from Chaucer to the Cavaliers* (N. Y., 1930), for discussion and illustrations of some aspects of this influence.
19. Schelling, *A Book of Elizabethan Lyrics*, pp. 24–26.
20. *Oxford Book of English Verse*, No. 240.
21. Aiken, *Selected Poems*, pp. 172–174 ("Senlin: A Biography," II, ii).
22. *Ibid.*, pp. 54–56 ("The Jig of Forslin," V, iv).
23. Schelling, *op. cit.*, pp. 31–33.
24. *Oxford Book of Greek Verse*, No. 573. A translation by John Addington Symons is available in Mark van Doren, *Anthology of World Poetry* (Blue Ribbon ed.), pp. 315–320.
25. *Oxford Book of Latin Verse*, No. 320. A translation is available in Van Doren (see previous note), pp. 444–449.
26. *Oxford Book of English Verse*, No. 105.
27. *Oxford Book of German Verse*, No. 366.
28. Nietzsche, *Gedichte* (Insel-Bücherei), pp. 6–7.
29. *Oxford Book of French Verse*, Nos. 25–29.
30. Untermeyer, *Modern British Poetry* (4th revised ed.), p. 84.
31. Chaucer has three other examples of the same form in "Merciless Beaute," *The Student's Chaucer* (Oxford, 1929), p. 121.

32. *Oxford Book of French Verse*, Nos. 15–17.
33. *Ibid.*, No. 40.
34. *Ibid.*, No. 46.
35. All the poems mentioned in this paragraph are to be found in Woods, *Poetry of the Victorian Period* (N. Y., 1930).
36. *Oxford Book of Italian Verse*, No. 130.

CHAPTER XIII

1. Gautier, "l'Art," *Oxford Book of French Verse*, No. 290. A translation by Santayana is available in Van Doren, *Anthology of World Poetry* (Blue Ribbon ed.), pp. 755–756.
2. Ferguson, *A History of Musical Thought* (N. Y., 1935), p. 217.
3. De Quincey, *Collected Writings*, ed. by David Masson (London, 1897), XIII, 270–327.
4. *Ibid.*, 318–327.
5. This evidence is presented in my essay, "The Musical Structure of De Quincey's *Dream-Fugue*," *Musical Quarterly*, XXIV, 341–350. The following discussion is based on that article.
6. De Quincey, *Collected Writings*, XIII, 328–330.
7. This diagram is adapted from a similar general scheme for a four-part fugue in Ferguson, *op. cit.*, p. 215.
8. "Dream-Fugue on the above Theme of Sudden Death," *Blackwood's Edinburgh Magazine*, LXVI, 750–755 (Dec., 1849).
9. A. H. Japp, *The Posthumous Works of Thomas De Quincey* (London, 1891), I, 323–325. A version of part of Section IV of the *Dream-Fugue*, evidently antecedent to its first publication, shows no changes of importance from the point of view of form.
10. Tennyson, "To Milton," *Poetic and Dramatic Works* (Student's Cambridge ed.), p. 268.
11. Moody and Lovett, *A History of English Literature* (N. Y., 1930), p. 179.
12. *Paradise Lost*, XI, 554–559.

13. Stanzas xii–xviii (Modern Library ed., pp. 89–90).
14. e. g., Delmore Schwartz, "The Repetitive Heart: Eleven Poems in Imitation of the Fugue Form," *In Dreams Begin Responsibilities* (Norfolk, 1938), pp. 91–104. Rumer Godden's *Take Three Tenses; a Fugue in Time* (Boston, 1945) succeeds in giving a contrapuntal texture to fiction by using different periods in the history of a family as the voices, but it makes no attempt to follow the specific form of the fugue.
15. Joyce, *Ulysses* (Modern Library ed.), pp. 252–286.

CHAPTER XIV

1. *Oxford Book of French Verse*, No. 285.
2. No. 15 of the *Nouvelles méditations poétiques*.
3. Sterne, *Tristram Shandy*, Book VI, Chapter xi.
4. Woods, *Poetry of the Victorian Period* (N. Y., 1930), pp. 788–793.
5. Plattensteiner, *Neue musikalische Gedichte* (Leipzig, 1928), pp. 36–37.
6. *Ibid.*, "Brahms, IV. Symphonie," pp. 42–43; and "Bruckner-Symphonie," pp. 46–49.
7. *Ibid.*, "Kreutzer Sonata," pp. 20–23 (first movement).
8. Grace Hazard Conkling, *Afternoons of April: a Book of Verse* (London, 1916), pp. 13–20.
9. These poems and others of the same type are to be found in Fletcher's *Preludes and Symphonies* (N. Y., 1930), which is a reprint of *Irradiations: Sand and Spray* (1915) and *Goblins and Pagodas* (1916).
10. *Goblins and Pagodas*, Preface, xx–xxi.
11. This and the two following quotations are from the Preface to *Preludes and Symphonies*.
12. *Preludes and Symphonies*, pp. 43–60.
13. Todhunter, *Sounds and Sweet Airs* (London, 1905), pp. 86–96.
14. *The Musical Opus in Poetry*, unpublished dissertation, University of Wisconsin, 1934.

15. *Poems of Sidney Lanier* (N. Y., 1884), pp. 60–70.
16. Legge, *A Symphony and Other Pieces* (London, 1913), pp. 1–47.
17. Plattensteiner, "Musikalische Begebenheit," *Musikalische Gedichte* (Leipzig, 1927), pp. 54–55.
18. *L'Héroïque* (Paris, 1921) and *La Pastorale* (Paris, 1924).
19. André Coeuroy (*Revue Musicale*, Feb., 1925, pp. 206–208) gives a brief account of the two novels already mentioned and says that Cadilhac is at work on a *Pathétique*.
20. *Ludwigs Werke* (ed. by Schweizer), I, 9–104.
21. André Coeuroy, *Musique et littérature* (Paris, 1923), pp. 68–72. The passage gives a good resumé of Ludwig's contrapuntal theory and of the play.

13. *Time in the Rock*, XCII, p. 132.
14. *Poetry: A Magazine of Verse*, XIV, 152–159.
15. *Blue Voyage* (N. Y., 1927), pp. 291–292.
16. See Gehring, *The Basis of Musical Pleasure* (N. Y., 1910).
17. *Nocturne of Remembered Spring and Other Poems* (Boston, 1917), p. 16.
18. *The Jig of Forslin*, I, vii.
19. *The House of Dust*, III, viii.
20. *The Jig of Forslin*, I, vi.
21. *Preludes for Memnon*, XVI.
22. *Time in the Rock*, LXXXIII.
23. p. 37.
24. The "Argument" printed as introduction to *The Pilgrimage of Festus* (N. Y., 1923).
25. *The Pilgrimage of Festus*, V, i.
26. *The House of Dust*, IV, iii.

CHAPTER XV

1. Whitman, *Song of Myself*, Sections 15, 13, 18, and 26, respectively.
2. *Ibid.*, Section 52.
3. "Come up from the Fields, Father," line 28.
4. See the entries in Whitman's *Specimen Days* under August 12, 1863; and under March 4 and April 16, 1865.

CHAPTER XVI

1. As other conspicuous examples we may mention "Variations," *Selected Poems* (N. Y., 1929), pp. 66–76, and *Time in the Rock* (N. Y., 1936), LXV, p. 95.
2. *The Coming Forth by Day of Osiris Jones* (N. Y., 1931), p. 37.
3. See *Preludes for Memnon* (N. Y., 1931), Sec. XXXV, for an excellent example.
4. *Senlin*, II, ii.
5. *Senlin*, II, x.
6. First published in *Poetry: A Magazine of Verse*, 1919. Included in *The House of Dust*, IV, iv.
7. *The Jig of Forslin*, V, iv.
8. *Senlin*, II, ii.
9. *Selected Poems*, pp. 3–6.
10. Goepp, *Great Works of Music*, I, 386.
11. III, i.
12. V, v.

CHAPTER XVII

1. Tovey, *Essays in Musical Analysis*, IV, 129–130.
2. Huxley, *Point Counter Point* (Harper's Modern Classics), pp. 293–294.
3. Oskar Walzel, "Leitmotive in Dichtungen," *Das Wortkunstwerk* (Leipzig, 1926), pp. 151–181.
4. Ronald Peacock, *Das Leitmotiv bei Thomas Mann* (*Sprache u. Dichtung*, Heft 55; Bern, 1934). G. Donati-Petténi, *D'Annunzio e Wagner* (Firenze, 1923).
5. Thomas Mann, *Stories of Three Decades* (N. Y., 1936), Preface, p. vi.
6. H. A. Basilius, "Thomas Mann's Use of Musical Structure and Techniques in *Tonio Kröger*," *Germanic Review*, XIX, 284–308 (Dec., 1944), gives a much more detailed analysis of both the sonata-form and the use of the Leitmotiv than that found in the following discussion. My own analysis was written before this article came to my attention; thus the two serve for mutual confirmation.

CHAPTER XVIII

1. See Newman, "The Small Poem in Music," *A Musical Motley* (N. Y., 1925), pp. 40–53.

2. *The Oxford Book of English Verse*, No. 27.
3. Güntter, *Walther von der Vogelweide, mit einer Auswahl aus Minnesang und Spruchdichtung* (Leipzig, 1899), p. 2.
4. *A Musical Motley*, p. 53.
5. Frederick Niecks, *Programme Music in the Last Four Centuries* (London, 1906), pp. 274–275 and 302–303.
6. *Ibid.*, pp. 280–281.
7. A. Kalisch, Art. "Strauss, Richard," Grove's *Dictionary*.
8. *Ibid.*
9. *Ibid.*, and Niecks, *op. cit.*
10. Niecks, *op. cit.*, p. 511.

CHAPTER XIX

1. The best account of both the history of program music and the views of its practitioners is Frederick Niecks, *Programme Music in the Last Four Centuries* (London, 1906).
2. For examples see: L. Hoffmann, *Ein Programm zu Beethovens Neunter Symphonie* (Berlin, 1870); Mme. Edgar Quinet, *Ce que dit la musique* (Paris, 1893), notes; Richard Plattensteiner, *Neue musikalische Gedichte* (Leipzig, 1928), pp. 31–34; and Jules Combarieu, *Les rapports de la musique et de la poésie* (Paris, 1893), p. 113.
3. Guy Albert d'Amato, *Beethoven Beethovenized* (privately printed: Boston, 1941).
4. Hadow, *The Place of Music among the Arts* (Oxford, 1933), p. 29.
5. Ambros, *The Boundaries of Music and Poetry* (N. Y., 1893), pp. 136–137.
6. Fuller-Maitland, *The Spell of Music* (London, 1926), pp. 100–101.
7. The edition used in the following discussion is that of Breitkopf & Härtel, Leipzig, 1922. The English translation bears the title of *The Beautiful in Music* (N. Y., 1891).
8. Hanslick, Ch. II.
9. *Ibid.*, Ch. III.
10. *Ibid.*
11. *Ibid.*
12. *Ibid.*, Ch. V.

13. Leonard, *Two Lives*, Part III, xxvi.
14. Busoni, *Entwurf einer neuen Ästhetik der Tonkunst* (Insel-Bücherei: Leipzig, n.d.), p. 16.
15. MacDowell, *Critical and Historical Essays* (N. Y., 1912), pp. 261–273.
16. Carl Spitteler, "Die Allegorie im Orchester," *Lachende Wahrheiten* (Leipzig, 1898), pp. 151–166.
17. Bar 454 ff.
18. Grove, *Beethoven and his Nine Symphonies* (London, n. d.), p. 361.
19. See Harry P. Weld, "An Experimental Study of Musical Enjoyment," *American Journal of Psychology*, Vol. 23; and Max Schoen, *The Effects of Music* (N. Y., 1927). Schoen's book is a collection of fourteen studies by different psychologists.
20. Printed with the miniature score, Munich, 1904.
21. *Ein Heldenleben . . . Erläuterungsschrift von Friedrich Rösch, nebst einer umschreibenden Dichtung von Eberhard König* (Leipzig, n.d.).
22. Tovey, *Essays in Musical Analysis* (London, 1936), IV, 3–16.
23. Written to Marc André Souchay, Oct. 15, 1842: *Briefe von Felix Mendelssohn Bartholdy* (London, 1887), p. 80.
24. Niecks, *Programme Music*, p. 190.

CHAPTER XX

1. Grove, *Beethoven and his Nine Symphonies*, p. 188. A good many points in the following discussion are based on Grove's account of this symphony, and individual references on this material are not given.
2. See Niecks, *Programme Music*, pp. 61–62.
3. Tovey, *Essays in Musical Analysis*, IV, 92.
4. Niecks, *op. cit.*, p. 175.
5. *Ibid.*, p. 176.
6. Robert Haven Schauffler, *Beethoven: the Man who Freed Music* (N. Y., 1935), p. 264.
7. Niecks, *op. cit.*, p. 176.
8. For a discussion of this type of poetry see E. D. Snyder, *Hypnotic Poetry* (Philadelphia, 1930).

CHAPTER XXI

1. Niecks, *Programme Music,* pp. 14–16.
2. *Ibid.,* pp. 501–502.
3. *Ibid.,* p. 499.
4. Richard Specht, *Richard Strauss und sein Werk* (Leipzig, 1921), I, 190.
5. Philip Hale, quoted by Lawrence Gilman, *Stories of Symphonic Music* (N. Y., 1907), p. 264. The passage is not in Burk's edition of Hale's program notes.
6. Tovey, *Essays in Musical Analysis,* IV, 158.
7. Upton & Borowski, *The Standard Concert Guide,* revised ed. (Chicago, 1930), p. 467.
8. Goepp, *Great Works of Music* (N. Y., n.d.), III, 278.
9. Richard Specht, introductory note to Eulenburg edition of miniature score.
10. Tovey, *Essays in Musical Analysis,* IV, 155.
11. Article on "Programme Music," Grove's *Dictionary.*

CHAPTER XXII

1. Deems Taylor, *The Well Tempered Listener* (N. Y., 1940), p. 238.
2. Goethe, *Conversations with Eckermann,* June 6, 1831.
3. Hanslick, *Vom Musikalisch-Schönen,* Ch. III.

Index

Except for a few works like *La Marseillaise*, works of music and literature are listed under the names of their authors or composers.

AABA formula, 125, 136 n., 196.

ABA form, as movement in larger work, 161; expanded in sonata-form, 162; in literature, 136–140, 166, 170, 175, 195–196; in music, 135–136, 140.

Absolute music, 229; poetry, 270.

Abstraction, in music and literature, 268–271.

Aeschylus, *Prometheus Bound*, 269.

Aesop, *Fables*, 241.

Aiken, Conrad, ABA form, use of, 137; *Blue Voyage*, 203–204; *Brownstone Eclogues*, 195; *The Charnel Rose*, 201; *The Coming Forth by Day of Osiris Jones*, 206; compared to A. Huxley, 210–211; *A Counterpoint*, 40, 197; *Disenchantment: A Tone Poem*, 203; *Earth Triumphant*, 203; *Evensong*, 198–199; *The House of Dust*, 196, 197, 201, 207; *The Jig of Forslin*, 196, 199–201, 204, 205; *Meditation on a June Evening*, 204–205; musical techniques in poetry of, 195–207; *The Pilgrimage of Festus*, 196, 204, 206; *Selected Poems*, 195; *Senlin: A Biography*, 142–143, 196, 201, 204; sonata-form, use of, 165, 172; stream of consciousness, use of, 269; *Time in the Rock*, 201; *Variations*, 196.

Allegory, moral, 171; orchestral, 236, 254.

Alliteration, 36, 104, 173.

Alma Mater songs, 85.

Annunzio, G. d', influenced by Wagner (*Trionfo della Morte*), 211–212; *Sopra un Adagio di J. Brahms*, 139.

Answer, in fugue, 150 n.

Antheil, George, *Ballet Méchanique*, 265 n.

Anthology, Greek, 222.

Architecture, 7; balance in, 114; "frozen music," 9; relation to other arts, 9.

Ariosto, L., 101.

Aristotle, 257; on episodic plots, 89–90; on poet as maker of plots, 89; on poetic justice, 5.

Art, and science, 1–6.

Arts, fine and useful, 7; static and dynamic, 10; temporal and spatial, 10; visual and auditory, 8.

Aside, in drama, 98.

Assonance, 36, 104.

Autonomous aesthetic of music, 244.

Avison, Charles, 60, 62; *Essay on Musical Expression*, 53–54; on musical imitation, 58.

Babbitt, Irving, on confusion of arts, 100.

Bach, C. P., 85.

Bach, J. S., 73, 149; ABA form, use of, 135; *Air for the G String*, 255; fugues, 255; motifs of, 67, 94; setting of texts, 63–64; *St. Matthew Passion*, 35.

Bagatelle, 110, 128.

Balance and contrast, 103; in literature, 114–122; in music, 122–127.

Ballad, 45; repetition in, 112.

Ballade, 106, 110, 128, 219; both musical and literary form, 128.

Banville, T. de, *Nous n'irons plus au bois*, 137.

Baroda, Old Whore of, 37.

Baudelaire, C., *Hymne*, 137.

Beauty, musical, defined, 232.

Becket, Thomas à, 186.

Beethoven, L. v., 5, 33, 72, 241; *Diabelli Variations*, 210; *Heiligenstadt Testament*, 249 n.; *Missa Solemnis*, 44; *Quartet, B Flat Major*, 210; *Sonata "Ap-*

passionata," 171, 230 n.; *Sonata, Kreutzer,* 128; *Sonata, Pathétique,* 148; *Sonata, "Moonlight,"* 230 n.; Symphonies, 102, 209, 259; *Symphony No. 3 (Eroica),* 128, 175, 186, 187; *Symphony No. 5,* 90, 131, 173, 194; *Symphony No. 6 (Pastoral),* 36, 174 n., 175, 230, 233, 238, 245, 246–251, 254, 257; *Symphony No. 7,* 166, 168 n., 230; *Symphony No. 9,* 11, 28, 128–129, 142, 143, 173, 175, 230, 235, 236, 253.

Benson, A. C., *Land of Hope and Glory,* 85.

Beowulf, 105, 108, 117.

Berlin, Irving, *God Bless America,* 86.

Berlioz, H., 246; on Beethoven's *5th,* 90; on Beethoven's *9th,* 236; *idée fixe,* 94, 173, 226; Leitmotiv, use of, 265; orchestra, influence on, 259; *Les Soirées de l'Orchestre,* 91.

Bible, King James, 114–117.

Bion, *Lament for Adonis,* 143.

Bird-imitations, in Beethoven's *6th,* 250–251.

Blake, W., *The Tiger,* 137.

Blank verse, 8, 221.

Böcklin, A., *Das Gefilde der Seligen,* 225; *Die Toteninsel,* 225.

Borodino, Battle of, 263–264.

Bourré, 168.

Brahms, J., 88; *Academic Festival Overture,* 263; poem on, by d'Annunzio, 139; symphonies, 255; *Symphony No. 2,* 173, 199; transcription from Gluck, 136.

Bridges, Robert, on text and music, 46–51; triolets, 144.

Brockes, B. H., descriptive poetry of, 245.

Browne, Sir Thomas, 159.

Browne, William, *A Welcome,* 141–142.

Browning, R., *Cavalier Tunes,* 23–24; *Charles Avison,* 53; dramatic monologues, 62; *Master Hughues of Saxe-Gotha,* 159; *The Ring and the Book,* 133–134.

Buck, Percy, on program music, 267.

Bürger, G. A., *Der Wilde Jäger,* as source for Franck, 225.

Burns, Robert, *Green Grow the Rashes, O,* 140–141; *Tam O' Shanter,* 107.

Busoni, F., on musical representation, 234, 257.

Byrd, William, musical description of battle, 257.

Byron, Lord, 266; as source for Liszt, 224.

Cadenza, in concerto, 162.

Cadilhac, Paul-Émile, symphonic novels (*La Pastorale*), 174–176, 209.

Calverly, C. S., *Ballad,* 146.

Campion, T., 45, 53.

Carnival of Venice, The, 130.

Catullus, use of ABA form, 136.

Caxton, W., 121.

Cazalis, Henri, as source for Saint-Saëns, 225, 260–261.

Cervantes, M. de, 112 n.

Chamisso, A. von, 137.

Chanting, 49.

Chant royal, 110.

Charles d'Orléans, rondeaux, 144.

Chaucer, G., *Book of the Duchess,* 104 n.; repetition in, 112; rondeau from *The Parlement of Foules,* 145.

Cherubini, L., *Non mi negate, no,* 85.

Chesterton, G. K., *Lepanto,* 26–27.

Chinese music, 66.

Chopin, F., 28; *Funeral March,* 109, 110, 135, 136, 138; *Nocturne, Op. 37, No. 1,* 137; poems on, by Ujejski, 138; *Prelude No. 15,* 136, 139; *Preludes,* 223; *Scherzo in B Flat Minor,* 109.

Christine de Pisan, *Rondeaux,* 145.

Cimabue, G., 118.

Circular development, 165, 193.

Civil War, American, 186.

Claudius, M., *Der Tod und das Mädchen,* 140.

Closing subject, 162.

Coda, 163, 192, 215.

Coleridge, S. T., 82, 162; *Christabel,* 27; *Kubla Khan,* 37; *Lines Composed in a Concert Room,* 90; on imagination, 101–102, 116; on logic of poetry, 81.

Color-organ, 10.

Combarieu, J., on text and music, 50.

Communication, in artistic process, 4.

Concerto, 128, 161.

Confidante, in French drama, 98.

Conkling, G. H., sonata form attempted (*Symphony of a Mexican Garden*), 165–169, 176; *Variations on a Theme,* 130.

Corneille, P., 98.

Cornelius, P., *Ein Ton* (*The Monotone*), 83–84.
Counter exposition, 150.
Counterpoint, 38–43; Aiken on, 202; Fletcher on, 169.
Counter-subject, in fugue, 150, 154.
Couperin, F., *Soeur Monique*, 241.
Cycles in art, 101.
Cyclical form, 173, 227.

Dactylic hexameter, 191 n.
Dance, 7, 10.
Dante Alighieri, 4, 255; *Commedia*, 101, 149, 225, 269; symbolism of rhyme, 104 n.
Daudet, A., 174.
Debussy, C., *Afternoon of a Faun* (*Prélude à 'L'Après-Midi d'un Faune'*), 32, 240, 241, 253–254, 255.
Declamatory settings, 49.
De Quincey, T., 177; *Dream Fugue*, 151, 153–160; *The English Mail-Coach*, 151; *The Glory of Motion*, 151; *Going Down with Victory*, 151; *The Vision of Sudden Death*, 151–152.
Descriptive music, 245–256; distinguished from narrative, 240–241.
Detective stories, logical flaw in, 80–81.
Deutschland über Alles, 85.
Development, of fugue, 150; of sonata form, 162, 165; of symbols, 178–207.
Diabolus in musica, 260, 263.
Dickens, C., 211.
Dimensions, of visual arts, 9.
Disney, Walt, *Fantasia*, 85.
Divisions, 54 n.
Dobson, A., rondeau, *In After Days*, 145; triolets, 144.
Donne, John, 42, 255.
Dorchain, A., *Chant Militaire*, 85.
Double concerto, 161.
Double fugue, in program music, 227, 228.
Drama, 110.
Dramatic monologue, 62, 117.
Dramatic setting, of texts, 62–86.
Dreiser, T., *American Tragedy*, 127.
Dresden Amen, use in religious music, 263.
Drink to me Only with Thine Eyes, 48, 83.
Dryden, J., on deaths on stage, 88.
Dukas, P., *L'Apprenti Sorcier*, 225, 239–240, 258.

Durchkomponiertes Lied, 48.
Dvořák, A., *New World Symphony*, 85.
Dynamic arts, distinguished from static, 10.

Ecclesiastes, 37.
Edinburgh Magazine, 158.
Elegiac couplet, 117, 191.
Elgar, E., 86; *Enigma Variations*, 128; *Falstaff*, 225, 242–243; *Pomp and Circumstance, No. 1*, 85.
Eliot, T. S., 202, 255.
Elizabethan, drama, 43, 108; lyric, 141; sonnet, 117; songs, 20, 141.
Emotion-masses, 202.
End-stopped lines, 72.
Epic, 110.
Exposition, of fugue, 150; of sonata form, 162.
Expression, distinguished from imitation, 53–54.

Fain Would I Have a Pretty Thing, 141.
Fiction, musical influence on, 208–218.
Field, Rachel, 85.
Fine arts, 7–14.
First-movement form, 161.
Fitzgerald, E., 107.
Flaischeln, Cäsar, *Silvesterlied*, 84.
Fletcher, J. G., *Blue Symphony*, 169; *Green Symphony*, 169; *Sand and Spray: A Sea-Symphony*, 170; sonata form, use of, 165, 169–170, 176; *Steamers*, 130, 170; *Violet Symphony*, 169; *White Symphony*, 169.
Folk-epic, 45.
Form, defined, 127–128; inseparable from substance, 101; term limited for literature, 221–222.
Foster, Stephen, *Swanee River*, 150.
Franck, César, *Le Chasseur Maudit*, 225; *Les Djinns*, 225; *Sonata in A*, 173; *Symphony in D Minor*, 173.
Fugue, 109, 111, 128, 149–160, 165, 231; defined, 150–151; diagram of, 157.
Furioso, 164 n.

Gautier, T., on difficulty in art, 150–151; *Symphonie en Blanc Majeur*, 163; *Variations sur le Carnaval de Venise*, 130.
Gavotte, 135.
Gerstenberg, H. W. von, 85.

Gide, A., influence on A. Huxley, 209; *La Symphonie Pastorale*, 174 n.

Gigue, 128.

Gilbert and Sullivan, patter songs, 20.

Gluck, C. W. von, 90, 248; *Gavotte* from *Iphigenia*, 136; on libretti, 92.

God Preserve Thy People, 263.

Goethe, J. W. von, *Erlkönig*, 70–83; *Faust*, 225, 269; songs of Mignon, 136; *Die Wahlverwandtschaften*, 211; *Der Zauberlehrling*, 225, 239, 240.

Gott Erhalte Franz den Kaiser, 85.

Grail, as pivot in Malory, 121.

Greek tragedy, 45; imitated in opera, 90.

Greene, Robert, *Sephestia's Lullaby*, 143.

Gregorian chant, 16.

Grieg, E., *First Peer Gynt Suite (Ase's Death)*, 110.

Grove, Sir George, on Beethoven's *6th*, 246, 248; on Beethoven's *9th*, 236.

Guillaume de Machault, triolet by, 144.

Haller, A. von, descriptive poetry, 245.

Handel, G. F., 70, 71 n.; *Harmonious Blacksmith*, 128; *Israel in Egypt*, 59; *Largo* (from *Xerxes*), 85; *The Messiah*, 52, 54–61 ("Every Valley Shall be Exalted," 55–59), 63, 69, 234.

Hanslick, E., 64; *Vom Musikalisch-Schönen*, 231–234.

Harald, King, 41.

Hardy, T., *Birds at Winter Nightfall*, 144.

Harmonic series, 31.

Harmony, 38–43.

Haydn, J., 86, 247 n.; *The Creation*, 59; *Emperor Quartet*, 85; *The Seasons*, 59, 233.

Heat, suggested in music, 248, 254.

Hebbel, C. F., *Requiem*, 143.

Hebrew literature, 114.

Henley, W. E., *London Voluntaries*, 164.

Herrick, R., 131, 222.

Heteronomous aesthetic of music, 244.

Hillyer, Robert, *Variations on a Theme*, 130.

Hoffman, E. T. A., 164, 209.

Hofmannsthal, H. von, 93.

Hölderlin, F., variant versions of poems, 132.

Homer, abstraction, lack of, 268–269; epithets, use of, 94, 211; repeated passages in *Iliad*, 106–107, 112; synonyms in *Iliad*, 105.

Housman, A. E., *Epitaph on an Army of Mercenaries*, 119; short lyrics, 222.

Houssaye, A., 165.

Hugo, Victor, *Les Djinns*, 225; on music, 98; source for Liszt, 224.

Human experience, 3.

Hundred Years' War, 229.

Hunt, Leigh, 132; *Serenade*, 85.

Huxley, A., *Point Counter Point*, 209–211.

Hypnotic poetry, 244–245.

Iambic pentameter, 17, 191 n.

Icelandic poetry, 41.

Ideal suggestion, 236.

Idée fixe, 94, 173, 226.

Imagists, 222.

Imitation in music, 35–36, 58–62, 231, 249–251, 262.

Impressionism, 253.

Impromptu, 110.

Introduction, in sonata form, 162 n., 168 n.

Italian sonnet, 41, 104, 117, 119, 127, 169, 221.

Job, 114–117, 122.

Johnson, R. U., poem on Chopin, 139.

Johnson, Dr. S., on iambic pentameter, 17; remarks of, 223.

Jonson, Ben, short lyrics of, 222; *To Celia*, 48.

Joyce, James, fugato passage in *Ulysses*, 159–160; stream of consciousness, 269.

Judges, 105.

Kalevala, The, 225.

Kaulbach, W. von, fresco by, 225.

Keats, John, 68, 132; *Bards of Passion and of Mirth*, 137; *La Belle Dame sans Merci*, 137; *Lines on the Mermaid Tavern*, 137.

Key, F. S., *The Star-Spangled Banner*, 85, 86.

Kleist, E. von, descriptive poetry of, 245.

Klopstock, F. G., *Geistliche Lieder*, 85.

Knecht, J. H., *Portrait Musical de la Nature*, 245.

König, E., verse-program for *Ein Heldenleben*, 242.

Körner, T., 85.

Kuhnau, J., *Bible Sonatas*, 258, 259.

Lamartine, A. de, *Préludes*, 163; source for Liszt, 224.
Lamb, C., *Dissertation on Roast Pig*, 209.
Lamentation, musical expression of, 68.
Landor, W. S., 222.
Lanier, S., 51; *The Centennial Cantata*, 46–47; on English metrics, 17; on "tunes" in speech, 29; *The Symphony*, 171–172, 176.
La Rochefoucauld, F. de, quoted, 189 n.; maxims of, 223.
Leacock, S., 42.
Lee, R. E., 186.
Legge, A. E. G., *A Symphony*, 165, 172.
Leitmotiv, 51; a musical word, 12, 217; use in literature, 99, 174, 211–218; use in music, 94–99, 226, 264–265.
Lenau, N., *Don Juan*, 225, 266–267.
Leonard, W. E., *Two Lives*, 21–22, 233.
Leonardo da Vinci, 4.
Liliencron, D. von, *Die Musik Kommt*, 34.
Lincoln, A., 186 ff.
Lindsay, Vachel, *The Congo*, 24–26; *General William Booth Enters into Heaven*, 26.
Linear development, 165.
Liszt, F., 246; *Faust-symphonie*, 225–229; *Festklänge*, 225; *Héroïde Funèbre*, 225; *Hungaria*, 225; *Hunnenschlacht*, 225; Leitmotiv, use of, 265; literary inspiration of, 241; *Sonnets of Petrarch*, 140; spinning-wheel pattern, 235; symphonic poems, 209, 224–226; *Symphonie zu Dante's Divina Commedia*, 225; transcription of Schubert's *Erlkönig*, 140.
Literal settings, 53–62.
Literature, an auditory art, 8; an exclusive term, 7.
Lodge, Thomas, *Phoebe's Sonnet* (*Rosalind*), 143.
Loewe, K., *Erlkönig*, 73, 82.
Longfellow, H. W., *Evangeline*, 20.
Longing, expressed by dissonances, 68.
Ludwig, O., *Der Erbförster*, 176.
Lyly, John, 141.

McCrae, John, *In Flanders' Fields*, 146.
MacDowell, E., literary titles, use of, 220; short compositions, 224; *Suggestion in Music*, 235–236, 237.
MacLeish, Archibald, *Panic*, 19.
MacPherson, J., Ossianic poems, 241.

Mallarmé, S., *L'Après-Midi d'un Faune*, 241, 253.
Malory, Sir T., balance in *Morte D' Arthur*, 121; stylistic repetition in, 106.
Mann, Thomas, *Buddenbrooks*, 213; Leitmotiv, use of, 211–217; *The Magic Mountain*, 213; on Wagner's *Tristan*, 98; *Tonio Kröger*, 177 n., 213–217; *Tristan*, 212.
March time, in poetry, 24–27.
Marot, C., 145.
Marseillaise, La, 263–264.
Marvell, A., *To his Coy Mistress*, 119–121.
Masefield, John, *Sea Fever*, 23.
Mathematics, and music, 5.
Meaning, 11.
Medici, Lorenzo de', *Trionfo di Bacco ed Arianna*, 146–147.
Memory, needed for temporal arts, 11.
Mendelssohn-Bartholdy, F., 246; *Hebrides* (*Fingal's Cave*) *Overture*, 36, 240, 241, 251–253; on Beethoven's *6th*, 245; on titles of *Songs without Words*, 243–244; *Spinning Song*, 235; *Trio, Op. 66*, 264; *Variations Sérieuses*, 128.
Meredith, G., *Love in the Valley*, 27; *Tardy Spring*, 139.
Merens-Melmer, M., sonata form in, 165; *Thème et Variations*, 130.
Metaphysical wit, 42.
Meter, defined, 16.
Metrical romances, Middle English, 254.
Metrics, Anglo-Saxon, 27; Early Germanic, 27, 92–93; French, 18, 38; Greek, 17; Latin, 17; modern European generally, 17 ff.; musical, 27–29; Persian, 29; special effects in Whitman, 191.
Middle Ages, 45, 222.
Millay, Edna, 33, 93; *Fatal Interview*, 118.
Milton, John, 112 n., 131, 159; influenced by music, 100; *On his Blindness*, 232; on rhyme, 38; *Paradise Lost*, 8, 38, 54, 93, 129, 247 n.; *Samson Agonistes*, 21, 42; sonnets, 119, 127.
Minuet, 161; as literary title, 129–130, 164.
Mitchell, M., *Gone with the Wind*, 122.
Mode, 125–126.
Mood, in poetry and music, 83.
Morris, W., *Two Red Roses across the Moon*, 146.

Motion, imitated in music, 60.
Movements, relationship of, 173; sequence in symphony, 161.
Mozart, W. A., 85, 126, 166, 168 n., 259, 266; additional accompaniments by, 55; *Sonata in A,* 123–125, 128, 136.
Mundy, John, *Fantasia,* 257.
Music, as ultimate reality, 205–208; defined, 11; distinguished from score, 8; epitome of universe, 195; measured and unmeasured, 16.
Musset, A. de, 85.

Napoleon, 186.
Narrative music, 257–268; distinguished from descriptive, 240–242.
National anthems, symbolically used, 263–264; text and music of, 85–86.
Nefertiti, Queen, 9.
Negatives, in literature, 13.
Nerval, G. de, 51.
Newman, Ernest, on singers, 91; on the small poem in music, 222, 223.
Nibelungenlied, balance in, 122.
Niecks, F., on early program music, 257.
Nietzsche, F., *Der Herbst,* 143.
Nocturne, 110, 128.
Novel, 110, 127, 219.
Novelette, 127, 220.
Noyes, A., *The Highwayman,* 137.

"Old Hundred," 264.
Omar Khayyám, 107.
O'Neill, E., *The Great God Brown,* 98; on associations of music, 51; *Strange Interlude,* 98, 99.
Onomatopoeia, 33–35.
Opera, 87–99.
Overtones, 31.

Paer, F., 85.
Painting, similar to sculpture, 9; as subject of music, 225.
Paisiello, G., 85.
Pantoum, 106.
Paragraphs, in music, 258.
Partials, 31.
Passacaglia, 111.
Passepied, 135.
Pater, W., on other arts' imitating music, 101, 194.
Patriotic songs, 85–86.
Pedal-point, 151, 156.

Peele, George, 131.
Pervigilium Veneris, 143.
Petrarch, F., 118–119; Liszt's use of sonnets of, 140.
Petrarchan sonnet (see Italian sonnet).
Pitch, in poetry, 29–30; symbolism of, in music, 235.
Plain-song, 16.
Plato, on instrumental music, 45.
Plattensteiner, R., sonata form, use of, 165, 176; *Ein Symphonisches Gedicht,* 166; *Wasser-Lied,* 130; *Wolken-Symphonie,* 130.
Poe, E. A., 82; *Dream Land,* 137; *The Philosophy of Composition,* 81; *The Raven,* 81.
Poet, broad sense of word, 112 n.
Poetry: A Magazine of Verse, 201.
Pope, A., 131.
Prelude, 110, 128, 153.
Pre-Raphaelites, use of refrain, 146.
Principal subject, 162.
Program music, 221–268; growth of, 219.
Prokofieff, S., *Visions Fugitives,* 224.
Proust, M., 269.
Proverbs of Solomon, 223.
Psalm VIII, 136.
Pure poetry, 12, 270.

Quintet, 161.
Quotations, musical, 263–264.

Rachmaninoff, S. V., *Die Toteninsel,* 225.
Racine, J., 98.
Ravel, M., *Bolero,* 24, 233.
Recapitulation, 162.
Refrain, use by Pre-Raphaelites, 146.
Renaissance, appearance of opera, 90; separation of poetry and music, 45.
Repetition, in literature, 103–109; in music, 109–113, 215 ff.
Rests, in poetry, 21 ff.
Rhyme, 37–38, 104.
Rhythm, 15–29.
Ritter, A., influence on R. Strauss, 226; verse-program for *Tod und Verklärung,* 242.
Rondeau, 106, 110; distinguished from rondo, 128; forms illustrated, 144–146.
Rondo, 109, 111, 128; adaptations in literature, 140–148, 197; definitions of form, 140, 148; frequent as last movement, 161; used programmatically, 227.

Ronsard, P., 49; on instrumental music, 45.
Rosseter, Philip, *A Book of Ayres*, 53.
Rossetti, D. G., *Sister Helen*, 146; *Troy Town*, 146.
Rossini, G., *William Tell Overture*, 257.
Russian (Czarist) Anthem, 263–264.

Saint Anthony of Egypt, 231.
Saint-Saëns, C., *Carnaval des Animaux*, 237–239, 240, 241; *Danse Macabre*, 225, 260–263, 264; *Rouet d'Omphale*, 225.
Sameness with difference, 102.
Sand, George, on Beethoven's 6th (*Lettres d'un Voyageur*), 247 n.
Sappho, 222.
Saraband, 168.
Scansion, explanation of symbols, 17.
Schauffler, R. H., on influence of Beethoven's 6th, 253.
Scherzo, 128, 161; as literary title, 164.
Schiller, J. C. F., as source for Liszt, 224; *Don Carlos*, 213.
Schönberg, A., *6 Kleine Stücken*, 224.
Schopenhauer, A., on descriptive music, 243, 246–247; on lack of particularity in music, 67; on music as autonomous art, 11; on music as epitome of universe, 195, 233; on opera, 87; on other arts' imitating music, 101, 194.
Schubert, F., *Die Allmacht*, 73; *Ave Maria*, 85; *Death and the Maiden Quartet*, 128; *Erlkönig*, 48, 70–83, 94. *Gretchen am Spinnrad*, 235; operatic efforts, 88; *Der Tod und das Mädchen*, 140.
Schumann, R., *Kinderszenen*, 230; on programs for music, 244, 267; short pieces, 223, 224; spinning-wheel pattern in, 235; symphonies, 173.
Schweitzer, A., 73; on Bach's motifs, 67, 94; on Bach's setting of texts, 63–64.
Science, and art, 1–6.
Scriabin, A., short pieces, 223.
Sculpture, similar to painting, 9.
Second subject, 162.
Semantics, 11.
Sentimentality, 5.
Serenade, 128.
Shakespeare, W., 4; *Hamlet*, 11; *King Lear*, 108; *Macbeth*, 43, 217; *The Merchant of Venice*, 30; *The Merry Wives of Windsor*, 243 n.; *Othello*, 46; *Sonnet 73*, 107–108; *The Tempest*, 122.
Shelley, P. B., 107.
Short story, 127.
Sibelius, J., 86; *Finlandia*, 85, 225; influenced by *Kalevala*, 225; *The Swan of Tuonela*, 255.
Sicilienne, 128.
Sidney, Sir Philip, *First Song (Astrophel and Stella)*, 137.
Sitwell, S., *The Cyder Feast and Other Poems*, 131; *On Hearing Four Bands . . .*, 40.
Skaldic poetry, 41.
Smetana, F., *The Moldau*, 225.
Soliloquy, 98.
Solomon, 223.
Sonata, 109, 161; vague use of term by poets, 163–164.
Sonata form, 110, 126, 128, 193, 247, 253; in literature, 163–178, 208, 214–215; in music, 161–163; refusal to repeat exposition in, 113.
Song-hits, form of, 136 n.
Sorantin, E., on formulae for musical expression, 67–69.
Spatial arts, distinguished from temporal, 10.
Speech-patterns, and emotional states, 66.
Spenser, E., 33, 101; *Faerie Queene*, 254.
Spenserian stanza, 221.
Spinning-wheel, imitated in music, 235.
Spitteler, Carl, on orchestral allegory, 236, 254.
Spohr, L., 244.
Squire, J. C., *The Exquisite Sonnet*, 12–14, 21, 36, 42–43.
Stamford Bridge, Battle of, 41.
Stanzaic song, 47–48, 72.
"Star" System, in opera, 90.
Static arts, distinguished from dynamic, 10.
Sterne, L., *Tristram Shandy*, 164.
Storm, Theodor, *Die Nachtigall*, 137 n.
Strauss, Johann II, waltzes, 233.
Strauss, Richard, 258; *Alpine Symphony*, 227 n.; *Also Sprach Zarathustra*, 225; *Aus Italien*, 226; *Don Juan*, 225, 266–267; *Don Quixote*, 227, 228, 229, 265, 266, 267; *Festive Prelude*, 227 n.; *Ein Heldenleben*, 227, 242; influence on orchestra, 259; narrative music of, 265–267; on program music, 227–228, 230;

Sinfonia Domestica, 226, 227, 247; *Till Eulenspiegel*, 16, 225, 227, 247; *Tod und Verklärung*, 242.
Stress, syllabic, 17.
Stretto, 151, 156, 158.
String quartet, 128, 161.
String quartet concerto, 161.
String trio, 161.
Stubbornness, imitated in music, 60.
Subject, of fugue, 150; of musical composition is a theme, 231.
Sub-plot, 43, 108.
Suite, dance, 168.
Suppé, F. von, *Light Cavalry Overture*, 74; *Poet and Peasant Overture*, 97.
Swinburne, A. C., 37, 121; *Atalanta in Calydon*, 255.
Swing Low, Sweet Chariot, 263.
Symbols, poetically used like musical themes, 178–194, 197–201.
Symphonic novel, 174–176, 209.
Symphonic poem, 209, 224–228.
Symphony, 128, 161; vague use of term by poets, 163–164.
Synonyms, poetic use of, 105.
Syrinx, associated with woodwinds, 236.

Taylor, Deems, on abstraction in painting and music, 268; on Antheil, 265 n.
Tcherepnin, A. N., II, *Bagatelles*, 255.
Temporal arts, distinguished from spatial, 10.
Tennyson, A., *The Lotus Eaters*, 255–256; *Morte d'Arthur*, 19, 33–34; on Milton, 159.
Tenses, used as keys, 174.
Theme, musical, analyzed, 123–125; imitated by Aiken, 197–201.
Theme and variations, as movement in larger work, 161; in literature, 129–134, 152, 166, 170, 196; in music, 128.
Theocritus, 236.
Three Blind Mice, 151.
Tieck, L., 164; *Die Verkehrte Welt*, 129–130.
Timbre, 31–38.
Time, musical, as repetition and variation, 103; compared with poetic, 18 ff.
Tirso de Molina, 266.
To Anacreon in Heaven, 85.
Todhunter, John, 165, 176; *Beethoven's "Sonata Appassionata,"* 171.
Tolstoi, L., *The Kreutzer Sonata*, 67.

Tonality, 125–126; a poetic problem, 165; suggested by tenses, 174.
Tone, distinguished from noise, 31.
Tone-painting, 257.
Tovey, Sir D., on Elgar's *Falstaff*, 242–243; on program music, 244.
Tragi-comedy, 117.
Trio, 135 n.
Triolet, 106, 110; defined and illustrated, 144.
Triplet, used in poetry, 27.
Tritone, in imitative effect, 252; symbolic use of, 260–263.
Tschaikowsky, P. I., *1812 Overture*, 229, 242, 263–264; *Hamlet*, 225; hysteria in, 102; *Romeo and Juliet*, 225; *Symphony No. 6 (Pathétique)*, 103.

Uhland, J. L., *Schäfers Sonntagslied*, 136.
Ujejski, K., poems on Chopin's music, 138, 139.
Useful arts, distinguished from fine arts, 7.

Van Dyke, Henry, 165.
Variation, in literature, 102–109, 196, 210; in music, 109–113; (See also Theme and variations).
Verdi, G., *Otello*, 45–46; *Rigoletto*, 89.
Vergil, 112, 236; *Eclogues*, 254.
Verlaine, Paul, *Chanson d'Automne*, 35.
Vialls, M. A., sonnets on musical compositions, 137–138, 140.
Vigny, A. de, *Le Cor*, 34.
Villanelle, 106; defined and illustrated, 147–148.
Villon, F., rondeau with reduced refrain, 145.
Visual arts, distinguished from auditory, 8 ff.
Vivaldi, A., concertos on seasons, 245.
Vocal music, 44–100; always programmatic, 229.
Voice, not necessarily vocal, 150 n.
Vowel sequences, 37.

Wagner, R., 90, 246; contributed Leitmotiv to literature, 211; development on large scale, 209; *Götterdämmerung*, 88–89; his own librettist, 46, 92–93; influence on orchestra, 259; Leitmotiv, use of, 98–99, 226, 265; *Der Ring des Nibelungen*, 92, 93, 96; *Siegfried (Waldweben)*, 253; *Siegfried Idyll*, 209; spinning-wheel pattern, 235; *Tannhäuser Overture*, 138; *Tristan und Isolde*, 92, 98–99, 212.

Waltz, 128.

Waterloo, 154.

Weingartner, F., *Das Gefilde der Seligen*, 225.

Whitman, Walt, *Crossing Brooklyn Ferry*, 179; *When Lilacs Last* . . . , 178–194.

Widor, C. M., 85.

Wilde, Oscar, *Theocritus*, 147.

Wittgenstein, Princess, affair with Liszt, 225.

Woodwind octet, 161.

Wordsworth, W., 4, 19, 107, 254.

Work of art, 4.

Yankee Doodle, 263.

Zola, Emile, imitation of Wagner (*Le Ventre de Paris*), 211; use of Leitmotiv 211.

Lightning Source UK Ltd.
Milton Keynes UK
UKOW051845220113

205217UK00001B/41/P